THE PRESIDENCY, CONGRESS, AND THE SUPREME COURT

Third Edition

Scholastic American Citizenship Program

THE PRE
CONGRES
SUPREM

Third Edition

By Steven Jantzen

Advisory Editor

James MacGregor Burns
Professor of Political Science
Williams College

Educational Consultants

Jean Tilford Claugus
Past President of the National Council For the Social Studies

Ann-Marie Brush
Principal, Edgewater High School
Brevard County, Florida

SIDENCY, S, AND THE E COURT

Titles in the
SCHOLASTIC AMERICAN
CITIZENSHIP PROGRAM:

Foundations of Our Government

The Presidency, Congress, and the Supreme Court

State and Local Government

Politic? and People

For reprint permission,
grateful acknowledgement is made to:

Houghton Mifflin Company for an excerpt from
THE LAW OF DELAY by C. Northcote Parkinson

Macmillan Publishing Co, Inc., for an excerpt from
ROBERT M. LAFOLLETTE by Belle and Fola
LaFollette, copyright© 1953 by Fola LaFollette.

William Morrow & Co., Inc., for an excerpt from
HARRY S TRUMAN by Margaret Truman, copyright
© 1972 by Margaret Truman Daniel.

The New York Times for "An Opinion of One of Those
Soft-Headed Judges" by Marvin Frankel,
copyright © 1973 by The New York Times Company.

The New York Times Magazine for "The Foreign Policy
Tussle" by Stephen V. Roberts, copyright © 1988 by
The New York Times Company.

Saturday Review Press/E.P. Dutton & Co., Inc., for
an excerpt from BELLA! MS. ABZUG GOES TO
WASHINGTON by Bella Abzug, copyright © 1972
by Bella S. Abzug.

Time, The Weekly Newsmagazine, for "We Shall Pay
Any Price," copyright © 1961 by Time, Inc.

Congressman Jim Wright for an excerpt from
YOU AND YOUR CONGRESSMAN.

Teaching Consultants:

Terry Erickson
Sylvan Middle School
Citrus Heights, California

Dean A. Woelfle
East Peoria High School
East Peoria, Illinois

Staff for the
AMERICAN CITIZENSHIP
PROGRAM

Publisher: Eleanor Angeles
Project Editors: Stephen M. Lewin, Charles L. Wrye,
  Penny Parsekian
Editorial Director: Carolyn Jackson
Production Editors: Nancy J. Smith, Jeanette Farrell
Art Editor and Designer: David Rollert
Art Director: Dale Moyer
Revision Art: Murray Belsky
Cover Art: Lee Renner
Maps: Hal Aber
Collages: Gary Friedman
Illustrations: Mario Jamora

ISBN-0-590-35311

13 12 11 10 9 8 7 6 5 4 3 2 1 — 8 9 0/9 1 2 3/9

CONTENTS

Unit I: The Presidency, 7
1: The Toughest Job, 9
2: Roles of the President, 23
3: Who's Qualified To Be President? 37
4: Running the Executive Branch, 39
5: Can a President Be Too Strong? 65
6: Replacing the President, 77
7: How To Judge a President, 91
Ten Good Books About the Presidency, 100

Unit II: Congress, 103
8: The People on Capitol Hill, 105
9: An Act of Congress
   (And a Look at Blood River), 121
10: How To Judge a Bill, 133
11: Power in Congress, 145
12: Does Congress Do Its Job? 157
13: How To Influence Congress, 169
Ten Good Books About Congress, 182

Unit III: The U.S. Courts, 185
14: John Doe in a U.S. Court, 187
15: Who Shall Judge? 200
16: The Nine Most Powerful Judges, 210
17: Taking a Case Through the Courts, 226
Eight Good Books About the U.S. Courts, 236

The Constitution of the United States, 238
Glossary of Key Words and Terms, 248
Index, 252

UNIT 1:
THE
PRESIDENCY

Mt. Rushmore, South Dakota. These 60-foot faces of Washington, Jefferson, Theodore Roosevelt, and Lincoln were carved in granite by artist Gutzon Borglum.

1: THE TOUGHEST JOB

Poof! The photographer's pan of chemicals exploded, gave off a flash of light, and briefly lit up the face of Abraham Lincoln.

In Lincoln's day, over 100 years ago, cameras were large and clumsy. To get your picture taken was a long and tricky process. But Lincoln "sat for his picture" several times during his career in politics. Two of these pictures, shown at the left, were taken at different times of his life.

Can you guess how old Lincoln was in each of the pictures? Write your guesses on a sheet of paper. (Your teacher has the answers in the Answer Key, which is in the Teaching Guide for this book.)

The two pictures of Abraham Lincoln tell us something about the job of being President. They suggest why some people have called the President's job the toughest in the world.

You may hear someone say: "I wouldn't take the President's job for a million dollars." Why not? What's so hard about being President?

To understand, you'll need to know about the President's duties as defined by the U.S. Constitution. Then you'll need to see the President's problems as a President himself sees them.

need to see the President's problems as a President sees them.

This chapter will tell you about two of the hardest problems American Presidents have ever faced. You will then have a chance to make a decision about each problem, as if you yourself were President. But first, what does the Constitution say about the President's duties?

The Constitution defines the President's job. The office of President was created in Philadelphia during one of the hottest summers that city has ever known. The year was 1787. Inside a red brick building, a small group of men met and argued together about a constitution—a new plan of government for the United States.

Most agreed that one *branch** of the new government should make the laws, while a second branch should enforce them. They decided to call the first branch *Congress.** And the leader of the second—or *Executive Branch** —would be called a *President.*

But, they asked, should one person have all the power to carry out the nation's laws? Or should there be two executives or three or maybe even four? And how long should the term of office be?

Finally, they agreed that one person should be in charge of the Executive Branch. The Constitution they wrote said: "The executive power shall be vested in a President of the United States of America. He shall hold his office during the term of four years."

You'll find the rest of the plan in Article II of the Constitution. (Look for it on page 241.)

The President's job, as described in Article II, includes these powers and duties:

- commanding the armed forces;
- appointing judges to U.S. Courts;
- presenting messages to Congress about the need for new laws;
- carrying out federal laws;
- making *treaties** (written agreements) with foreign countries.

The President is responsible for the Executive Branch. Today he has hundreds of advisers and many thousands of government workers to help him. But he is responsible for what they do. If they make a mistake, then it is his mistake as well. If they give him bad advice, he must take the blame for following it.

What are the President's problems? The Constitution lists the President's duties. But it does not mention the single most important and difficult job—the job of giving leadership to the nation.

The President often has to decide what is best for the United States. The President must try to answer hundreds of difficult questions. Should this nation spend more money or less on health and education? If an American ship is attacked at sea, what should the United States do about it?

Think how hard it must be to make an important decision as President. First, you need to know the facts that bear on the problem. But you are so

AMERICA IN 1803

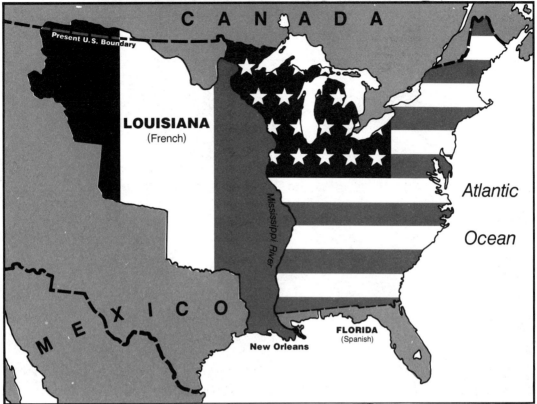

busy you don't have time to consider all the facts. You therefore ask your advisers to look into the problem and suggest what to do. But your advisers often disagree.

What then do you decide to do? Do you (a) take the opinion held by *most* of your advisers, (b) listen to the one adviser whom you trust the most, or (c) follow your own judgment?

Case study: What should the President do about Louisiana?

Find out why it is so hard and even painful to make decisions as President. Put yourself in the place of one of our Presidents, Thomas Jefferson. Ask yourself what you would have done about the Louisi-

ana Territory in the year 1803.

First, look at the map above. Notice the borders of the United States and the territories in the West and South. Our nation is still young and fairly weak. We're surrounded by lands held by different European nations.

But now, in 1803, President Jefferson has just heard that France wants to sell to the United States the Louisiana Territory. This includes the port of New Orleans and millions of acres of wild country stretching for a thousand miles west from the Mississippi River to the Rocky Mountains.

Jefferson wants to buy the Louisiana Territory. Having it would give the United States control of the Mississippi River. The French now control

Thomas Jefferson

the river. If they close the river to trade, U.S. farmers in the West will not be able to ship their crops to market. If that happens the Western settlements will suffer great losses of income.

Also, think of what could happen to the Louisiana Territory if the United States fails to control it. It could become a separate nation — perhaps a strong rival and enemy of the United States.

If we buy the Louisiana Territory, it will greatly increase the size and power of our country. Jefferson himself has dreamed of spreading the United States westward to the Pacific. The French are offering millions of acres of land for pennies per acre. It could be one of the greatest bargains in the history of the world.

But . . . there's a catch.

Does the Constitution allow the U.S. government to buy the Louisiana Territory? Jefferson has strong doubts. Many times, Jefferson has said that the U.S. government has the power to do only those things listed in the Constitution. Jefferson has said that a President should follow the words of the Constitution strictly. Otherwise, the people's liberties may be in danger.

Is there anything in the Constitution about buying new lands, rivers, and cities for the United States? No. Therefore, according to Jefferson's own words, the United States does not have the power to buy the Louisiana Territory.

However, it is possible to change

DECISION CHART

"What should I tell the Senate?"

Choices	Risks	Advantages
1. Tell the Senators about your doubts. But ask them to approve the treaty anyway because the country needs it.	The Senate might not approve the treaty if you say you aren't sure it is legal. Thus, by following your own view of the Constitution, you might harm your country's future.	It is the most honest course to take.
2. Tell the Senate the treaty is important. Say nothing about your doubts.	You would be going against your own ideas about the meaning of the Constitution. Also, this might cause Congress and the people to have less trust in your leadership in the future.	The Senate would be most likely to approve the treaty.
3. Tell the Senate to pass an amendment to the Constitution which would clear up any doubts about the treaty.	It would take a long time. France might call off the deal.	You could be absolutely sure that the Constitution allows this treaty to be made.

or add to the Constitution. To do this, you must get both houses of Congress and three fourths of the state *legislatures** to approve an *amendment** to the Constitution.

Jefferson wonders if he should ask Congress to approve an amendment allowing him to make the deal with France. His advisers tell him no. They say it will take too long to get an amendment passed. The French are already saying they will take back their offer if the U.S. government does not soon sign a treaty agreeing to the purchase.

What should Jefferson do? If he is to buy the Louisiana Territory, he must present a message to the *Senate** asking them to vote on a treaty with France.

The Constitution says two thirds of the Senate must approve a treaty before it is legal. Jefferson knows how hard it is to get even a majority of the Senate to vote a certain way. To get a two-thirds vote is of course even more difficult. He must now decide what kind of message he should send to the Senate.

If you were Thomas Jefferson, what would you tell the Senators? The chart above lists three choices. Notice that each choice has both risks and advantages.

You're the President. You're the leader of the Executive Branch. It's your responsibility to decide.

After you have made your decision, your teacher can tell you what Jefferson decided.

ACTION PROJECT

You've now seen how a President must choose between several courses of action. As Thomas Jefferson, you had to make up your mind which values were more important to you — being true to your own views about the Constitution and being frank with Congress and the people; or carrying out your desire for a larger and stronger American nation.

Your choice was probably not an easy one. All courses of action involved risk and the sacrifice of one value for another.

Now you will be challenged to make another choice as President. It is perhaps the most difficult choice any President has ever made. It too involves a choice between two values:

● the need to avoid war;
● the need to keep the U.S. one nation.

Which is more important to you?

You'll have a chance to find out after reading about Abraham Lincoln's first great problem as President.

The question of Fort Sumter.

Washington is cold and gray in March 1861. As Abraham Lincoln, you have just moved into the White House as the 16th President of the United States. Right away you must deal with the fact that the United States is no longer united.

For the past 30 years, the nation has been torn with bitter quarreling. Groups of Northerners have been demanding new laws to end slavery. Southerners who depend on slaves to harvest their crops feel that their way of life is under attack.

As a Northerner from Illinois, your dislike of slavery is well known. Many Southerners cannot stand the idea

Confederate cannons aimed at Fort Sumter

that you are now President. As a result, several Southern states have declared their independence from the United States. Still others may also decide to leave the Union.

People in the North and the South are worrying about what you will do as President. Will you use force against the Southern states? Or will you allow them to become a new and separate nation?

You hope that peace can be preserved. But at the same time, you believe it is your duty as President to keep the United States together as one nation.

Some Southern states are not only withdrawing from the Union. They are also beginning to take military action against U.S. property in the South.

By mid-March there are only four U.S. forts in the South that are still in the hands of the U.S. One of them is Fort Sumter, in South Carolina. But Fort Sumter too may be taken by Southern troops at any moment.

Should you try to defend Fort Sumter? If you do, there will probably be a terrible civil war between the North and the South.

Can Fort Sumter be saved?

You ask an old military man, General Winfield Scott. No, says Scott. It is hopeless. Fort Sumter is on an island in the harbor of Charleston, South Carolina. No ship can reach it because Southern cannons guard the entrance to the harbor. The fort should be abandoned, he says.

Four days later, you hold a *Cabinet** meeting. You ask the members if they think it is wise to send supplies to Major Robert Anderson at Fort Sumter.

One Cabinet member says that supplying the fort will anger the South. He advises you to surrender it. Five other members agree.

Another says he is worried about the Southern and "border" states that have not left the Union. If you use force to try to save Sumter, they may leave. Give the Southerners time to cool off, he says.

Montgomery Blair, Postmaster General, disagrees. Blair argues: What will the world think if you give up Sumter without a fight? People will say the President is weak. It will en-

courage rebellion in the South.

By the end of March, the fort is still holding out. But Union troops are down to their last barrels of food. You are aware that there can be no more delay.

You must send a message to Major Anderson. What should you say: That you are sending food by sea and the men should hold out? That you are sending troops to drive away the Southerners? That the men should surrender?

To help you make a choice, copy the chart below on a separate sheet of paper. Fill in the risks and advantages of each course of action.

Make your decision. Then compare it with the decisions of other student-Lincolns. (Your teacher can tell you what actually happened in April 1861.)

DECISION CHART
"Should I risk war?"

Choices	Risks	Advantages
1. Tell Major Anderson that food supplies are on their way. But there will be no troops to help him save the fort.		
2. Tell Major Anderson that a fleet of warships is being sent to rescue the fort.		
3. Tell Major Anderson to surrender the fort.		

THE SITUATION

Four Southern forts 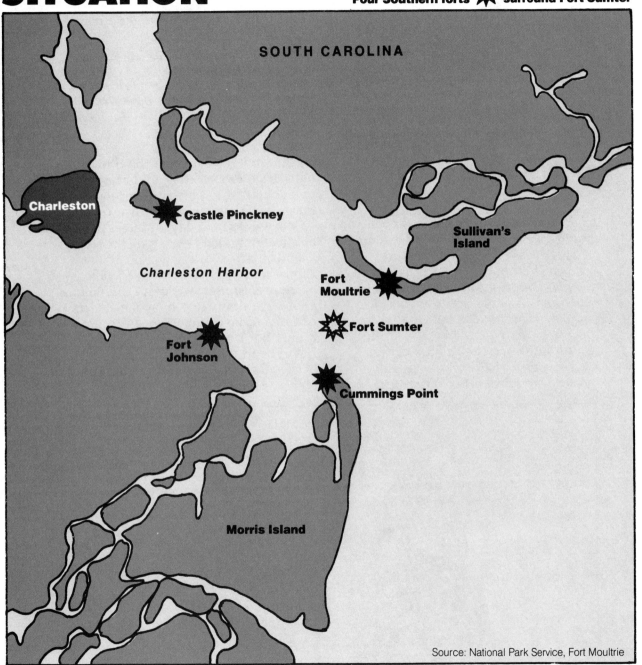 surround Fort Sumter

SOUTH CAROLINA

Charleston

Castle Pinckney

Sullivan's Island

Charleston Harbor

Fort Moultrie

Fort Sumter

Fort Johnson

Cummings Point

Morris Island

"THE LAST WORD"

by Alexander McClure

A President has to worry about how the public reacts to his or her decisions. It is far easier to be a successful leader if you have the support of the people, Congress, and the newspapers. But Lincoln never had this kind of support. Throughout the Civil War, people in the North as well as in the South bitterly criticized his actions.

Alexander McClure, a newspaper reporter who knew Lincoln, wrote a book about the President's troubles after Fort Sumter. He remembered how the public reacted to the awful losses General U.S. Grant suffered at the Battle of Shiloh in April 1862. Here is a passage adapted from McClure's book. Does it help you to understand why Lincoln aged so fast as President?

The first reports from the Shiloh battlefield created fear and alarm throughout the country. There was a flood of criticism against Grant.

Throughout the loyal states, the public demanded Grant's dismissal from the army. His victories at Forts Henry and Donelson seemed to have been forgotten. It was quite common to hear Grant denounced on the streets as unfit to hold important military command. I can recall only a single Republican member of Congress who boldly defended Grant after his troubles at Shiloh.

Abraham Lincoln and an adviser

18

I did not know Grant at that time. But I shared the common belief that the President should remove Grant from command. I had many talks with Lincoln's closest friends, all of whom agreed that Grant must be removed.

I was so impressed with the need for prompt action that I called on Lincoln at 11 o'clock at night and sat with him alone until after one o'clock in the morning. He was, as usual, worn out with the day's heavy duties. But he did not allow me to leave until the Grant problem had been gone over. I urged him to remove Grant because his own support from the public depended on it. As was his custom, he said but little. He sat before the open fire in the old Cabinet room. Most of the time he had his feet up on the high marble mantel. He showed unusual distress over his military problems. They seemed to be getting worse every day. He had gone through a long winter of terrible strain with McClellan and the Army of the Potomac. And for many months, he had had only trouble and confusion from among his generals in the West.

I appealed to Lincoln, for his own sake, to remove Grant at once. I told him how strongly the loyal people of the land felt about this issue. They wanted Grant removed. During the conversation, I could not tell what effect my arguments had upon him. He was, however, greatly distressed. When I had said everything that could be said from my standpoint, we fell into silence. Lincoln remained silent for what seemed a very long

time. He then raised himself in his chair and said in a tone of strength that I shall never forget: "I can't spare this man; he fights."

(YOU HAVE THE LAST WORD)

In a *democracy,* * government officials are supposed to pay attention to the wishes of the people. Some people, like McClure, believe a President should try, above all, to please the public.

But President Lincoln thought a true leader should do something else. What is Lincoln's idea of leadership? Do you agree with Lincoln or with McClure? Or do you think there is a middle ground? Why?

U.S. Grant

"CHECKOUT"—1

Key terms

President	state legislatures	military
Constitution	amendment	Cabinet
treaty	majority	democracy

Review

1. Name two of the duties of the President described in the U.S. Constitution.

2. What is "tough" about the duties of the President?

3. Describe a tough decision that Thomas Jefferson had to make as President.

4. Describe a tough decision that Abraham Lincoln had to make as President.

5. What are *choices, risks,* and *advantages?* What part do they play in decision-making?

Discussion

1. Is the President's job too tough for one person? If so, how could the duties be lightened? Should there be a shorter term of office? Should there be two — or more — Presidents at the same time, to share the duties of the office? Think about possible answers to these questions — and to others that may occur to you.

Then think of how well, on the whole, the institution of the Presidency has functioned for our country for more than 200 years. What risks might be involved in changing that institution in the ways you might be considering?

After the class discusses these issues, see if you can agree on answers to these two questions: **(a)** *Does the Presidency need changing?* **(b)** *If it does need changing, how should it be changed?*

2. President Truman wrote in his memoirs: "A man who ... is afraid to make decisions which may make him unpopular is not a man to represent the welfare of the country." There is another view of the duty of the elected official, however. It is that in a democracy, an elected official should follow the will of the people. Suppose polls show that 60 percent of the people are against a particular action. Should the President decide in favor of this action if he or she believes it is the right thing to do? Would your answer be the same if 90 percent of the people are against the action? Explain your answers.

20

3. Comment on — attack, defend, or change (until it expresses your view) — this statement: *The President should be held responsible for anything that goes wrong in the Executive Branch.*

Activities

1. You might draw up a decision chart for a problem that concerns you. It may be a problem in your own life, in your school, or in your community. List the different choices you have for dealing with the problem. Then, for each choice, list at least one risk and one advantage. Finally, decide which choice seems to give you the greatest advantage with the least risk. If your problem is one that you can share with your classmates, you might be helped in coming to a decision by discussing it with others in your class.

2. Some students might read about other difficult Presidential decisions and report to the class on them. Among those that might be researched are: Truman's decision to drop the A-Bomb, Nixon's decision to resign, Carter's decision to recognize the People's Republic of China, Reagan's decision to bomb Libya. Some students might read *Thirteen Days* by Robert Kennedy, about his brother's toughest decision as President. This was the blockade of Cuba in 1962, when the Soviets installed missiles there.

3. "My movements to the chair of government will be accompanied by feelings not unlike those of a culprit who is going to his execution," wrote George Washington shortly before he became our nation's first President in 1789.

"If you're as happy ... on entering this house as I am in leaving it and returning home," retiring President James Buchanan said to incoming President Abraham Lincoln in 1861, "you are the happiest man on Earth."

Some of you might be interested in assembling other views of Presidents and would-be Presidents about the job of being President and about life in the White House. (Not all viewed the job as an ordeal; some loved it.) You could research collections of quotations, biographies of Presidents, or memoirs of people who worked with them.

You could post your findings on the bulletin board or read them aloud and discuss them in class.

4. You might want to start your study of the Presidency in this unit of *American Citizenship* by choosing one President to learn about in detail. Each member of the class could choose a different President — or, if your teacher concurs, you might choose your favorite. You should read at least one biography about your chosen President. You might look in the card catalog at the school or public library for additional readings. You could also look for portraits or photographs to copy. As you go through this unit, you may find other information — and suggestions for further research — that will make your study more rewarding. You might put all your data about your President into a notebook or an album.

2: ROLES OF THE PRESIDENT

What do you have in common with a President of the United States?

Like the President, you spend your daily life moving from one role to another.

Roles people play. A role is a special way of behaving. It's often the way other people expect you to behave at certain times.

For example, just walk into a store —any store—and you will automatically step into the role of Customer. In this role, you can handle and examine almost anything on the store shelves. But you can't operate the cash register. Only someone in the role of Store Clerk or Shop Owner can operate the cash register.

Go from store to school and you instantly step into the role of Student. Here, you know enough about roles not to sit at the Teacher's desk. You can't even eat a meal at home without behaving in another role—the role of Son or Daughter.

All of us play roles throughout our lives. What other roles do you know about? Make a list of 10 roles, besides those mentioned here.

The roles Presidents play. The President has more roles to play than most people. For example, President Ronald Reagan often spent vacations at his ranch in California. Photographs of the President in his riding gear frequently appeared in the press. The ranch also happened to be the setting from which, in July 1983, President Reagan issued a statement to commemorate the signing of the Non-Proliferation Treaty. (He was on vacation there at the time.) It said the U.S. would continue to try to reach an agreement with the Soviet Union on nuclear disarmament.

What was President Reagan up to in each of these incidents? To understand his actions, you should know the many different roles that a President is expected to play. These are explained in the chart on pages 28–29.

After reading the chart, identify the role that explains the President's appearance in the photograph. Then find a role that explains his issuing the statement on nuclear weapons.

A President changes roles not only from day to day, but also from hour to hour and even from minute to minute. You could see how often these changes occur by following a President through a single day of his life in the White House.

Whole books have been written on the subject of what a President does from the hour he wakes up in the morning to the hour he goes to bed at night. One such book is *A Day in the Life of President Johnson,* by Jim Bishop. Bishop followed Lyndon Johnson for a day in 1966, from 7 A.M. until after midnight. A summary of his book is given below in two parts.

As you read, look for examples of these four roles:
- Chief Executive;
- Chief of Party;
- Commander-in-Chief;
- Chief Legislator.

PART 1
The President's Day
7 A.M. The day begins, naturally enough, in the bedroom. President Johnson is in his pajamas, reading through a pile of newspapers stacked on his bed. In one hand, he holds a remote-control switch that controls the three television sets in his room. This allows him to watch the morning news on three channels at once.

Now the President reaches for the

telephone. He wants to know what's happening in Congress with some *bills** he supports. "How about that housing bill?" he asks someone at the other end. "Did you get to the Hill [Capitol building] yet and see the *committee**? It's never going to get out of committee unless you fellows learn to go over there and talk for what you want."

8 A.M. The President is still making phone calls and leafing through the papers while a television set is on in the background. Mrs. Johnson comes into the room and joins him for breakfast. His two daughters, Lynda and Luci, follow close behind.

9 A.M. The President picks up the phone again and calls one person after another. He makes calls even while getting dressed. While straightening his tie, he has a thought, picks up the phone, and calls an assistant for the second time in 10 minutes. "This bill must be signed by midnight. Now you get in touch with these people, Jake. I mean now."

10 A.M. The President leaves his bedroom and walks down the hall to a large oval-shaped room — the President's Oval Office, it is called. Here, the President, through more than 200 assistants, directs the affairs of the U.S. government.

The President finds a large stack of letters on his desk. They're from strangers — citizens who for many reasons have written to the President. The President can look at only a fraction of the thousands of letters that are sent to him every week. But he is reading one of them now. It is from

a woman who wants to tell him how proud she is that her son was admitted to Harvard College. The President tells his secretary: "Remind me to write a letter of congratulations to this boy's mother."

The President walks out of the office into another room where 20 people are seated, waiting for him. They are all government officials in the U.S. Department of Defense. He tells them: "I want you to make certain that the American fighting man is the best-equipped soldier in history." There is loud applause at the end of the speech.

The President returns to his office. There are now a number of phone messages and lengthy reports on his desk. Hurriedly he scans the reports while making two phone calls.

11 A.M. Fifteen people are seated at a long oak table in the Cabinet room. Eleven of them direct the major de-

Lyndon Johnson

partments of the Executive Branch of government. A 12th person is the Vice-President, Hubert Humphrey. The other three people are the President's chief advisers. They all stand as the President enters the room and sit after he sits.

Everyone has a sheet of paper listing what will be discussed at this Cabinet meeting. First, the Secretary of Health, Education, and Welfare presents a report on his department. Then someone gives a report on how tough it will be to get an important *foreign aid** bill through Congress.

The President calls for action. Pointing a pencil at each person in the room, he tells them to speak to Congressmen. "If all of us know who has the ball, we're pretty sure to get the 10 votes we need, and maybe a few more. Don't phone them. Go over there."

12 noon. The Cabinet meeting continues into a second hour. Economic experts report the *economy** is strong. The Attorney General, who runs the Department of Justice, reports on what's being done to control riots in the cities. That's the final report on the list.

Now the President has the final word. He reminds everyone that an election is coming up soon. Democratic Congressmen will need help. There are a lot of Democratic accomplishments the voters want to know about, he says. "Go tell them," says the President, looking hard at each person at the table. "Remember, they don't pay you to come in second. We don't want to fail in November."

The President leaves the room.

1 P.M. A labor leader is waiting for him in the Oval Office. The President talks with him for 10 minutes. Then he returns to the Cabinet room to give a short speech to 41 state governors who have come to the White House for a meeting on highway safety.

Back again in his office, he glances through a stack of 50 letters and signs his name to all of them. A British political leader is brought in for a 10-minute chat. Two reporters from a Boston newspaper then get a 10-minute interview.

2 P.M. The President meets with three top assistants in private. Then there is a meeting on the Middle East situation with officials from the State Department. When they leave, the President returns to his desk for a few minutes — to try to catch up with the heavy stack of reports and notes that keep piling up on his desk.

3 P.M. The President has been working now for eight hours. He is tired and hungry. It is his habit to eat lunch in the middle of the afternoon and then nap for two hours. Joining Mrs. Johnson in the family dining room, he eats a plate of lamb chops and a bowl of tapioca pudding. Then he goes to bed.

PART 2
The President's Day

The President naps for two hours. He wakes at five, picks up the phone, and starts another seven hours of work. How many different roles can you find in this second half of the President's day?

5 P.M. The President spends 15 minutes greeting school children from Cotulla, Texas. He tells them about the days, early in his career, when he taught school in Cotulla.

6 P.M. The President asks two of his economic advisers: "Can't we get at least a few million dollars cut from this thing?" He is talking about the government budget for 1967.

7 P.M. There are more reports to be read about different problems in the Executive Branch. Johnson carries a stack of them into his bedroom and gets dressed for dinner.

8 P.M. A Marine band plays "Hail to the Chief" as the President and Mrs. Johnson enter a ballroom in the White House. Here they greet their two guests of honor — Ferdinand Marcos, President of the Philippines, and Mrs. Marcos.

9 P.M. The Marcoses and over 100 guests of the President take their seats in two White House dining rooms. An orchestra plays softly in the background.

10 P.M. After dinner there is a full hour of dancing and entertainment.

11 P.M. The Marcoses and most of the other guests leave. The Johnsons join a small group of friends from Texas, overnight guests in the White House.

12 P.M. In his bedroom, the President looks at the stacks of reports that he brought from the office. But he's too tired to read them. After two more telephone calls, the President settles back and falls asleep.

End of a day in a President's life.

SEVEN ROLES FOR ONE PRESIDENT

This chart is adapted from Clinton Rossiter,
The American Presidency (Harcourt, Brace & Co., 1960).

Roles	Examples of Behavior In Roles
1 Chief of State This role requires a President to be an inspiring example for the American people. In some nations, the chief of state is a king or a queen who wears a crown on special occasions, celebrates national holidays, and stands for the highest values and ideals of the country. As the American Chief of State, the President is a living symbol of the nation. It is considered a great honor for any citizen to shake the President's hand.	• Awarding medals to the winners of college scholarships. • Congratulating astronauts on their journey into space. • Greeting visitors to the White House. • Making a patriotic speech on the Fourth of July.
2 Chief Executive The President is "boss" for millions of government workers in the Executive Branch, deciding how the laws of the United States are to be enforced and choosing officials and advisers to help run the Executive Branch.	• Appointing someone to serve as head of the Central Intelligence Agency (CIA). • Holding a Cabinet meeting to discuss government business. • Reading reports about problems of the Federal Bureau of Investigation (FBI).
3 Chief Diplomat The President decides what American *diplomats** and *ambassadors** shall say to foreign governments. With the help of advisers, the President makes the *foreign policy** of the United States.	• Traveling to London to meet with British leaders. • Entertaining Japanese diplomats in the White House. • Writing a message or a letter to the leaders of the Soviet Union.

Roles	Examples of Behavior in Roles

4 Commander-in-Chief
The President is in charge of the U.S. armed forces—the Army, Navy, Air Force, and Marines. The President decides where troops shall be stationed, where ships shall be sent, and how weapons shall be used. All military generals and admirals take their orders from the President.

- Inspecting a Navy yard.
- Deciding, in wartime, whether to bomb foreign cities.
- Calling out troops to stop a riot.

5 Chief Legislator
Only Congress has the actual power to *make* laws. But the Constitution gives the President power to influence Congress in its lawmaking. Presidents may urge Congress to pass new laws or *veto** bills that they do not favor.

- Inviting members of Congress to lunch in the White House.
- Signing a bill of Congress.
- Making a speech in Congress.

6 Chief of Party
In this role, Presidents help members of their *political party** get elected or appointed to office. The President campaigns for those members who have supported the President's policies. At the end of a term the President may campaign for reelection.

- Choosing leading party members to serve in the Cabinet.
- Traveling to California to speak at a rally for a party nominee to the U.S. Senate.

7 Chief Guardian of the Economy
In this role, the President is concerned with such things as unemployment, high prices, taxes, business profits, and the general prosperity of the country. The President does not control the economy, but is expected to help it run smoothly.

- Meeting with economic advisers to discuss ways to reduce unemployment.
- Meeting with business and labor leaders to discuss their needs and problems.

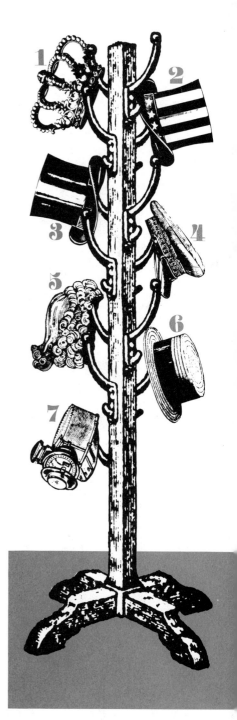

29

ACTION PROJECT

Almost every day, there are headline stories in the newspaper about the President's latest actions and decisions. These stories make greater sense if you know about the President's many roles.

These clippings are adapted from *The New York Times*. Each clipping shows President Ronald Reagan performing not just one role, but several roles at once. From reading and thinking about these clippings, you'll discover that the President's roles often overlap and support each other.

In each clipping, look for at least two roles that the President is carrying out. You may even find as many as three roles. Compare your answers with other students and then ask your teacher for the answers.

Later, at home, you could watch the evening news on TV and collect current examples of the President's roles.

39 AMERICAN HOSTAGES FREE AFTER 17 DAYS

Reagan Seeks Drive to Raise Productivity of U.S. Agencies

WASHINGTON, Feb. 19—In a draft report to Congress, President Reagan calls for a broad drive to achieve major increases in the productivity of all Federal agencies.

The President recommends that legislation be approved to give the Office of Management and Budget sweeping new authority to establish performance standards for a variety of Government tasks, thus setting the pace for Federal agencies.

The proposal was contained in the Reagan Administration's first "Overview Report on the Management of the U.S. Government," to be submitted Wednesday to Congress. Last year Congress ordered that such a report be produced annually to parallel the budgets that Presidents have been submitting to Congress for decades.

Disparity in Increases Cited

Available studies suggest that, Governmentwide, productivity increases have been only 1.5 percent a year since 1967, well below those achieved by many private corporations, the report says.

By 1992, it says, the President hopes to achieve a 20 percent increase in productivity in certain Government functions, which would help reduce the Federal deficit and contribute to a more prosperous national economy.

Reagan Apology to Backer

LOS ANGELES, Feb. 19 (AP)
President Reagan tried to apologize to an 84-year-old pensioner who ended up rummaging through trash in search of food because he could not say no to conservative groups seeking contributions.

The pensioner, Gerald Colf, believed he was being a good Republican last year when he gradually mailed all his savings, more than $4,200, to 27 conservative groups that sent him solicitations.

Mr. Colf's granddaughter, Judy Kerrigan, took action to stop the donations and get her grandfather's money back last fall. That was when Mr. Colf told her he had run out of money and had resorted to combing trash cans for food.

Mr. Reagan heard about Mr. Colf's plight this week and telephoned Mrs. Kerrigan on Monday morning. Robin Gray, a White House spokesman, confirmed the President's call today.

Mrs. Kerrigan was vacuuming her teenage daughter's room when the telephone rang in their home in the San Fernando Valley area of Los Angeles.

The operator said, " 'Hold on for the President,' and my reaction was, 'What president?' " Mrs. Kerrigan said.

Mr. Reagan's voice then came over the phone and he apologized for what happened to Mr. Colf, she said. She said the President told her that he appreciated Mr. Colf's support, but that if Mr. Colf got any future mail, "he should throw it in the trash."

Mr. Reagan did not talk to Mr. Colf, who entered a retirement home Sunday, Mrs. Kerrigan said.

At Mrs. Kerrigan's request, some groups have returned the contributions. So far $1,500 has been returned, she said.

REAGAN HAILS MOVE

In White House Talk, He Also Warns Terrorists 'We'll Fight Back'

WASHINGTON, June 30—President Reagan welcomed the release of the American hostages today, but said the United States "will not rest until justice is done" in Beirut as well as El Salvador.

"Terrorists be on notice," Mr. Reagan said in a nationally televised speech from the Oval Office as the freed Americans left Syria for West Germany. "We will fight back against you in Lebanon and elsewhere. We will fight back against your cowardly attacks on American citizens and property."

It was not clear from Mr. Reagan's strong words about hijackers and terrorists that he was hinting at the possibility that the United States would retaliate militarily for the Beirut hostage crisis.

But a ranking Administration official, who asked not to be identified, seemed to indicate that the United States had ruled out military retaliation against the Lebanese Shiites who seized Trans World Airlines Flight 847 on June 14, taking the passengers hostage and later killing one, a Navy diver named Robert Dean Stethem.

Knowledge of Terror Groups

Shortly after Mr. Reagan spoke, Secretary of State George P. Shultz appeared in the White House briefing room, where he emphasized what he said was the Government's determination to respond to terrorism.

"THE LAST WORD"

by Margaret Truman

Margaret Truman

What would happen to you if you became a star or celebrity overnight? How would your life change? This actually happened to a college youth, Margaret Truman (shown above launching a ship), and to her parents, Harry and Bess Truman.

President Franklin Roosevelt died suddenly in April 1945 and Vice-President Harry Truman took over as President.

Margaret quickly learned that there was a huge difference between the importance of President and Vice-Pres-

ident. In a book about her father, Margaret described the shock of stepping into the role of President's Daughter. The passage below is adapted from her book. It describes events that occurred when she was a college student at George Washington University.

At nine in the morning, Eddie McKim, an old friend of the family, arrived at the White House. Dad had called him the night before to ask for his help.

Eddie stood in front of Dad's desk, completely at a loss for words for the first time in his life.

Dad stared at him in astonishment.

"Do you have to stand there?" Dad asked.

"Well, Mr. President, I suddenly find myself in the presence of the President of the United States and I don't know how to act!"

It was Dad's first glimpse of the tremendous awe with which so many people regarded the Presidency. "Come on over here and sit down," he said.

A few days after Dad became President, I went back to school. It was terrible. I was followed by a mob of reporters and photographers everywhere I went. I was also trailed by the Secret Service man assigned to me, John Dorsey.

At first the photographers almost reduced me to tears. But after I had retreated to a private room and pulled myself together, my Truman common sense returned. I decided to let them take pictures until they wore themselves or their lenses out.

Then, I hoped, they would go away and stop bothering me and the rest of George Washington University. It worked beautifully.

I remained calm and invited my sorority sisters and even my professors to say cheese and let the photographers click away. They were satisfied by the end of the day. I have used this approach ever since.

There is really no point in trying to fight off the picture boys. If you try to beat them at their game, they will go out of their way to take bad pictures of you.

My father worried a good deal about the problems he was creating for the rest of the family. "It is a terrible — and I mean terrible — nuisance to be kin to the President of the United States," he told his mother and sister. "Reporters have been haunting every relative I ever heard of. And they've probably made life miserable for my mother, brother, and sister. I am sorry for it, but it can't be helped."

(YOU HAVE THE LAST WORD)

Imagine yourself living in the White House as a member of the President's family. How would people expect you to behave as either the President's Son or Daughter? Would you change your habits in order to fit the new role?

"CHECKOUT"—2

Key terms

Congressional bill
committee
foreign aid
economy

budget
Chief of State
Chief Executive
Chief Diplomat

Commander-in-Chief
Chief Legislator
Chief of Party
Chief Guardian of the Economy

Review

1. Name three of the President's roles.

2. When and how did Lyndon Johnson's day begin as President? Which of the following people did he talk with in the course of the one day: officials of the Defense Department, members of the Cabinet, a labor leader, state governors, reporters, school children, the President of the Philippines?

3. What role does a President play when making an official visit to a foreign country?

4. What role does a President play when greeting visitors to the White House?

5. How did Margaret Truman get photographers to stop bothering her for pictures?

Discussion

1. Your class might have a panel discussion of this question: Which of the President's roles is most important? You could have seven panel members, one to speak for each role. After questions and discussion, the class could vote on which they think is most important.

2. In 1988 the President had a salary of $200,000 a year. He was also allowed up to $170,000 a year for official expenses. In view of the President's duties, do you think this amount is fair? Too little? Too much? How does it compare with the salaries of sports stars, TV personalities, motion-picture actors, or corporation and union executives you may know about? After your class has discussed these questions, you might decide on a word or a number to complete this sentence: *The President of the United States should be paid* _____ .

3. What roles do you think members of a President's family should play? Should they take part in official ceremonies? Tell the President their opinions on political issues? Express these opinions publicly? Disagree openly with the President? Explain your answers.

4. Look back at the Seven Roles chart. It is unlikely, isn't it, that any person could be equally good in all seven roles? Suppose you were President. Which of the roles do you think you would perform best? Which would you have the most trouble with? Now, think about the current President. Which of the roles does he perform best? Which does he have the most trouble with?

5. Some Americans believe that the President, in addition to the roles already described, should be the moral leader of the nation. In other words, the President's behavior should set a good example for all Americans to follow. Decide whether you agree with this belief. Then prepare two arguments either supporting or attacking it. Be ready to present your arguments in class.

Activities

1. You might look through your daily newspaper for one week for stories about actions that the President has performed. Clip the most interesting and note on the clipping which of the seven roles it represents. Try to get examples of at least four different roles. A group of representative clippings from the class could be posted on the bulletin board.

2. You might imagine that you are the President of the United States. Write an imaginary hour-by-hour log or diary about your activities for one day. Include as much colorful detail as you wish. You might enjoy reading aloud parts of your account in class — as well as hearing those of other students.

3. If you have some drawing skill, you might try your hand at sketching a political leader — or someone else — playing a particular role.

4. You might research the experiences of the family members of one or more Presidents. For example, you might read such books as *Harry S. Truman* by Margaret Truman or *A White House Diary* by Lady Bird Johnson. Or you might look through newspapers and magazines for reports of the activities of members of the current President's family. You could prepare a report on your reading for the class.

5. You might imagine that you are the President's daughter or son. Write a short story, an essay, or a diary entry about one experience in this role.

6. Lyndon Johnson began his day by reading the newspapers and watching the news on TV. Later Presidents have kept in touch with the news in much the same way. You might imagine you are the President. You could watch the TV news this evening and make notes to help you in your Presidential duties. You might write the notes under these three headings: **(a)** *Things to keep an eye on,* **(b)** *Action to take,* **(c)** *What people are saying about me.*

Louis James

Helen Swift

Henry Rosenthal

Susan Dorf

3: WHO'S QUALIFIED TO BE PRESIDENT?

You've now seen what the President must do. You've seen the roles the President plays and the types of decisions that must be made. Knowing all this, what kind of person can best do the job of being President?

Think of the four people pictured on the opposite page as candidates for President. Which of them, in your judgment, would be best qualified for the job?

Briefly, this is the life story of each candidate:

Susan Dorf. Born in Michigan 18 years ago. Was graduated from a private school for girls. Plans to go to college,
get married, and raise six children. Her mother is president of a university. Her father is vice-president of a major corporation.

Henry Rosenthal. Born in Nuremberg, Germany, in 1931. Moved with family to United States to escape anti-Jewish laws of Nazi government. Became American citizen in 1951. Was graduated from Harvard College where he made highest grades. Became a professor of government. Has published many books on U.S. foreign policy. In 1979 the President appointed him to important post in U.S. government.

Helen Swift. Born in Melbourne,

Australia, in 1949. Rose quickly to stardom as a singer. Came to United States in 1974 and became American citizen six years ago. She is interested in politics and supports candidates who believe in equal rights for women.

Louis James. Born in Boston. Won national fame playing for his high school basketball team. Led college team to championship. Entered politics 8 years ago at the age of 25 and campaigned unsuccessfully for a seat in Congress.

Constitutional requirements for President. Have you made your choice? Could your candidate meet the legal requirements for President as written in the Constitution? Article II of the Constitution says:

"No person except a natural born citizen . . . shall be eligible to the office of President; neither shall any person be eligible to that office who shall not have attained to the age of 35 years, and been 14 years a resident within the United States."

Which two of our "candidates" can never be President (unless the Constitution is amended)? Which two are not now qualified, but must wait until they're old enough?

Many Americans today are like Susan Dorf and Louis James. They're too young to be President. In 1980, when the U.S. government last counted the population, 132 million Americans were under 35. 14 million were disqualified because they were born outside the United States to foreign parents.

Still, we are left with approximately 89 million people who *are* American born and who *are* old enough to be President, according to the Constitution. Out of those millions, whom will we choose to lead the nation?

Political requirements for President. Obviously, some citizens over 35 would make better candidates than others. But which ones stand a fairly good chance of actually being chosen as candidates?

In America's two-party system, a person is chosen as a candidate at either the Republican party convention or the Democratic party convention. Every four years, politicians from these two major parties seek a candidate who they think can win the most votes in the November election. A third-party candidate *could* be elected President. But as a practical matter, it would be difficult.

History tells us what qualifications a candidate seems to need to win the race. From 1789 to 1987, there were

38

WHO CAN BE PRESIDENT?

50 elections for President, but only 39 people held the job. The chart on pages 40–41 gives facts about the backgrounds of these 39 Presidents.

From it, you can discover that most Presidents so far have been well-educated (even though neither George Washington nor Abraham Lincoln got more than a few years of schooling). Thirty former Presidents went to college and 24 of these were graduated. It seems, therefore, that people with a college degree stand a better chance of being President than people who quit school early.

What other things did Americans look for in these 39 Presidents? Did they think a person's religion was important? Was it important whether a President was male or female? Did it matter whether the person came from a large state or a small one? The chart gives us the answers. Studying this chart, you can discover for yourself some of the standards Americans have used to select their leaders.

Using the chart, answer these questions on a separate sheet of paper.

1. Sex of the Presidents:
How many Presidents were men?
How many were women?

2. Religion of the Presidents:
How many Presidents were Protestants?
How many were Roman Catholics?
How many were Jewish?
How many did not belong to any organized religion?

3. Ancestry of the Presidents:
How many Presidents had ancestors who lived in England, Scotland, or Wales?
How many Presidents had ancestors who were *not* from England, Scotland, or Wales?

4. Early career of the Presidents:
How many Presidents were trained as lawyers?
How many Presidents were experienced in politics early in life?
How many Presidents were neither politicians nor lawyers?

5. Home state of the Presidents:
How many Presidents came from one of the largest states in the country?
How many Presidents came from one of the smallest states in the country?

6. A typical American President:
Complete this sentence: An American President is usually _____ (male or female); belongs to the _____ religion; has _____ (ancestry) ancestors; has experience as both a _____ and a _____ (career); and comes from a _____ (large or small) state.

WHO ARE THE PRESIDENTS?

President	Sex	Higher Education	Religion	Ancestry	Size of Home State*	Early Career
George Washington (1789–1797)	Male	No	Protestant	British	Large (Virginia)	Politician & Military leader
John Adams (1797–1801)	Male	Yes	Protestant	British	Large (Massachusetts)	Lawyer
Thomas Jefferson (1801–1809)	Male	Yes	No church	British & Irish	Large (Virginia)	Lawyer & politician
James Madison (1809–1817)	Male	Yes	Protestant	British	Large (Virginia)	Politician
James Monroe (1817–1825)	Male	Yes	Protestant	British	Large (Virginia)	Lawyer & politician
John Quincy Adams (1825–1829)	Male	Yes	Protestant	British	Large (Massachusetts)	Lawyer
Andrew Jackson (1829–1837)	Male	No	Protestant	British & Irish	Medium (Tennessee)	Lawyer, politician, & military leader
Martin Van Buren (1837–1841)	Male	No	Protestant	Dutch	Large (New York)	Lawyer & politician
William Henry Harrison (1841)	Male	Yes	Protestant	British	Large (Ohio)	Military leader
John Tyler (1841–1845)	Male	Yes	Protestant	British	Large (Virginia)	Lawyer & politician
James Polk (1845–1849)	Male	Yes	Protestant	British & Irish	Medium (Tennessee)	Lawyer & politician
Zachary Taylor (1849–1850)	Male	No	Protestant	British	Medium (Louisiana)	Military leader
Millard Fillmore (1850–1853)	Male	No	Protestant	British	Large (New York)	Lawyer & politician
Franklin Pierce (1853–1857)	Male	Yes	Protestant	British	Small (New Hampshire)	Lawyer & politician
James Buchanan (1857–1861)	Male	Yes	Protestant	British & Irish	Large (Pennsylvania)	Lawyer & politician
Abraham Lincoln (1861–1865)	Male	No	No church	British	Medium (Illinois)	Storekeeper, lawyer, politician
Andrew Johnson (1865–1869)	Male	No	No church	British & Irish	Medium (Tennessee)	Tailor & politician
Ulysses S. Grant (1869–1877)	Male	Yes	Protestant	British	Large (Illinois)	Military leader
Rutherford B. Hayes (1877–1881)	Male	Yes	Protestant	British	Large (Ohio)	Military leader, lawyer, & politician
James A. Garfield (1881)	Male	Yes	Protestant	British & French	Large (Ohio)	Carpenter, teacher, & lawyer

President	Sex	Higher Education	Religion	Ancestry	Size of Home State*	Early Career
Chester A. Arthur (1881–1885)	Male	Yes	Protestant	British & Irish	Large (New York)	Teacher & lawyer
Grover Cleveland (1885–1889; 1893–1897)	Male	No	Protestant	British & French	Large (New York)	Clerk & lawyer
Benjamin Harrison (1889–1893)	Male	Yes	Protestant	British	Large (Indiana)	Lawyer & politician
William McKinley (1897–1901)	Male	Yes	Protestant	British & Irish	Large (Ohio)	Lawyer & politician
Theodore Roosevelt (1901–1909)	Male	Yes	Protestant	Dutch & French	Large (New York)	Author & politician
William Howard Taft (1909–1913)	Male	Yes	Protestant	British	Large (Ohio)	Lawyer
Woodrow Wilson (1913–1921)	Male	Yes	Protestant	British & Irish	Medium (New Jersey)	Teacher & lawyer
Warren Harding (1921–1923)	Male	Yes	Protestant	British & Dutch	Large (Ohio)	Newspaperman & politician
Calvin Coolidge (1923–1929)	Male	Yes	Protestant	British	Medium (Massachusetts)	Lawyer & politician
Herbert Hoover (1929–1933)	Male	Yes	Protestant	Swiss-German	Large (California)	Engineer & business leader
Franklin D. Roosevelt (1933–1945)	Male	Yes	Protestant	Dutch & French	Large (New York)	Lawyer & politician
Harry S. Truman (1945–1953)	Male	No	Protestant	British & Irish	Medium (Missouri)	Storekeeper & politician
Dwight D. Eisenhower (1953–1961)	Male	Yes	Protestant	Swiss-German	Large (New York)	Military leader
John F. Kennedy (1961–1963)	Male	Yes	Roman Catholic	Irish	Medium (Massachusetts)	Author & politician
Lyndon B. Johnson (1963–1969)	Male	Yes	Protestant	British	Large (Texas)	Teacher & politician
Richard M. Nixon (1969–1974)	Male	Yes	Protestant	British & Irish	Large (New York)	Lawyer & politician
Gerald R. Ford (1974–1977)	Male	Yes	Protestant	British	Medium (Michigan)	Lawyer & politician
Jimmy Carter (1977–1981)	Male	Yes	Protestant	British	Medium (Georgia)	Farmer & politician
Ronald Reagan (1981–1989)	Male	Yes	Protestant	Irish & Scots	Large (California)	Actor & politician

*Size when President elected.

We know from the chart that religion, education, and occupation have been important to American voters in the past. But are they important to you and other students in the class? This Action Project will help you pinpoint some of *your* values in choosing leaders.

Tear a sheet of paper into four pieces. Each piece of paper will be a secret ballot on one of the following questions. Mark your ballots **A, B, C,** and **D.** Write your answer to each question on the matching ballot.

Ballot A. Suppose you were given a choice between a male and a female candidate for President. Both candidates seem to have the same ability. Which would you probably prefer?
- The male candidate.
- The female candidate.
- The sex of the candidate would not matter.

Ballot B. Suppose you were given a choice between Protestant, Catholic, and Jewish candidates for President. All candidates seem to have the same ability. Which would you probably prefer?

- The Protestant candidate.
- The Catholic candidate.
- The Jewish candidate.
- The religion of the candidate would not matter.

Ballot C. Suppose you were given a choice between candidates for President who have had different careers. All candidates seem to have the same ability. Which would you probably prefer?
- The candidate who has been both a lawyer and a politician.
- The candidate who has been a military leader.
- The candidate who has been a business leader.
- The candidate who has been a teacher, a farmer, or a labor leader.
- The occupation of the candidate would not matter.

Ballot D. Suppose you were given a choice between candidates for President who came from different regions of the country. All candidates seem to have the same ability. Which would you probably prefer?
- The candidate who comes from the Far West.
- The candidate who comes from the Northeast.
- The candidate who comes from the South.
- The candidate who comes from the Middle West.
- The home state of the candidate would not matter.

Collect and count all ballots. Write the results on the chalkboard. Do you think other classes of students throughout the country would vote as you did? Do you think that, in the future, Americans should continue to use

PRESIDENTS SHOULD BE...

shrewd   honest   brave
kind   strong   firm
patient   fair   healthy
determined   intelligent   good-looking
wise   friendly   hard-working

the same standards for choosing Presidents? Or should they use different standards?

The personality of a leader. We still have not dug down very deeply as we've tried to discover what Americans look for in their Presidents. We know what the Constitution says about who can be President. We also know the kind of background Americans prefer in their President. But what about the personality of the candidate? What about his or her character?

Above is a list of 15 personality traits. Suppose a President should have at least five of these qualities.

Which ones do you consider the most important? Study the list of words several times before deciding. Then write your five choices on a separate piece of paper.

Compare your choices with those of other students. Which qualities does everyone think are the most important? Which ones are the least important?

The person you have just described in five words is an ideal type. He or she may or may not exist in real life. It is helpful to know what your ideal is. But you must remember that all people, no matter how strong they are in some ways, have their faults and weaknesses.

"THE LAST WORD"

by Robert Sherwood

Many people think Franklin D. Roosevelt was one of the best qualified of all American Presidents. They believe this even though he had a serious physical handicap. A victim of polio, he could not walk in all the years that he was President. Nevertheless, he was an active leader. The photo on the next page shows him asking Congress to declare war on Japan in 1941.

In the reading below, Robert Sherwood, an author and close friend of the President, explains why this leader was loved and admired by so many Americans. His description was written shortly after Roosevelt's death in 1945.

To those of us who knew and loved President Roosevelt, the greatest memory we hold today is the memory of his good humor, his great courage, his love for our country, his faith in our country.

In the depths of the Depression—in the blackest hours of war—there was nothing strong enough to shake that faith.

I shall always remember the true quality and character of Mr. Roosevelt in the hours and days that followed the sudden attack on Pearl Harbor. [The Japanese had bombed American ships at Pearl Harbor, Hawaii, in December 1941, destroying most of our Navy.]

That was a body blow against this nation. For a lesser nation, it might have been a knockout punch.

And yet—when the attack came—Mr. Roosevelt showed the iron that was in him, the iron that is in the heart and soul of our country, the iron that has made the United States of America great.

In those hours and days that followed Pearl Harbor, the city of Washington was troubled with jitters. Some people who knew about the terrible damage to our Navy were talking of "disaster."

But—when I went into the White House in those hours and days, when I saw the President himself—I heard no talk of "disaster," no jitters. I knew then that I was back in America. The President knew—better, perhaps, than any man who ever lived—he knew what Americans are and what Americans can do.

The President knew people. And, precisely because he knew them, he loved them and had faith in them.

I hesitate to speak now of my personal feelings at his death. I had the honor to be numbered among his friends. But that was a very large company—a company large enough to include the entire human race.

He was a good man. He was a decent man. He was a friendly, patient, supremely tolerant man. I never saw him lose his temper with anyone who was working for him and working for

Franklin Roosevelt

our country. I have seen him insulted and driven beyond what seemed to me the limits of human endurance. But I have never seen him to be anything less than great under pressure. I have never in my life known anyone to be so consistently kindly, so downright sympathetic and understanding.

Mr. Roosevelt was a serene person. He took things in his stride. He took economic crisis in his stride; he took Adolf Hitler in his stride; he took Pearl Harbor in his stride. He took his whole awesome job in his stride.

I don't know about the final minutes of his life. But I'm certain of one thing: He took Death in his stride too.

(YOU HAVE THE LAST WORD)

How does Franklin Roosevelt (as Sherwood saw him) compare with today's President? Does today's President have all the traits that Sherwood says Roosevelt had? A sense of humor? A strong belief in the American people? Patience and tolerance? Are these the *most* important qualifications for being President? What other qualifications do you think a President should have?

"CHECKOUT"—3

Key terms

constitutional requirements
ballot

candidate
qualifications

convention

Review

1. List the three constitutional qualifications for the Presidency.

2. Choose the word that best fits the following sentence: *Most Presidents of the U. S. have had* (uninteresting, different, poor, similar) *backgrounds.*

3. Describe three features of a "typical" President from 1789 to 1987.

4. What feature of a "typical" President was shared by all of the Presidents listed?

5. Besides background and experience, what other traits are important in a President?

Discussion

1. Think about the Constitution's three requirements — concerning age, citizenship, and residence — for qualifying to be President. What do you think of these requirements? Are there any you think should be changed or dropped? What requirements, if any, would you add? Be ready to give reasons for your answers in class.

2. The typical President is male, Protestant, of British ancestry, has experience as a lawyer and politician, and comes from a large state. Why do you think Americans have usually chosen Presidents of this type? Are different types of Presidents more likely to be elected today? Which categories could most easily be changed? Which might be the last to change? Are there any categories you think should *not* be changed?

3. You've been taking separate looks at different kinds of Presiden-

tial qualifications. Now it's time to bring them all together. What is your picture of an *ideal* President?

4. How important in winning an election do you think a candidate's views on issues are — compared to a candidate's background? Compared to a candidate's personality?

Activities

1. You might select a book about the President or Presidents from the bibliography at the end of this unit. Read the short review after each title to see which one sounds the most interesting to you. After you read the book, you could prepare a class report on the qualifications and personality of one of the Presidents described.

2. Using encyclopedias or biographies, you might write brief profiles of any two Presidents and their chief rivals for election. Make sure you include the same kind of information for each: ancestry, religion, experience, home state, personality, age (at election), views on the issues of their day. Also, you might look for photos or portraits and include your opinion of each person's looks. To what extent do you think the differences you found between rival candidates led to the election result? You could report your findings to the class.

3. You might take your own public opinion poll on Presidential qualifications. Each question should be on the lines of: *Would you vote for a Presidential candidate who ...?* Complete the questions on the basis of the qualifications and standards discussed in

the chapter. For example, two questions could be: *Would you vote for a Presidential candidate who was a woman? Would you vote for a Presidential candidate who was a black person?*

You could take the poll among other students, friends, or family members. After you add up the *Yes, No, Not sure* answers to each question, you could present the results to the class.

4. A section of the classroom might be set aside for a display, perhaps titled "Gallery of Our Political Leaders." A committee of students could prepare letters to the offices of the President and Vice-President of the United States, asking for pictures of them for the classroom display.

5. Some students might be interested in researching this topic: *Women who might have made great Presidents.* Each student could focus on one woman in the past and prepare a report for class discussion. Other students could report on: *Women who might become President.*

6. If a Presidential election campaign is in progress, you might analyze the backgrounds and personalities of all the major candidates. Consult the factors discussed in this chapter of the text. Arrange your findings and put them on a chart. Based on only these factors — the backgrounds and personalities of the candidates — come to your own conclusions on which candidates have the best chance of winning.

You might discuss your findings with others in the class.

4: RUNNING THE EXECUTIVE BRANCH

The President is in charge of a giant organization called the Executive Branch of the U.S. government. Nobody has seen this entire organization —although everybody has seen parts of it. Nobody really knows what the Executive Branch looks like. It's much too big to be seen and much too complicated.

An artist once pictured the Executive Branch as a series of pipes feeding into the White House. (See the illustration on the opposite page.) The pipes reach out to every federal *agency** in the country, every social security office, every military base.

In this chapter, you'll learn how this huge network of offices and government services is organized and controlled.

Two parts of the Executive Branch. Let's look first at two of the biggest and best known parts of the Executive Branch. One of these is the Defense Department. To understand the size of this organization, ask yourself these questions:

Which is greater?
(a) The population of Los Angeles.
(b) The number of Americans working for the Defense Department.

Which is greater?
(a) The population of the whole state of Wyoming.
(b) The number of Americans wearing an Army uniform.

Which is greater?
(a) The number of offices and telephones in the Empire State Building.
(b) The number of offices and telephones in the Pentagon (above; a five-sided building on the outskirts of Washington where the Department of Defense has its headquarters).

In every case the answer is **(b)**.

In 1985 the U.S. Department of Defense employed about three million people. More than one million of these were in the Army. The rest were either serving in the other branches of the armed forces or working in the Pentagon. The telephone system in the Pentagon is the largest in the world with more than 45,000 phones.

Because the Defense Department is so large, it may be more difficult to manage than most nations of the world. The person who tries to manage it every day cannot, by law, be in military service. His or her title is Secretary of Defense.

The Defense Department—large as it is—is only one part of the Executive Branch of government. Another part is called the Social Security Administration.

Every month, this huge organization mails checks to about 22 million retirees. It sends another 15 million checks to disabled workers, widows, orphaned children, and mothers of children without fathers. In 1985 the total *benefits** paid to people who qualified under the law was 186 billion dollars.

How do you take part in the social security system? First, by receiving a card with a nine-digit number on it like this: 070–34–4441. Throughout your working life, you and your employer pay taxes regularly to a special social security fund. When you retire after a certain age, you may collect monthly checks.

The law that creates this system of social security is complicated. And it changes almost every year.

The *administrator** in charge of seeing that the system runs correctly has a challenging job. So do hundreds of other administrators who run other systems and try to enforce other federal laws. But all of their problems (problems of the Secretary of Defense + problems of the Social Security Administrator + problems of all other administrators in the Executive Branch) finally become the problems of the Chief Executive, the President of the U.S.

Managing the bureaucracy.

Historian Clinton Rossiter points out the trouble Presidents sometimes have in getting government bureaus to carry out their programs. "I wonder how many thousands of times some stubborn or fainthearted official has made a mockery of the President's good intentions," he says. And he quotes President Franklin Roosevelt, who said:

"The Treasury Department is so large and far-flung and ingrained in its practices that I find it almost impossible to get the action and results I want. . . .

"But the Treasury is not to be compared with the State Department. You should go through the experience of trying to get any changes in the thinking, policy, and action of the career diplomats and then you'd know what a real problem was.

"But the Treasury and the State Departments are nothing compared with the Navy. . . . To change anything in the Navy is like punching a feather bed. You punch it with your right and you punch it with your left until you are finally exhausted. Then you find the bed just as it was before you started punching."

Roosevelt was complaining about something called a *bureaucracy.**

To understand this term, think of a pile of cardboard boxes. Think of each box as a government office. Many boxes or offices are placed side by side at the bottom of the pile. One box or office is on top. In between are rows of offices that get fewer in number as you move to the top. In other words, the pile looks like a pyramid.

The person in the top office commands the people in the next row of offices. The second row commands the third row and so on.

The diagram on the opposite page shows how the federal bureaucracy is organized. Imagine that you are one of the unit chiefs at the bottom of the bureaucracy. What department are you in? Who is your boss? Who is the boss of your boss? Who is the boss of your boss's boss? Follow the diagram all the way up to the President's office.

The diagram leaves out more offices than it shows. Each department head has a string of bureau chiefs under him or her. And under each bureau chief, there exists a string of division chiefs.

There is no room to show all of this on one page of a book. You must try to imagine what the total structure looks like.

The Cabinet and the Civil Service.
The diagram shows only four department heads reporting to the Chief Executive. In 1988 there were 13. They make up the President's Cabinet. The Secretary of Defense is one department head. Others and the work of their departments are described in the Guide to Government Services (pages 55–57). Every week, the department heads meet together to report to the President on government business.

How does a person get to be a member of the President's Cabinet? Politics plays a big part. A Republican President usually chooses Republican politicians to serve in the Cabinet. A Democratic President usually chooses Democrats.

To please different sections of the country, the President may try to appoint at least one Southerner, one Easterner, one Westerner, and one Midwesterner. Cabinet members are often expected to help the President keep his own political party in power.

When a President takes office, his first task is to appoint a team of people to help him. He has the power to fill over 4,000 government jobs with members from his own party. This may seem like a lot. In fact, it's only a fraction of what it used to be.

One hundred years ago, almost all government workers were chosen for their politics. Today, over 85 percent are chosen for their special skills.

A Civil Service Commission — not the President — controls the hiring of most government workers. If you want to work for the Executive Branch, you'll probably have to take a civil service test. The kind of test depends on the kind of job you're seeking.

If you score 70 or better on the test, your name will go on a long list of qualified people. You'll be hired, however, only if you score higher than most of the other qualified candidates. The salary you receive and future promotions are also strictly controlled by civil service laws.

Outside the giant bureaucracies.
Most civil servants work for one of the 13 departments—Department of the Treasury, Department of Defense, etc. Each of these is headed by a Cabinet member. Even the smallest of these

LOOKING AT THE BUREAUCRACY

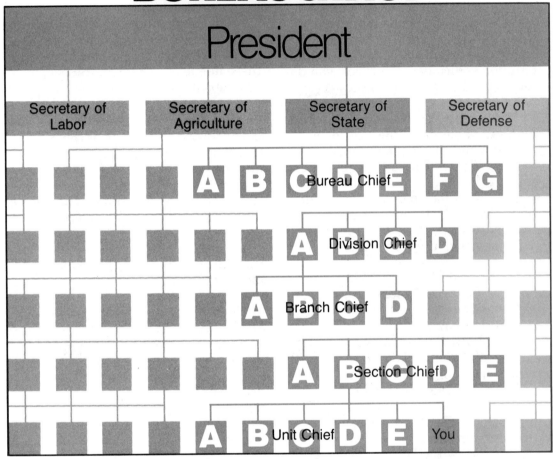

The colored boxes in this diagram of the federal bureaucracy help you to trace one branch of the organization.

great organizations employs almost 5,000 people and spends more than 16 billion dollars a year. But within the Executive Branch there are more than a million additional employees who do not work for any of the 13 departments.

• **The Office of Management and Budget,** which helps the President make the budget for the government.

• **The White House Office,** which employs the President's personal *staff.** A staff member can be assigned to almost any task—answering the President's mail, preparing speeches, giving advice and information.

• **The Federal Reserve System,** which controls the flow of money in the nation's banks.

• **The U.S. Postal Service,** which employs 744,000 workers to deliver 140 billion pieces of mail every year.

Notice the dividing line between the first two offices and the last two. The offices above the line take orders directly from the President. The agencies below the line do not take orders from the President. We call them *independent agencies.**

Some independent agencies have the power to make rules over various activities of American life. We call these agencies *regulatory agencies.** For example, the Federal Communications Commission makes rules about radio and television broadcasting. The Food and Drug Administration makes rules about the content of the food, medicine, and other products we

buy. The Interstate Commerce Commission makes rules about transporting goods from one state to another.

The President's only power over these agencies is to pick the people who run their governing boards.

Boss's orders: Should they be questioned? All parts of the Executive Branch are supposed to carry out laws passed by Congress. Each bureau and office is supposed to do only those things that the law allows. But sometimes government officials disagree about what the law allows.

For example, suppose you work for the FBI, which is part of the Department of Justice. Your boss tells you to collect information about college students suspected of being "disloyal" Americans. Your boss tells you to listen in on their telephone conversations and to read their mail.

You wonder whether these methods are permitted by law. But you're afraid to ask your boss about it. The boss goes into a rage whenever his orders are challenged.

What then should you do?

(**a**) Carry out your orders, assuming your boss knows best.

(**b**) Tell your boss your doubts about the assignment.

(**c**) Write a note to the Director of the FBI, complaining about your boss's orders.

(**d**) Write a note to the Attorney General, who is the head of the Justice Department.

(**e**) Write a note to the President.
Explain your choice.

GUIDE TO GOVERNMENT SERVICES

Every American citizen is entitled to seek services from the Executive Branch. After all, government was created for your needs, not the other way around. This chart tells you what services are available from the 13 departments in the Executive Branch.

Department	Services	People Most Often Helped
Department of Agriculture 14th St. and Independence Ave. SW Washington, D.C. 20250 **Head:** Secretary of Agriculture	Helps provide electricity and telephone services in rural areas. Inspects plants and animals for evidence of disease. Finds markets for farm crops. Pays farmers *subsidies** when their crops bring too low a price.	Farmers Conservation groups
Department of Commerce 14th St. between Constitution Ave. and E St. NW Washington, D.C. 20230 **Head:** Secretary of Commerce	Collects information on U.S. industries. Helps find foreign markets for American goods. Protects and develops ocean's resources. Runs National Weather Service. Issues *patents** for new inventions. Counts the population and gathers other *statistics** to aid in business and government planning.	Business people Scientists Professors Lawyers
Department of Defense The Pentagon Washington, D.C. 20301 **Head:** Secretary of Defense	Plans defense of U.S. against possible attack. Builds new weapons systems. Runs Army, Navy, and Air Force. Advises President on military problems.	Aircraft and weapons manufacturers Friendly foreign governments
Department of Education 400 Maryland Ave. SW Washington, D.C. 20202 **Head:** Secretary of Education	Oversees all federal assistance to education and compliance to civil rights laws in schools receiving assistance. Promotes improvements in education by collecting and disseminating information on successful school programs and encouraging state and local government involvement.	Teachers School administrators Students

Department	Services	People Most Often Helped
Department of Energy 1000 Independence Ave. Washington, D.C. 20585 **Head:** Secretary of Energy	Researches new ways of generating energy. Promotes energy conservation. Runs the nuclear weapons program. Regulates energy production, use, pricing. Tries to protect environment, safeguard consumers.	Oil and gas producers Scientists
Department of Health and Human Services 200 Independence Ave. SW Washington, D.C. 20201 **Head:** Secretary of Health and Human Services	Supports research in health. Operates Centers for Disease Control. Helps states fight drug abuse and alcoholism. Inspects food and drugs for health hazards. Helps disabled citizens find work. Collects social security tax and sends monthly checks to those who qualify. Helps pay for medical care for elderly.	Doctors and patients Old people Blind and disabled people Retired workers Unemployed people Poor people
Department of Housing and Urban Development 451 Seventh St. SW Washington, D.C. 20410 **Head:** Secretary of Housing and Urban Development	Provides low-interest loans for construction of housing for the poor, the elderly, and the handicapped. Helps finance community services construction. Helps low income families pay rent and get *mortgages*** for housing. Gives grants for fixing up run-down neighborhoods.	Homeowners Apartment dwellers Local governments State governments Savings and loan banks Minority groups Real estate people Neighborhood associations
Department of Interior C St. between 18th and 19th Sts. NW Washington, D.C. 20240 **Head:** Secretary of the Interior	Runs the national parks. Protects fish and wildlife. Searches the U.S. for new mineral resources. Provides information on all lands and waters in U.S. Helps Indians meet needs of health, education, and employment. Manages 450 million acres of mineral and forest lands. Supports programs of outdoor recreation. Irrigates arid lands.	Tourists and vacationers Indians Conservation groups Mining companies Lumber companies Farmers Scientists
Department of Justice Constitution Ave. and 10th St., NW Washington, D.C. 20530 **Head:** Attorney General	Employs FBI to search out violators of federal law. Argues cases of federal law to the courts. Defends the U.S. government against legal suits. Runs federal prisons. Controls *immigration*** to the U.S. and the granting of citizenship. Assists state and local police with problems of law enforcement.	Civil rights groups *Consumer*** groups Conservation groups Law enforcement groups Lawyers Local and state police Persons seeking citizenship

GUIDE TO GOVERNMENT SERVICES

Department	Services	People Most Often Helped
Department of Labor 200 Constitution Ave. NW Washington, D.C. 20210 **Head:** Secretary of Labor	Supports employment bureaus, run by the states. Provides job training for youth, veterans, and unemployed workers. Pays the states for giving workers unemployment benefits. Helps to settle disputes between unions and businesses. Sets up standards of safety in factories and office buildings. Gathers statistics on nation's labor force.	Wage earners Labor unions Unemployed people Youth Business people
Department of State 2201 C St. NW Washington, D.C. 20520 **Head:** Secretary of State	Advises President on foreign policy. Negotiates treaties and agreements with foreign nations. Collects information about foreign nations. Issues passports to Americans traveling abroad. Represents U.S. abroad and in international agencies.	Business people with interests in foreign trade Tourists Foreign governments
Department of Transportation 400 Seventh St. SW Washington, D.C. 20590 **Head:** Secretary of Transportation	Runs the Coast Guard, which makes ports and harbors safe for navigation. Controls planes, airports, and air traffic through Federal Aviation Administration (FAA). Builds federal highways and aids building of state highways. Gives financial help to the nation's railroads. Gives money to states and cities for mass transit systems (buses and subways). Sets up standards of highway safety.	Airlines Railroads Road construction companies State governments Boat owners Shipping companies
Department of the Treasury 1500 Pennsylvania Ave. NW Washington, D.C. 20220 **Head:** Secretary of the Treasury	Collects income taxes through Internal Revenue Service (IRS). Coins and prints money (Bureau of the Mint). Runs Secret Service for guarding President and Vice-President and protecting money against *counterfeiting.** Sells U.S. Savings Bonds. Supervises national banks. Collects *duty** on *imported** goods. Enforces regulations and laws on all foreign goods brought into the U.S.	Bankers Accountants Law enforcement groups Importers

A B C D

ACTION PROJECT

What can the federal bureaucracy do for you? You will get some ideas by matching the government services on pages 55–57 with the needs of the eight citizens listed here. Imagine that all eight people have written letters asking the government for help. But they don't know which of the 13 departments would best be able to help them. Therefore, they don't know how to address the envelopes.

Write the letters **A** to **H** on a piece of paper. Then, for each person, write the name and address of the department that's most likely to help. (In some cases, a citizen could be helped by more than one department.)

E F G H

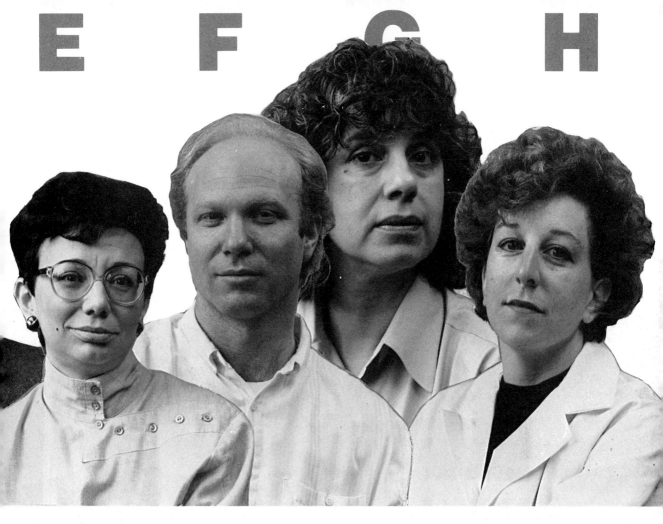

A. Carl Babbit. Owns chain of quality grocery stores in Oregon. Wants to put a gourmet food section of mostly imported items in each of his stores.

B. Angela Wickes. Computer scientist from New Jersey. Wants to protect her invention of a computer hardware component against copying by competitors.

C. Jim Lopez. Community health officer from Wisconsin. Seeks latest information on AIDS virus.

D. Anthony Scarpula. High school principal from Colorado. Needs help solving vandalism problem in his school.

E. Nancy French. Mother of four children from Tennessee. Wants to know about accommodations in national parks for family vacation.

F. Alan Skolnik. *Political activist** from Vermont. Seeks federal aid for a community clean-up and repair project.

G. Helen Pappas. Moved to Ohio with her family from Greece. Wants to know how she and her family can become U.S. citizens.

H. Bonnie Dawson. Professor of marine biology from California. Seeks government aid to continue her research on the migration patterns of whales in the Pacific.

"THE LAST WORD"

by C. Northcote Parkinson

What can go wrong with an organization as large as the Executive Branch? The problems of a bureaucracy have been studied by many people, including a British writer, C. Northcote Parkinson. The following passage is adapted from Parkinson's book, The Law of Delay.

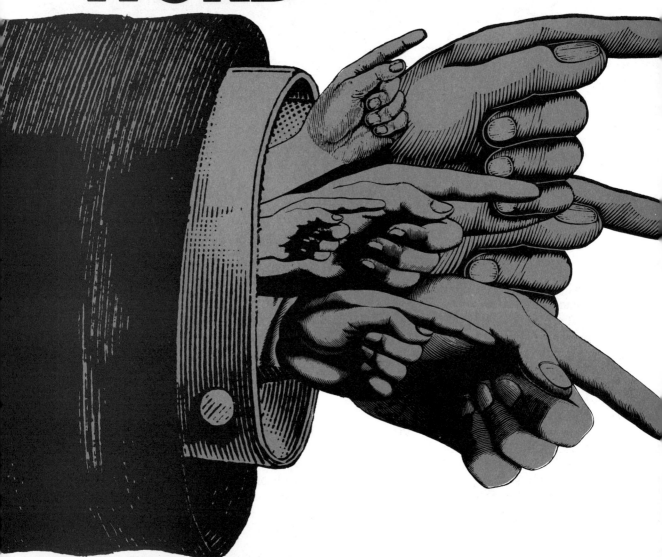

The phrase "passing the buck" is commonly heard in both the United States and Great Britain. It means that one person, the "buck-passer," shifts the responsibility for making a decision to another person. Doing so, he tries to avoid all possible blame for having given the wrong answer. This is, of course, a common practice in the over-organized world of today.

Buck-passing is practiced in every large organization. But it is especially common in the Civil Service. Most lower-level decisions in government almost always need to be approved by an upper-level official.

The process begins, let us say, with a project idea that lands on the desk of a young official named Bottomley. Although very inexperienced, he sees right away that the answer to the application must be either "Yes" or "No." Fearing the "Yes" may involve him in a lot of extra work, he suggests the answer "No." He does this lightheartedly because he knows that the final decision is made on a higher level. So Bottomley sends the file to his boss, Underleigh.

Underleigh is thinking of something else that day and fails to form an opinion of any sort. Absentmindedly, he notes on the file that he agrees with Bottomley. He passes it on to Middlebloke, knowing of course that the final decision will not be his. Middlebloke, with other things on his mind, repeats the "No" of others and passes the file to Upperman. But Upperman has come to rely upon Middlebloke, whose ability has been tested over the years. He writes a formal nega-tive reply and sends it to Topdog for his signature.

It is one of the weaknesses of the pyramid process that nearly everything is sent up to Topdog's desk. He can do no more than glance at the papers he has to sign, relying on Upperman to see that each decision is the right one. Out goes the reply and the answer is "No."

What is wrong with the paper-passing process is that everyone relies upon everyone else. The person at the top assumes that the whole subject has been thoroughly studied by the people at the bottom. In the imaginary case described, each executive assumed that the work would be done or had been done on another level. Instead, no work had been done by anyone.

(YOU HAVE THE LAST WORD)

Is it so unusual to "pass the buck"? When you fail at something or make a bad mistake, what are you more likely to say:

(a) "Sorry, my mistake. I take full responsibility for it."

(b) "It's not really my fault. Other people talked me into it."

If you were in charge of a group of employees, what, if anything, could you do to discourage "passing the buck"?

"CHECKOUT"—4

Key terms

Executive Branch	administrator	independent agencies
agency	bureaucracy	regulatory agencies
social security	Civil Service	Federal Reserve System
benefits	staff	subsidies

Review

1. Who is the head of the Executive Branch? Who chooses the heads of the departments and independent agencies of the Executive Branch?

2. President Franklin Roosevelt complained about the difficulty of bringing changes into the departments of the Executive Branch. What feature of these departments makes them resist change?

3. Describe the difference between the departments and independent agencies of the Executive Branch.

4. How many departments are there in the Executive Branch?

5. Name two departments that help the unemployed and two that have dealings with foreign governments.

Discussion

1. What departments and agencies of the Executive Branch had some effect on your daily life this week? For example, did you use any money? Did you send or receive any mail? Did you travel on an interstate highway? Check the Guide to Government Services in this chapter to see how many departments came into your life.

All the departments and agencies could be listed on the chalkboard, and the class might discuss which affected your lives most often.

2. Why do you think the Secretary of Defense has always been a civilian? Is this a constitutional requirement—or a result of custom? Do you think it is a good idea? Why or why not?

3. Having read in this chapter about the trouble Presidents sometimes have in getting government bureaus to carry out their programs, would you now hold to—or change—your response to the following statement (from Chapter 1's Checkout)? *The President should be held responsible for anything that goes wrong in the Executive Branch.* Why or why not?

4. President Franklin Roosevelt complained that it was practically impossible to change the bureaucracy of the Executive Branch. What are the signs of a bureaucracy? Do you think that these signs are found only in big government departments, or could they happen in any organization? Think of organizations you belong to or are familiar with. Do they have anything in common with a bureaucracy?

5. Have you ever made a request, suggestion, or complaint to a department or an agency of the Executive Branch? What happened? Did you

come across any buck-passing or other signs of a bureaucracy? Did you feel reasonably satisfied with the response you got?

Activities

1. You might choose the department of the Executive Branch whose services interest you most. Write a letter to this department asking for information about a particular subject, or for help in solving a problem.

2. You might look in your local telephone book under the *U.S. Government* listings. Which of the departments of the Executive Branch have offices in your city or county? Which independent agencies have offices? Choose three departments whose services are of interest to you, and make a note of the numbers you would call for information.

3. The departments of the Executive Branch could form the basis of a classroom quiz game. This might be played with a panel of individual contestants, two teams of four to five students each, or teams made up from the whole class. You could prepare matching lists of six departments and the services or topics they cover. These lists will be your contribution to the questions. The questioning team reads out a service or topic. The answering team has 20 seconds to name the department which handles that service or topic.

4. You might research each of the heads of Executive Branch departments who serve in the President's Cabinet. You—or teams of two—might share responsibility for finding pertinent biographical information about each of the department heads. You might make charts similar to the "Who Are the Presidents?" chart (in Chapter 3) which would include information under the six categories listed there. (Under the heading "Size of Home State When Elected," you should, of course, change "Elected" to "Appointed.") The charts could be posted on the bulletin board and discussed in class—along with other research findings.

5. For the Gallery of Our Political Leaders, students might prepare a letter to each Cabinet member, requesting a picture of him or her and explaining the purpose of the request.

6. In March 1979, President Jimmy Carter proposed a plan calling for a new Department of Natural Resources that would absorb the present Department of Interior and parts of the Commerce and Agriculture Departments. Some of you might research this plan and report to the class on it—with recommendations that it be approved or rejected. Or you might play the role of Senator and prepare a speech for or against the plan to be delivered to the "Senate" (class). Afterward, the class could vote on the plan.

7. Some department or agency of the federal government probably has an office in your community—or nearby. Someone from one of these agencies might be invited to speak to the class about his or her work and about the advantages—and disadvantages—of working for the federal government.

5: CAN A PRESIDENT BE TOO STRONG?

Can a President be too strong? "Of course not," most people would answer. "It's always better to be strong than weak."

Perhaps. But can a President be so powerful that he or she threatens the nation's freedom? Should a President be allowed to violate the rights of the American people? Or to ignore the rights of other nations?

In recent years, many people think that the President has become too strong. They say that the President has taken so much power from the other branches of government that this threatens our democratic system.

Are there rules to tell a President how far he or she can go? The U.S. Constitution is supposed to prevent the President from using power in the wrong way. Article II states all the things that a President may do and some of the things that he or she may not do.

The growing power of the President.
The Constitution was written 200 years ago. The people who wrote it did not know about nuclear weapons or rockets to the moon or com-

puters or television. They didn't know that the U.S. would some day be the richest, most powerful nation on Earth, with the power to destroy other nations in minutes. They didn't know that our economy would become so complicated and so big that it would require constant attention to keep it running smoothly.

Therefore, the rules that they wrote in the Constitution say little about a modern President's real power. George Washington would be shocked to know the following facts:

• **The President today has the power to command the instant destruction of entire cities.** The U.S. has thousands of missiles with nuclear warheads. Only the President can give the signal to launch them. How much military power did President Washington command in 1789? A few cannons and 718 soldiers.

• **The President's power is felt all over the world.** The President travels by jet from one nation to another. Foreign leaders often come to the White House. If Washington had tried to visit Europe or Asia, he would have been on a ship at sea for months at a time.

• **The American people expect the President to deal with a huge number of problems.** If there is economic trouble, they expect the President to cure it. Modern Presidents don't just try to administer the laws passed by Congress. Nor do they merely "recommend measures" to Congress as required by the Constitution (Article II, Section 3). Through

staff members, they often bring pressure on Congress to pass favored bills, including some actually written in the Executive Department. In Washington's day, many people thought the President's powers were only those directly mentioned in Article II of the Constitution.

Does the Constitution allow a "strong" President? How much power *should* the President have? How much does the Constitution set limits to the President's actions? These are very old questions.

Throughout American history, there have been many kinds of Presidents. But a number of them have tended to fall into two very different groups in their attitudes toward Presidential power.

The first believed that the powers of the President were few and limited. Presidents of this type thought they could — or should — do no more than follow the exact words of the Constitution and carry out the laws of Congress. You might call them "weak executive" Presidents.

That doesn't mean that they were weak people. It means only that they believed their actions were strictly limited by the Constitution. Modern examples of such Presidents were Warren Harding (1921–23), Calvin Coolidge (1923–29), Herbert Hoover (1929–33), and Dwight Eisenhower (1953–61).

Some others have been "strong executive" Presidents. They believed the Constitution gave them enough power to be strong leaders. In their view, a

President could act in ways not specifically mentioned by the Constitution.

Almost all our most famous Presidents since Abraham Lincoln have believed in a strong Presidency. Lincoln, Theodore Roosevelt (1901–09), Woodrow Wilson (1913–21), and Franklin Roosevelt (1933–45) all acted in bold new ways. Their critics were sometimes shocked by their actions and complained that the Constitution was ignored. But the "strong executive" defended himself with arguments like those in the Last Word (page 72).

The question of how strong a President should be may be more important now than ever before. After all, the President has gained enormous power in recent years. Some scholars who once favored a strong President now believe that the trend has gone too far. They believe that we should go back to the days when the President and Congress were more or less equal in power.

What do you think? Below are arguments on either side of the question. Decide which argument is strongest.

The case against a strong President. We often treat our Presidents as if they were royalty. Presidents live in a big mansion. They have servants and assistants whose only job is to make sure the President has everything he or she wants.

They don't get much personal contact with the American people because the Secret Service fears they may be attacked. As one critic says: "No one speaks to him unless spoken to first. No one ever tells him to go soak his head when his demands become unreasonable."

The President has taken more and more power at the expense of Congress. The people who wrote the Constitution believed in *checking and balancing** power between Congress and the President. But today, the President is more powerful than Congress.

One example of what has happened is in the power to declare war. The Constitution clearly gives that power to Congress only. Yet recent Presidents have been able to fight wars without a formal declaration of war by Congress.

Take, for example, Vietnam. Though

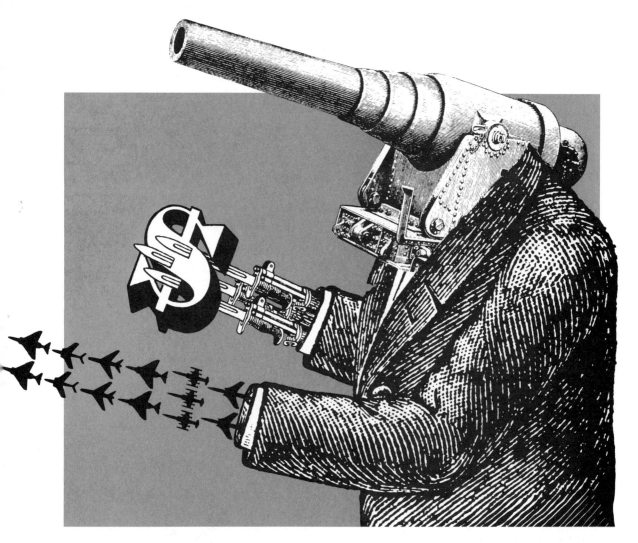

the President never asked Congress for a declaration of war against anyone in Southeast Asia, Congress allowed the President to conduct a war there.

Congress passed a resolution allowing the President "to take all necessary measures to . . . prevent aggression [in Vietnam]." Then, over the course of the years, it consistently gave the President the money that he said he needed to do so. It may be said that by doing this Congress willingly gave up its exclusive power to declare war.

So run the arguments of those who are against the idea of a strong President.

The case for a strong President.
The growth of the President's power is necessary. Presidents *should* be strong and powerful.

The U.S. today *needs* a strong President. Who else can give the nation leadership? Who else can make the quick decisions that are needed in a national emergency?

In the old days, an army could move only as fast as its horses and sailing ships. There was plenty of time for Congress to debate issues of war and peace. But not today. Only the President can act fast enough in an emergency.

Furthermore, only the President can give real leadership on the many national problems. Congress cannot lead as well as the President simply because there is only one President, but there are 435 Representatives and 100 Senators. Members of Congress seldom agree on what to do.

Unlike members of Congress, the President is elected by *all* the voters. The President does not represent just one part but the whole of the country. And if the people think that the President has taken too much power, they can always elect someone else every four years.

So run the arguments of those who believe in the need for a strong President.

ACTION PROJECT

narrow strip of land called Panama. *(The drawing on the next page shows the type of jungle through which the canal will have to be dug.)* This canal would mean ships would not have to sail all the way around South America to get from the Atlantic to the Pacific.

The trouble is that Panama is part of the Republic of Colombia. It belongs to the Colombians just as much as Florida belongs to the United States. What is the best and cheapest way to get a canal

Imagine yourself in the role of President.

What kind of President would you be: One who believes his powers are strictly limited to those set forth in the Constitution? A strong President? Very strong? Super-strong? Do you think you could be a strong President and still be fair? Could you be deeply concerned about respecting the duties and rights of other government branches and of other people—and still be strong?
Test yourself with the following problem.

The problem of Panama. The year is 1903. The airplane has not yet been invented. The only way to cross the oceans is by ship. For many years, the United States government has wanted to build a canal through a

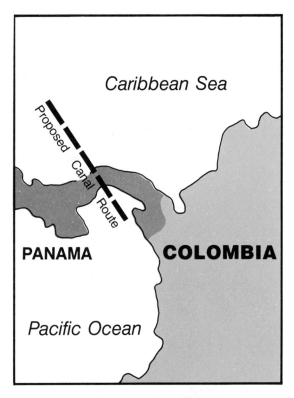

PANAMA
IN 1903

built through this foreign territory? That is your problem as President.

You have already worked very hard to make a deal with the government of Colombia. You have offered to pay Colombia 10 million dollars for the right to dig a canal through Panama. A week ago, you were told that the Colombians would accept your deal. But then, all of a sudden, they called it off. They've decided to hold out for a higher price. It is a price very much higher than you're willing to pay.

But, as you know, there are many ways to skin a cat. Suppose, for example, that Panama became an independent country. You're sure that this new country would sell you canal rights for the 10-million-dollar price.

You've been told that the people of Panama will revolt against the Colombian government on a certain day in November. The revolt will be successful only if the Americans help out. The Colombian government is very weak. All that's needed is three American warships to guard the major harbor of Panama. You are quite sure that the plan will work. But is it right?

As Commander-in-Chief, you have the power to order American ships to sail for Panama. If you are going to act, you must act now. What would a "strong" President do in this situation? What might a "weak" President do? What would a "fair" President do? Which would you rather be?

Now make up your mind. Are you going to support the revolt in Panama—or not? (After deciding, ask your teacher what actually happened in Panama in 1903.)

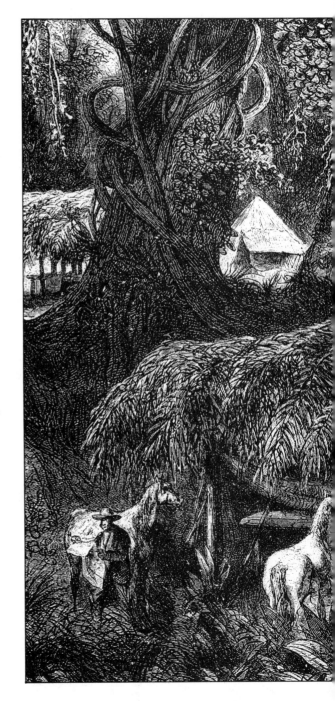

"THE LAST WORD"

by James MacGregor Burns

Theodore Roosevelt

The man sitting in the crane in the photo is Theodore Roosevelt, in the jungles of Panama. He was the President who actually made the decision about the Panama Canal. For his day, Teddy Roosevelt was a new kind of President — a very strong President. He also had firm ideas about how a modern President should use his power. Read about Roosevelt in the passage below. It is adapted from Presidential Government, *a book by a historian and professor of government, James MacGregor Burns.*

Theodore Roosevelt, as one scholar has said, will be remembered as the "first great President of modern times." Like many other Presidents before him, he *wanted* to be a great President. But unlike many of them, he had a clear idea of how a great President should behave. He had learned from history that great Presidents were strong Presidents. He tried to follow the example of Presidents like Washington and Lincoln — especially Lincoln.

He had a clear view of Presidential power. In his words: "My view was that every high government official was obliged to do all he could for the people. He should not just keep his talents undamaged in a napkin. My belief was that it was not only his right but his duty to do anything that the needs of the nation demanded. Under this view of executive power, I did many things not previously done by other Presidents. I did not usurp [steal or seize] power. But I did greatly broaden the use of executive power."

Roosevelt was also frank about how he lived up to this theory. He stated in a letter to a friend: "While President I have *been* President — very much so. I have used every ounce of power there was in the office. And I have not cared a rap for those who criticized me for my usurpation of power. I knew that the talk was all nonsense. I believe in a strong executive. I believe in power. But I believe that responsibility should go with power."

(YOU HAVE THE LAST WORD)

Think about two imaginary Presidents:

(a) A President who places no limits on his power.

(b) A President who sees so many limits to his power that he gives weak leadership.

Which would have bothered Theodore Roosevelt more? Which bothers you more?

Of course most Presidents have not viewed their powers in the extreme ways suggested by (a) and (b) above. Their uses of power have fallen somewhere between these two extremes.

Think about how our current President uses his powers. Is he closer to (a) or (b)? Or is he about midway between the two extremes? Give reasons for your answer.

"CHECKOUT"—5

Key terms
nuclear weapons   strong executive
weak executive   checks and balances

Review

1 Where does the Constitution mention the powers of the President?

2. Describe two ways (mentioned in the chapter) in which the power of any U.S. President today has changed from George Washington's time.

3. Name three past Presidents who were considered "weak" and three who were considered "strong."

4. List two arguments against a strong Presidency and two arguments in favor of it.

5. Explain what decision had to be made about Panama in 1903.

Discussion

1. The chapter lists some of the ways that the U.S. and the world have changed since the Constitution was written. Can you think of other changes that might have affected the powers of the President? What do you think is the most important difference between the world in which George Washington lived and the world of today's President? Two students might role-play a conversation between President Washington and the current President about these changes.

2. Read through the sections of the Constitution that deal with the powers of the President (Article II, Sections 2 and 3). Do these sections support the arguments in favor of a "weak" executive? A "strong" executive? Or do they allow either?

3. Do you think the President has too much power today? Just enough? Too little? Give examples to support your view.

4. If the President is thought to be

too powerful, could anything be done to reduce this power? If so, what? Can you give examples of occasions when action *was* taken to curb a President's power? What happened?

Activities

1. When President Jimmy Carter recognized the government of mainland China in 1979, he announced that the mutual defense treaty with Taiwan would be terminated in one year. Under the terms of the treaty, the U.S. government (as well as Taiwan) had the right to terminate the treaty in this way. But Congressional critics, led by Senator Barry Goldwater, charged that the President was assuming powers that he did not rightfully have. They said that, since the Constitution required a two-thirds vote of the Senate to put a treaty into effect, only a two-thirds vote of the Senate could terminate a treaty. Senator Goldwater filed suit in a U.S. district court because he felt that the treaty termination was unconstitutional.

The Justice Department, upholding the President's action, argued that the Constitution said nothing about how a treaty should be terminated and that other Presidents had exercised the right to end treaties without the approval of the Senate.

Some of you might research this issue and the outcome of Senator Goldwater's suit. You could report your findings to the class for discussion.

2. The drawing at the beginning of the chapter suggests that great strength may be destructive, but it doesn't say anything directly about Presidential power. You might make a drawing or cartoon of your own that shows your views about Presidential power—whether too much, too little, or just right. If you feel your artistic ability is not up to this task, you could write a brief description of such a drawing.

3. You might imagine it is the year 2001. You could suggest three technological advances or other major changes that may have taken place in the past decade or so. Then decide how these changes might have affected the power of the President. On the basis of these imaginary changes, you could write a news report that would be telecast in the year 2001.

4. Using encyclopedias, biographical dictionaries, or other sources, you might find out how each 20th-century President made use of Presidential power. In other words, you could decide which Presidents were clearly "weak," which were clearly "strong," and which were "in between." You might rate each President on a scale from 1 (weakest) to 10 (strongest).

5. In 1978 President Jimmy Carter proposed a treaty with Panama that would return the Panama Canal to that country by the year 2000. Some of you might research the long debate in the Senate that preceded its approval of the treaty. Afterward, you might report your findings to the class in oral or written reports. Or you could form teams and debate this question: *Should the Panama Canal Treaty have been approved?*

6: REPLACING THE PRESIDENT

Presidents are human beings. Like all of us, they can make mistakes. They get sick. They die. And the Constitution says that no person can be elected more than twice to the office of President. Therefore, every person who becomes President knows that sooner or later he or she will be leaving the office. Who will replace him or her?

Throughout human history, replacing a leader has been a major problem. All over the world, people have fought each other over the question of who will govern when a leader dies or leaves office.

The U.S. has a pretty good record in changing its leaders without bloodshed. The Constitution provides the rules for changing Presidents. It says that after a Presidential election (in November) the winning candidates for President and Vice-President will be sworn into office at noon on the following January 20.

But what happens if a President dies in office? According to the Constitution, the Vice-President immediately becomes President. This has happened seven times in U.S. history. The last time was in 1963, when President John F. Kennedy was murdered (photo at left shows his flag-draped coffin). Vice-President Lyndon Johnson automatically became President.

You can see how the U.S. changes its Presidents in the short play that follows.

ACTION PROJECT

Harry, Bess, and Margaret Truman

This play could be acted out in class, with volunteers to read the following parts:

Narrator
Sarah: elderly woman
Ralph: Sarah's husband
Harry Truman: U.S. Vice-President
Bess Truman: Harry's wife
Chief Justice: Supreme Court judge
Ike Eisenhower: President-elect
Mamie Eisenhower: Ike's wife

ACT ONE
The Death of a President

The time: April 1945.

The situation: The United States is at war. Franklin Roosevelt is President.

The scene: Sarah and Ralph's apartment.

Sarah: Go get the paper, will you, Ralph.

Ralph *(He goes to the apartment door, bends down, and starts to pick up a newspaper.):* Oooooh noooooo!! *(He reads headline aloud.)* PRESIDENT ROOSEVELT IS DEAD; TRUMAN TO CONTINUE POLICIES. My God. I don't believe it, Sarah! Roosevelt is dead!

Sarah: Let me see that. *(She takes the newspaper from him.)* I thought he was a very sick man. I could see it in his pictures.

Ralph: How did it happen? Read it to me.

Sarah: It says here: "President Franklin D. Roosevelt's last words were 'I have a terrific headache.' Mr. Roosevelt was sitting in front of a fireplace in the Little White House when he died. The President's servant carried him to his bedroom. He was unconscious at the end. It came without pain."

Ralph: Well, I'm glad he didn't suffer. Sarah! I just thought of something. Truman is going to be our new President. Can you imagine that? Harry Truman. He can't handle it. The job's too big for him. What does he know about being President? And at a time like this? There's a war going on. He can't handle the job.

(Curtain.)

Narrator: We now go to the Cabinet room of the White House. The room is crowded with people. They look at each other with tears in their eyes.

Harry Truman stands at one end of the room with the Chief Justice and Bess Truman. Eleanor Roosevelt, the President's widow, is one of those present in the room. She was the one who had to tell the Vice-President the news. Only an hour before, she had put her arm around Truman's shoulder and said softly: "Harry, the President is dead." He had answered, after a long pause, "Is there anything I can do for you?" And she replied warmly and sincerely: "Is there anything *we* can do for you? For you are the one in trouble now."

It is early evening. The clock on the wall shows the time to be exactly 7:09.

Chief Justice: Will you stand here between us, Bess, like so?

Bess Truman: Yes. Is this all right? *(She stands between her husband and their daughter, as shown in the photo at left. Harry Truman picks up a Bible, raises his right hand, and faces the Chief Justice of the United States.)*

Chief Justice: Repeat after me . . . I, Harry S Truman . . .

Harry Truman: I, Harry S Truman . . .

Chief Justice: . . . do solemnly swear . . .

Harry Truman: . . . do solemnly swear . . .

Chief Justice: . . . that I will faithfully execute the office of the President of the United States . . .

Harry Truman: . . . that I will faithfully execute the office of the President of the United States . . .

Chief Justice: . . . and will to the best of my ability . . .

Harry Truman: . . . and will to the best of my ability . . .

Chief Justice: . . . preserve, protect, and defend . . .

Harry Truman: . . . preserve, protect, and defend . . .

Chief Justice: . . . the Constitution of the United States . . .

Harry Truman: . . . the Constitution of the United States . . .

Chief Justice: . . . so help me God.

Harry Truman: . . . so help me God.
(*He shakes hands with the Chief Justice. He is the President of the United States.*)
(*Curtain.*)

ACT TWO
Inauguration

Narrator: The time is almost eight years later. It is January 20, 1953, a day for *inaugurating** a new President. In a hotel room in Washington, D.C., Dwight Eisenhower (Ike) and his wife Mamie are preparing for the Inauguration.[1]

Mamie: What's taking you so long, Ike? We have to go. There's a crowd out there waiting for us.

Ike: Let them wait. I want to ask you something, Mamie. Will you give me an honest answer? Do I look like the 34th President of the United States to you?

[1]The dialogue in this part of the play is imaginary. But the schedule of events — the drive to church, the drive to the White House, etc. — is real.

Mamie: No, you don't. To me, you look like plain old Ike Eisenhower.

Ike: Good. But at noon today, when I take that oath in front of the world, I will be the 34th President of the United States. Will I look like the President to you then?

Mamie: No. You'll still be Ike Eisenhower.

Ike: Wonderful. Then there will be someone in this world who will remember that I am just a human being. Promise that you won't ever call me "Mr. President," even in fun.

Mamie: OK, I promise. Now are you ready to go?

Ike: Not yet, not yet. We still have five minutes. Will you quiz me on the events of the day? I want to make sure this day goes right.

Mamie: OK, here's a quick quiz. What do we do first?

Ike: We go to church for a special Inauguration service.

Mamie: Correct. What next?

Ike: We drive to the White House to pick up Harry and Bess Truman. Harry joins me in the back seat of one car while you and Bess get into a second car. (*Photo at right shows Truman, on left, and Eisenhower riding to the Inauguration.*)

Mamie: Good. Then we drive slowly down Pennsylvania Avenue to the Capitol building. How long will that take?

Ike: Not long, I hope. I'm afraid Harry and I don't have much to talk about. We said some angry things about each other in the campaign. Well, I'm sure we'll be polite.

Mamie: What happens when we get

Harry Truman and Dwight Eisenhower

to the Capitol building?

Ike: The Marine Band will play "Hail to the Chief," and Harry will walk out there to his seat in the front row. Then a little later, I follow.

Mamie: OK, next question. Name three things that will happen before you take your oath of office.

Ike: Well, there are prayers. Then the Vice-President takes his oath of office. Then "The Star-Spangled Banner." Then I take the oath.

Mamie: What's next?

Ike: Then I read my speech. My Inaugural Address. After that, there will be another prayer and another chorus of "The Star-Spangled Banner." By this time, I guess I've been President of United States for about half an hour.

Mamie: You'll never be President unless we hurry. Let's go, Ike. You passed the quiz with flying colors, Mr. Pres—oops. I forgot.

(Curtain.)

Who takes the oath? In the first act, you saw how power passed to the Vice-President, Harry Truman, after the death of President Franklin Roosevelt. Because of this, the government continued to do its job without any big break. There was not a long time while the people wondered who would be the next President because only one person could become President—the Vice-President. The Constitution said so.

But consider this: Many other countries have their own constitutions. Yet in some of them, the rules of their constitutions are not always followed. Americans obey their Constitution because they believe in it—or because it has become habit to do so.

After Roosevelt's death, Americans accepted the fact that Harry Truman would be the next President. It did not matter that many Americans, like Ralph in the play, did not think Truman could do the job well. Never, not for a moment, did anyone suggest that someone else should be President.

There is, of course, a happier way to replace the President. And that was the subject of the second act of the play. It showed the Inauguration of Dwight Eisenhower on January 20, 1953.

After Inauguration Day, the new President is aware that he has only so much time in the office. He has been elected to lead the nation for four years. He may decide to run for a second term. But he can have only two elected terms as President. The 22nd Amendment to the Constitution sets two elected terms as a limit. This amendment was passed in 1951.

All Presidents take an oath when they enter office. You can find this oath of office on pages 79–80. In the oath, the President promises to obey the laws of the U.S. and to defend the Constitution.

The impeachment process. What happens if the President doesn't live up to his oath of office? Suppose many people think he has broken a law? Or not obeyed the Constitution? Or both? Is there any way to replace the President before his term of office is up?

There is. The process is called *impeachment.** If a President is suspected of violating his oath of office, charges may be brought against him in the *House of Representatives.** These charges are called a Bill of Impeachment. The House then votes on these charges. If a majority of the members of the House of Representatives vote for the Bill of Impeachment, the bill passes and goes to the Senate.

The Senate sits as jury in the case. It hears the charges and debates the evidence. Then it votes. If two thirds of the Senators vote against the President, he is found guilty. He is no longer President. The Vice-President becomes President.

The process of impeachment is very unusual. It has been used against Presidents only twice in U.S. history. In the first case, in 1868, President Andrew Johnson was accused of breaking a law. The House passed a Bill of Impeachment against him and the case went to the Senate. The vote in the Senate fell one vote short of the two-thirds majority. Andrew Johnson stayed in office until the end of his term.

The second case occurred more than 100 years later. It involved President Richard Nixon (below, right).

The case of Watergate. In 1972 Richard Nixon was a popular President. He had improved U.S. relations with China and the Soviet Union. He had won reelection in 1972 by a wide margin. As he began his second term, Nixon seemed on top of the world. But then things fell apart.

Nixon's troubles began during the 1972 campaign. The Democratic party had its headquarters in a high-rent building in Washington, D.C. The name of the building was Watergate.

One night a guard at the Watergate noticed someone had taped a door lock. He called the police. They found five men in the Democratic headquarters. The men were arrested for burglary.

It looked like some spy mission against the Democrats. The President said that his aides had nothing to do with the burglary.

But many people thought the President and his assistants were trying to "cover up" the burglary. Investigations showed that several persons working for Nixon had been involved. It seemed that they were trying to cover their tracks. But was Nixon involved too?

Other questions were also raised. "Watergate" came to stand for more than just a burglary. It even meant more than a "cover-up." It also came to mean:

- receiving secret campaign gifts from big companies; these gifts were against the law;
- playing "dirty tricks" on Demo-

cratic candidates during the 1972 election campaign;
- attempting to use the FBI and other government agencies against political enemies;
- setting up a secret group to carry out unlawful activities against political enemies.

For more than a year, Watergate stayed in the news. Investigators kept uncovering new facts. President Nixon said again and again that he had never tried to keep the truth from the American people. But many people came to believe that the President was not telling the truth.

Richard Nixon after resigning

A Bill of Impeachment was introduced in the House of Representatives. The next step was for a committee of the House to examine the charges. After months of study, the House Judiciary Committee voted to recommend that President Nixon be impeached. Now it was up to the full House to decide whether the President should be impeached—charged with crimes and put on trial in the Senate.

Before the vote could be taken, a bombshell hit. In July 1974, the U.S. Supreme Court ruled that the President had to give up tapes of conversations about Watergate he had made two years before. In August the President released these tapes to the public. They showed that Nixon had known about the cover-up all along.

Even many people who supported Nixon were shocked. It appeared certain that he would be impeached by the House. It also looked as if the Senate would vote to remove him from office. On August 9, 1974, Nixon gave up his office. He became the first person ever to resign as President of the United States.

Vice-President Gerald Ford replaced Nixon as President. Ford was an appointed Vice-President, having been named to the office almost a year before when the then Vice-President Spiro Agnew resigned under pressure. Agnew himself had been accused of misconduct and was found guilty of tax evasion shortly after his resignation. Ford was the first President to serve who was not elected either to the office of President or Vice-President.

RULES FOR REPLACING A PRESIDENT

A President's term is *usually* four years long. But who will be President if any of the following things happen?

1. If a President dies, the Vice-President will then become President.

2. If a President is too sick or for some other reason is unable to carry out his duties, one of two things could happen:

The President, if he is able, could send a written statement to leaders of the Senate and the House of Representatives. The

message would inform them that he is disabled and the Vice-President will act in his place.

Or the Vice-President could write the same kind of message and send it to the leaders of the Senate and the House. But before he takes over as President, he must have his message signed and approved by a majority of the President's Cabinet.

3. If the President says he is fit to carry on his duties, but the Vice-President and the Cabinet say that he is not fit, then Congress will decide who is right.

4. If both the President and the Vice-President die at the same time, then the Speaker of the House of Representatives shall become President. A law of Congress lists a number of other officials who are in line to become President in case the Speaker also dies. After the Speaker come the following: *President pro tempore** of the Senate, *Secretary of State,** other members of the Cabinet.

"THE LAST WORD"

from TIME Magazine

It was cold and snowy in Washington, D.C., when John F. Kennedy took the President's oath of office on January 20, 1961. In the first row of seats on either side of Kennedy were three other people who also took that oath. One of these had taken it before Kennedy. Two others were destined to take the oath after Kennedy died. Can you identify the four Presidents in the picture? How did each get to be President? (Your teacher can tell you the answer.)

After studying the picture, read about the Inauguration of President Kennedy adapted from Time *Magazine.*

Foul weather and a fine speech provided the most memorable moments of a historic week.

It was the week of changeover in the U.S. government, and for only the fifth time in the 20th century a new President moved into the White House in place of an outgoing President of the opposite party. A blizzard threatened to turn the whole momentous occasion into a farce—but President John Kennedy, delivering his Inaugural Address, more than saved the day.

Message of hope. Kennedy's Inauguration speech went beyond old truths from the U.S. past; it had deep meaning for the U.S. future. In clear, short phrases, the nation's new President pledged the U.S. to remain faithful to its friends and firm against its enemies.

Passages from the speech were compared with the inspiring quality of Franklin Roosevelt's Inaugural in 1933. Here are some examples:

• Let every nation know, whether it wishes us well or ill, that we shall pay any price, bear any burden, meet any hardship, support any friend or oppose any foe, to assure the survival and success of liberty.

• Let us never negotiate out of fear. But let us never fear to negotiate.

• Ask not what your country can do for you—ask what you can do for your country.

Reaction to the speech was immediate. From all shades of political outlook, from people who voted for Kennedy in November and people who had voted against him, came a surge of praise and congratulation.

Sense of history. In his address, John Kennedy told the nation and the world: "I have sworn before you and Almighty God the same solemn oath our forebears prescribed nearly a century and three quarters ago." This sense of history, this understanding of the U.S. and its government as continuing institutions, gave strength to the Kennedy speech. It underlined the orderly change of Presidential power that took place last week.

During the time between election

Kennedy Inauguration

and Inauguration, members of the Eisenhower Administration, at the President's orders, cooperated fully with Kennedy and his appointees. Eisenhower and Kennedy met for three hours in early December. The day before Inauguration, they talked again, then met with Cabinet officers of the old and new Administrations.

One nation. The cooperation brought into focus the fact that while much changed on Inauguration Day, 1961, much remained unchanged. The Eisenhower-Kennedy changeover could well serve to remind the Communist world that, despite conflicts of political parties and viewpoints, the U.S. is one nation, indivisible. "A new page in U.S. history begins," proclaimed the Soviet newspaper *Trud* just before the Inauguration. But if the page was new, it was a new page of the same book—the book that began on July 4, 1776.

(YOU HAVE THE LAST WORD)

Think of the years that lie ahead for you and the American nation.

In your lifetime, (let's say, for the next 60 years), how many times do you expect to see a change of Presidents? Do you expect the change from one President to another will always be as peaceful and hopeful as the Inauguration of 1961? Or do you think there will be more moments of violence such as the Kennedy assassination? Do you predict that a President and Vice-President will ever again be forced to resign?

"CHECKOUT"—6

Key terms

oath
Inauguration
impeachment

Speaker of the House
President pro tempore

Review

1. Describe the two common ways one President is replaced by another.

2. Whom did Harry Truman replace as President? What happened to that earlier President? Why was it Truman who replaced him?

3. Whom does the President notify if he feels too sick to continue in his duties? Who becomes President if both the President and the Vice-President die at the same time?

4. How many Presidents have been impeached? How many other Presidents have had impeachment proceedings begun against them? Give the names of each President.

5. Fill in the missing word: President Nixon resigned as a result of his involvement in the _____ affair.

Discussion

1. The 22nd Amendment states that no President may be elected to more than two terms in office. Since the people are free to vote against a President running for reelection, why do you think that this amendment was considered necessary? Do you agree with it? Why or why not?

2. In Act Two of the Action Project, you saw how Harry Truman rode with Dwight Eisenhower to the latter's Inauguration. It is the custom for the outgoing President to ride with his successor, even if they are bitter political rivals. What do you think is the reason for this custom? Do you think it is a good one? Why or why not?

3. Look again at the Rules for Replacing a President. Do you think that these cover all the possibilities? Can you think of any accidents that are not covered? If so, how likely are these accidents? Would you change the rules in any way? If so, how and why?

4. Who is the current Vice-President? How much do you know about this person? What can you remember about the Vice-President's latest speech or public action? Most Vice-Presidents have had little influence on how the government is run. If you were President, how much power —if any—would you share with your Vice-President? Why?

5. Do you think the procedures for impeaching a President are too difficult? About right? Too easy? Explain your answer.

6. If a nuclear attack wiped out Washington, D.C., how do you think the U.S. government would be ruled until new elections could be held? What problems do you think the nation would have if there were no President, Congress, or Supreme Court?

7. Would you favor a constitutional amendment stipulating that if a President dies or steps down, a Presidential election would be held immediately? What would be the advantages and disadvantages to such a system?

Activities

1. The 1961 Inauguration Day photo in The Last Word shows four Presidents (past, present, and future) together. You might choose one of these Presidents or one of their wives to role-play. But first, of course, you should do some research on the four Presidents and their wives. Then think about what you might say to the other Presidents and their wives. Afterward, you could hold a 1961 Inauguration Day conversation.

Other students might role-play conversations among the four Presidents and their wives that might have taken place if they had somehow surmised what the future held in store for them.

2. A President's Inaugural Address does not usually deal with any specific problems. It usually aims to be inspiring, or to set a mood of hope for the future. You might imagine that you have just been inaugurated President. People throughout the U.S. and the world are waiting to hear what you have to say. Write one paragraph of your Inaugural Address.

3. Using *The World Almanac,* an encyclopedia, or other sources, some students might find out how many Presidents did not complete their terms of office and were succeeded by Vice-Presidents. Then they could work out what percentage of Vice-Presidents have suddenly had to take over the Presidency.

You might use these statistics to open a class discussion on the topic: *The importance of the Vice-Presidency.*

4. Some students might research the assassinations of Presidents Abraham Lincoln, James Garfield, William McKinley, and John F. Kennedy. They could report their findings to the class for discussion.

5. You might research the names of the people who are in direct line of succession to the present U.S. President. You could put these names and their titles on a chart which could be posted somewhere in your classroom.

6. Some students might role-play a Cabinet meeting where the President is absent. One Cabinet member suggests that the President is ill and will have to be replaced. Some Cabinet members agree with this view, but others do not. Various participants can try to convince the others of their points of view and suggest actions to be taken.

7: HOW TO JUDGE A PRESIDENT

Imagine this scene.

A young person stops you on the street one day and says: "Hi. I'm Jackie Hunt. Sorry to bother you. I'm taking a survey of *public opinion** for a college course I'm taking. Could you help me out?"

You say: "OK."

She says: "Here's my question. How would you rate the job the President of the United States is doing today? Answer either 'excellent,' 'pretty good,' 'fair,' or 'poor.' If you don't know or can't decide, answer 'no opinion.' "

You ask her: "Can you give me some time to think about it?"

She says: "All right. I'll give you two minutes."

You now have two minutes to decide what sort of a rating to give the President. Your opinion, combined with other opinions, carries a lot of weight. It may not seem so, but the future of a President may depend upon it.

Much of the President's power depends on how many people approve of the President's actions. If most don't approve and say so in the polls, the President will lose some influence in Congress and the ability to lead.

Sixty percent or more say President is doing "good" or "excellent" job	**A very strong, popular rating.** With such overwhelming support for President, Congress will be **less** likely to oppose Presidential programs.
Between 50-60 percent say President is doing "good" or "excellent" job	**Satisfactory rating.** President has enough popular support to govern effectively.
Under 50 percent say President is doing "good" or "excellent" job	**Poor rating.** With such poor support, Congress will be **more** likely to oppose Presidential programs.

Your time is up. How would you rate the job the President is doing today? On a slip of paper, write either "excellent," "pretty good," "fair," or "poor." If you can't decide, write "no opinion."

Consider your answer carefully. Before writing your answer, ask yourself what the President has done to deserve a high or low rating.

After each student has written his or her opinion, you may want to have one person in the class collect all the opinions and sort them into three piles. Slips marked either "excellent" or "pretty good" should go in one pile. Slips marked either "fair" or "poor" should go in a second pile. The third pile is for "no opinion" slips.

From the percentages, you can tell whether the President is generally popular or unpopular with your class. Use the chart above to decide how well the President rates.

Discuss the reasons for your opinion of the President. When you wrote your answer, were you thinking mainly of the President's personality? Or were you thinking of the actions and decisions this person made as President? Or were you thinking of your parents' opinion? Why do your parents either like or dislike the President? Do you feel the same way about the President as your parents do?

There are many ways to judge a President. From your discussions, you may have discovered some of these ways. You may discover others in the following short skit.

This play could be acted out in class, with volunteers to read these parts.

Jackie Hunt: a professional poll-taker
Angela Miranda: a policewoman
Ann Grant: an unemployed airplane pilot
Fred Morrow: a wealthy businessman
Tony Smarts: a history professor

Scene: The mall of a shopping center in your town. Robert Q. Leedwell has been President of the United States for two years. The date is 2002. As the play begins, Jackie Hunt is speaking with three shoppers in a waiting area of the mall.

Hunt: Thank you very much for your opinions.

Grant: That's OK. I'm glad my opinion is being counted. I just hope it does some good. Leedwell is about the worst President this country has ever had. If I were in Congress, I would impeach him.

Hunt: Yes, I know that's your opinion. Of course, there are people who disagree with you.

Smarts: In my opinion, it's really much too early to judge whether Leedwell is a good President or a poor one. That's why I answered "no opinion."

Morrow: Excuse me, Ms. Grant. But I really think you're expecting miracles of the President. He's got a tough job. The toughest in the world. In my opinion, he has done a pretty good job so far.

Grant: You have to be kidding. Two years ago, I had a good job. It paid me $40,000 a year. Two months after Leedwell became President, the economy went into a slump. Now I'm looking for work.

Morrow: That's ridiculous. You can't blame the President for your misfortunes.

Smarts: Why can't she blame the President? Everyone else does. When times are good, a President will always try to take credit for it. Well

then, when the economy slumps, the people have every right to blame the President.

Miranda: Personally, I think Bob Leedwell is wonderful. Don't you love to watch him on TV? He's got such a great sense of humor! We need that in a President. When he talks to

"DOES PRESIDENT LEEDWELL LEAD WELL?"

"HE'S GOT SUCH A GREAT SENSE OF HUMOR!"

"HE'S DONE GOOD THINGS, BUT WHAT HAS HE DONE FOR ME?"

you, I get this feeling that here is someone I can trust.

Smarts: That's a silly way to judge a President. A President should be judged for his accomplishments, not for his personality. As I see it, he has performed well in three areas. First, in the area of foreign policy—

Grant: Excuse me. I have to fix lunch for my kids. Hot dogs. Can't afford steak or hamburgers anymore. Thanks, President Leedwell. I've always wondered what it's like to be out of a job. Now I know. Sure he's a nice person. But he's a lousy President! (*She walks off.*)

Smarts: As I was saying, President Leedwell has done well in the area of foreign policy. After all, he succeeded in improving relations in the Middle East.

Miranda: Yes, and he has done great work for the poor in America. That new bill he signed. Er. What's it called?

Smarts: The Burns-Post Act. What a wonderful step forward. . . .

Morrow: Now just a minute. That act is the most unfair, shameful law that this country has ever known. It's doubled the tax on everything I own. I still can't understand why Leedwell signed that awful law. In fact, Ms. Hunt, I think I should like to change my answer from a "pretty good" to "fair."

Hunt: I'll make the change, Mr. Morrow. Professor, what were you saying about the President's accomplishments?

Smarts: Thank you for asking. I was going to say that one way to judge a President is to look at the company he keeps. What appointments has he made to high office? And you must admit that—

Miranda: Oh, of course, I agree. Good point, Professor. Leedwell has made some wonderful choices. I am especially happy that he chose a woman to be his running mate and has placed women in key positions in his administration.

Smarts: As I was saying, Leedwell had the courage to choose a black American to be his Secretary of State. A very fine choice. I am much impressed by the President's record so far. I must confess that I like Leedwell but—

Hunt: But what? I don't understand. You told me you had "no opinion" of him.

Smarts: I did so for two reasons. First of all, as I said, a President cannot be fairly judged while he is in office. Harry Truman, as you know, did very badly in the opinion polls. But now, in 2002, many people think he was one of our great Presidents.

Hunt: What's your second reason for answering "no opinion"?

Smarts: I hate to say this but . . .

"SURE HE'S A NICE PERSON, BUT HE'S A LOUSY PRESIDENT!"

Can I trust you? Two months ago, I lost my job. Fired from the university. I appealed to the President. Wrote him a long letter and asked him to do something for me. So far, I haven't heard a word. Not one word. I am deeply disappointed in him. He's done good things, but what has he done for me?

Miranda: But Professor, shouldn't you try to forget about yourself? Shouldn't you think only of the good of the country?

Smarts: That is easy for you to say, Ms. Miranda. You still have a job. I don't. I'm sorry. I have an appointment at the unemployment bureau. Good-bye! *(He runs off down the mall. Jackie Hunt is so surprised that she drops her clipboard into Mr. Morrow's shopping bag.)*

That's the end of the play. But the question still has not been answered. "Does President Leedwell lead well?" As you saw, opinions about him changed as people discussed all that he had done as President. From what you have heard about him, how would you judge Leedwell?

Here is a summary of the points that were made about him:

- He has a good sense of humor.
- It is easy to like and trust him.
- He signed a law that taxed the rich heavily while aiding the poor.
- He improved relations in the Middle East.
- The economy has become worse and unemployment has increased.
- He has appointed women to key posts in his administration.
- His Secretary of State is a black American.
- His White House staff failed to answer a letter about the personal problems of an individual citizen.

Of course, Leedwell is an imaginary President. But you may use the same standards for rating the President today. You should be able to answer these four questions:

1. What important law or laws have been passed under the President's leadership?

2. What has the President achieved —or failed to achieve—in foreign relations?

3. Has the President chosen good men and women to help administer the government?

4. How would you describe the President's personality?

Think again about your answer to the opinion poll. How would you rate the job today's President is doing? **(a)** Excellent. **(b)** Pretty good. **(c)** Fair. **(d)** Poor. **(e)** No opinion.

Is your opinion the same or different from what it was at the beginning of this chapter?

"THE LAST WORD"

by Robert K. Murray and
Tim H. Blessing

How good have America's Presidents been? Which ones were the most successful? Robert K. Murray, a history professor at Penn State University, and his colleague, Tim H. Blessing, wanted to know the answers to these questions. They asked 970 historians to rate the Presidents on how they handled foreign policy, the economy, the Congress, and other matters. Their survey was the most extensive ever conducted on this subject. The survey results summarized below come from the Journal of American History, *December 1983.*

What conclusions did the survey draw on our country's greatest leaders? It identified those who have left an enduring mark on our history, and those who were the failures. It also explained what qualities made some Presidents stand out above all the rest.

According to the survey results, our greatest Presidents were those who led the country at a critical moment in American history. By timely action, each achieved lasting results.

Washington made the Constitution into a practical system of government. Jefferson enlarged the United States and gave America the huge region from the Mississippi to the Rockies. Lincoln saved the Union from destruction. Franklin Roosevelt preserved the country in the time of its worst Depression. He led it to victory in World War II.

Every one of these men left the Executive Branch stronger and more influential than he found it. Each expanded those powers granted to him by the Constitution.

While most people agree on who should be at the top of the list, the rankings for the rest of the Presidents have varied according to the poll takers and the era. Dwight D. Eisenhower is a good example. The Penn State survey ranked him 11th, an above-average President. Twenty-one years ago, shortly after Eisenhower left office, a group of historians put Eisenhower 10th from the bottom.

(YOU HAVE THE LAST WORD)

How do you think future historians will rate the Presidents from Ronald Reagan onward? What must a President do to be considered great? How can a President be a failure?

96

RESULTS OF POLL*

Great
1: Abraham Lincoln
2: Franklin D. Roosevelt
3: George Washington
4: Thomas Jefferson

Near Great
5: Theodore Roosevelt
6: Woodrow Wilson
7: Andrew Jackson
8: Harry S Truman

Above Average
9: John Adams
10. Lyndon Johnson
11. Dwight D. Eisenhower
12. James K. Polk
13. John F. Kennedy
14. James Madison
15. James Monroe
16. John Quincy Adams
17. Grover Cleveland

Average
18. William McKinley
19. William Howard Taft
20. Martin Van Buren
21. Herbert Hoover
22. Rutherford B. Hayes
23. Chester A. Arthur
24. Gerald Ford
25. Jimmy Carter
26. Benjamin Harrison

Below Average
27. Zachary Taylor
28. Millard Fillmore
29. Calvin Coolidge
30. Franklin Pierce

Failures
31. Andrew Johnson
32. James Buchanan
33. Richard M. Nixon
34. Ulysses S. Grant
35. Warren G. Harding

*Jimmy Carter was the last president included in the survey. It did not include William Henry Harrison, who served only 31 days, and James Garfield, who served six months.

"CHECKOUT"—7

Review

1. In the short play about public opinion, do all of the people polled agree about President Leedwell? Do any of them change their opinions in the course of the play? Which of the four has the most favorable opinion of Leedwell?

2. Which of these statements about President Leedwell is shown *not* to be true in the play? **(a)** He chose a woman as his Vice-President. **(b)** He chose a black person as his Secretary of State. **(c)** He has reduced unemployment.

3. Describe two questions that should be considered in judging a President.

4. Suppose 65 percent of the people polled about the President say he is doing a good job. What kind of rating would this be?

5. Name three of the Presidents that a group of historians judged "great."

Discussion

1. The chapter suggests four questions people should ask themselves in order to rate a President. Do you think most people who take part in opinion polls *do* ask themselves such questions? If not, do you think the poll is still valid? Why or why not?

2. In the Action Project play, what standards are used by each of the four characters being polled? Are some of the characters using better standards than others? If so, which character do you think has the fairest standards? Explain your answer.

3. Comment on — attack, defend, or change (until it expresses your view) — this statement by Smarts: *When times are good, a President will always try to take credit for it. Well then, when the economy slumps, the people have every right to blame the President.*

4. Do you think the results of opinion polls have too much, too little, or just enough effect on the power of the President? Explain your answer.

5. President Lyndon Johnson was widely praised for spurring civil-rights legislation, but widely criticized for his handling of the Vietnam war. President Ronald Reagan, praised for his economic policies that reduced inflation and unemployment, was severely criticized for his foreign policy in Central America. Which should count for most on a President's record, the achievements or the weaknesses? Explain your answer.

Activities

1. You, with others in your class, might plan and take an opinion poll on the current President. Include questions similar to the four listed at the end of the Action Project, and end with a question asking the interviewee's overall opinion of the President. For your interviewees, you might choose a sample of fellow students, teachers, family members, and neighbors. Tabulate the results by working out the percentages of interviewees who think that the President is doing an *excellent, good, fair,* or *poor job,* and who have *no opinion.*

The class could discuss the results and compare them with those of national polls.

2. You might read "*The Presidency,*" a collection of essays from *American Heritage.* You might take particular note of any information which changes your views of past Presidents or of the rating of Presidents in general. You could prepare a brief report on the essays for the class.

3. Using *Reader's Guide* or newspaper indexes, you could research other rankings of Presidents and compare them with the ranking in this chapter. You could report your findings to the class for discussion.

4. (This activity is a follow-up to a research project suggested for Chapter 6.) You might compare your list of Vice-Presidents who succeeded to the Presidency with the ranking of Presidents at the end of this chapter. Would you say that these Vice-Presidents, as a group, are rated *above average, average,* or *below average?* Your findings could serve as the basis for a class discussion of the topic: *Are Vice-Presidents ready for the Presidency?*

5. You might research the record of the current President, using newspapers and magazines with stories and articles about his performance — his achievements and his failures. You could make a list of each. Then the class might discuss what they have learned about the President and vote on a ranking for him or her among the Presidents ranked in the chapter.

TEN GOOD BOOKS ABOUT THE PRESIDENCY

Presidential Campaigns
by Paul F. Boller, Jr.
Join the Presidential campaign trail and find out about the lighter side of politics —the songs, slogans, and rallies. From Washington to Reagan, discover that politics can be fun! Oxford University Press, New York, 1988.

Keeping Faith: Memoirs of a President
by Jimmy Carter
"These last few days have been among the worst I've ever spent in the White House . . ." Jimmy Carter wrote in his diary in February, 1980. Find out the reasons why and more in this candid account of exhilaration and solitude in the Oval Office. Bantam Books, New York, 1983.

Lincoln
by Gore Vidal
Here is Abraham Lincoln in all his grandeur. A fictional account about the legendary President as well as the human one. Random House, New York, 1984.

Presidential Wives

by Paul F. Boller

Learn all about the first ladies, from Martha Washington to Nancy Reagan, in this collection of anecdotes. Oxford University Press, New York, 1988.

Speaking Out: The Reagan Presidency From Inside the White House

by Larry Speakes and Robert Pack

If you're the least bit curious about what goes on behind the scenes at the White House, this book by a former Reagan aide is for you. Speakes looks back on his years with the administration a year after he left. Scribner's, New York, 1988.

Harry S Truman

by Margaret Truman

A warm personal story of life in the White House. Especially enjoyable are the President's frank letters to his daughter "Margie" and other members of the family. William Morrow, New York, 1984.

Choosing the President 1984

by the League of Women Voters Education Fund

It may be small but there's much information here—this pamphlet is crammed with details about how we elect a President, how campaigns are financed, and how delegates to the conventions are selected. You'll also find out about the duties and powers of the President. Schocken Books, New York, 1984.

Franklin Roosevelt, Gallant President

by Barbara Feinberg

Roosevelt, our thirty-second President may have been handicapped with polio but he served the longest in office—twelve years, from 1932 until his death in 1945. Lothrop, Lee & Shepard, New York, 1981.

Herblock Through the Looking Glass: The Reagan Years in Words and Pictures

by Herbert Block

If cartoons make you laugh, read this book by one of America's famous cartoon commentators. Block shows Reagan's world in cartoon views—from Lebanon to Grenada. A book that's sure to amuse! W.W. Norton, New York, 1984.

America in Search of Itself: The Making of the President 1956–1980

by Theodore H. White

What kind of people are we? Who leads us? Where are we now and where are we going? Theodore White asks these questions and also discusses the events in Iran and their impact on Carter's and Reagan's election. Harper & Row, New York, 1982.

UNIT II: CONGRESS

8: THE PEOPLE ON CAPITOL HILL

The most important hill in America is not very steep. It is a gentle slope about 80 feet high in the center of Washington, D.C. People who work here call it "Capitol Hill" or just "The Hill."

The Hill is important because of the white stone Capitol building on top of the slope. Inside this building, the Congress of the United States meets to make the nation's laws.

Five hundred thirty-five people with different ideas. Congress, like the nation itself, is made up of people who differ from each other. Some members of Congress agree with each other most of the time. Others disagree most of the time. But no two individuals in Congress either agree or disagree all of the time. This is the first important fact to keep in mind about the nation's lawmakers.

Look, for example, at Cardiss Collins and Orrin Hatch. They are as different as two people can be. In 1987 Cardiss Collins was a Democratic member of the House of Representatives. Orrin Hatch was a Republican member of the Senate.

The majority of citizens in Collins's Chicago, Illinois *district** were black.

105

Most of Hatch's Utah *constituents** were white. Collins believed in women's rights and more government aid for minorities. She consistently voted for legislation to protect the environment. Hatch believed in limiting government control and keeping taxes down. Hatch wanted more government funds to go to defense and less to social welfare programs. Collins preferred just the opposite.

And yet, as different as they were, Representative Collins and Senator Hatch sometimes voted for the same laws. Not very often, but once in a while.

There are 435 Representatives in one wing of the Capitol building—the House of Representatives. One hundred Senators are in the other wing—the *Senate.* Together, these two groups are called *Congress.* No law can be passed unless a majority of these lawmakers in both houses agree on it.

Despite all their differences, the people in Congress realize the need to *compromise.** They bargain and trade with each other until enough votes can be found to pass a law. Every year, this process of give-and-take between 535 politicians creates over 500 laws—either new laws or changes in old laws.

Major questions about Congress.
The Constitution gives the Legislative Branch (Congress) first place in the United States system of government. It is the first branch to be mentioned (Article I). It receives more than twice as many words as the Executive Branch (Article II) and over four times as many words as the Judicial Branch (Article III). Most questions about the organization and powers of Congress can be answered by studying Article I of the Constitution (see page 238).

But first, before turning to the back of the book, you should know the answers to four major questions:

1. Why do we have both Senators

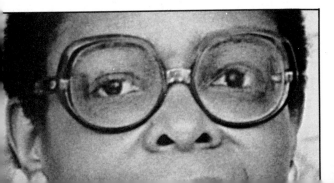

and Representatives — not just one or the other? There are two reasons. First, the people who wrote the Constitution were used to a two-house system of lawmakers. In England, the legislature had two houses. So did most of the American colonies.

Second, the writers of the Constitution saw this as a way of balancing the powers of the small and the large states. In the Senate, a state with a small population, such as Vermont, has two Senators. A state with a large population, such as California, has exactly the same number—two. But Vermont sends only one Representative to the House of Representatives, while California sends 45.

In other words, in the House, the voting power of a state depends on its population. In the Senate, however, the voting power of all states is the same.

2. Are there other differences between the Senate and the House? There are several very important differences. One house is much smaller than the other, and its members are elected for longer terms. One house has some power over treaties and Presidential appointments, while the other house has none. The house that lacks this power makes up for it with its special power over taxes and government spending.

The Vice-President presides (acts as chairperson) over one house. The *presiding officer** in the other house is the Speaker. Which house is which? The chart on page 108 gives the answers. The chart also shows in what ways the House and the Senate are alike.

3. How do Congresspersons spend their time? The Constitution says nothing about this question. Members of Congress are not required to sit all day in their seats in the Capitol building. In fact, on most days, less than a third of their time is spent in the Senate or House chambers. That's why tourists see so many empty seats when they visit the nation's Capitol.

107

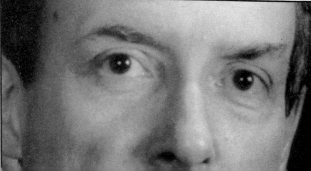

THE TWO HOUSES

HOUSE OF REPRESENTATIVES

SENATE

HOUSE OF REPRESENTATIVES	Question	SENATE
435.	**How many members are there?**	100.
According to population. In 1987 smallest states sent one Representative. Largest state sent 45 Representatives.	**How is membership *apportioned** among the 50 states?**	Each state sends two Senators.
Two years.	**How long is each member's term of office?**	Six years.
Yes. No limit to number of terms a member may serve.	**Can a member be reelected?**	Yes. No limit to number of terms a member may serve.
Yes. Representatives are elected in even-numbered years (1984, 1986, 1988, etc.).	**Are all members elected at the same time?**	No. Terms of different Senators expire at different times. One third of Senators are elected in each even-numbered year.
Must be American citizen for at least 7 years, 25 years or older, and a resident of state in which elected.	**What are the qualifications for membership?**	Must be American citizen for at least 9 years, 30 years or older, and a resident of state in which elected.
Speaker of the House.	**Who is the presiding officer?**	Vice-President of the U.S.
House may decide its own rules.	**What are the rules for conducting business?**	Senate may decide its own rules.
• Considers all revenue bills (taxes and *appropriations**) first. • Decides who shall be President in case no candidate receives majority vote. • Votes on impeachment of federal officials.	**What are its special powers?**	• *Confirms** treaties by two-thirds vote. • Confirms President's appointments by majority vote. • Votes on whether to remove from office federal officials impeached by House.

Senators and Representatives spend most of their time in the office buildings that surround the Capitol. They may be in their private offices answering letters or, more often, they are attending *committee meetings.** While in these meetings, they usually discuss the need for new laws.

When members of Congress are needed in the Capitol for a vote, bells and buzzers go off in every room of the office buildings. Then the lawmakers leave committee rooms and rush to catch a special underground train that takes them to the Capitol. Usually, they're on time to cast their vote or make a short speech.

4. Whom do Representatives represent? They represent the people who elected them to office. Senators represent all the people from their home state. Representatives represent people from their home districts. A district is an area within a state. The Constitution says the district may contain *no fewer than* 30,000 people. In 1987 the average district had a population of 519,000.

The people in a district are sometimes called a Representative's *constituency*. Within a constituency, there are different groups with different needs and opinions. A member of Congress tends to pay more attention to the needs of those groups that have the most voting power.

Compare (below) the constituencies of Representative Collins and Senator Hatch. Then you can better understand why these two members of Congress disagreed with each other on most issues.

Case study: Bob LaFollette's choice. Members of Congress serve many masters. Sometimes, they vote for laws their constituencies favor. Sometimes, they vote the way powerful leaders in Congress tell them to vote. And

WHOM THEY REPRESENT

	Hatch's Constituency	Collins's Constituency
	State of Utah	7th Congressional District of Illinois
People living in cities	1,262,000	519,034
People living outside cities	382,000	0
White people	1,540,141	150,445
Black people	9,225	347,007
People of other groups	94,634	21,582

Sources: *Politics in America: Members of Congress in Washington And At Home, 1986.* and *Statistical Abstract of the U.S., 1987*

sometimes they vote according to the way they personally feel about an issue.

Deciding how to vote is easy when your opinions happen to agree with the voters and party leaders. But what happens when these opinions don't agree?

The story of Bob LaFollette (shown in photo at right as a young Senator), a famous member of Congress, is a good example of what can happen. They used to call LaFollette "Fighting Bob." He grew up on a farm in Wisconsin. He worked his way through the University of Wisconsin, graduating in 1879. His first experience in politics was running for county *district attorney.**

Later in life, he wrote about his first campaign. He remembered riding out into the country in a horse and buggy and asking farmers to vote for him. LaFollette wrote:

"I remember how I often tied my horse, climbed the fences, and found the farmer and his men in the fields.

" 'Ain't you over-young?' was the objection chiefly raised.

"I was short and thin—at that time. I looked even younger than I really was.

"But there were a number of things that helped me. I knew farm ways and farm life. Many of the people who did not know me personally knew well from what family I came — and that it was an honest family."

Bob LaFollette was 25 years old when he won an election for district attorney. Four years later, he was elected to represent the farmers of Dane County, Wisconsin, in the U.S. Congress.

His early career in politics was a great success. But he was still young and inexperienced, compared with

Robert LaFollette

other politicians in Congress. He was entering a new job and he wondered how he should behave in it.

Imagine for a minute that you are LaFollette, a young politician serving your first term in the House of Representatives. Imagine that two letters have come to you from citizens who supported your campaign for election. Each letter gives you different advice about your role in Congress.

If you were LaFollette, would you be likely to take the advice given in Letter Number One? Or would you follow the advice of Letter Number Two?

Letter Number One
December 5, 1884

Dear Bob:

I believe you have a great future ahead of you. You have great ability as a public speaker. You're hard-working and intelligent and eager to move ahead in this world.

But I must warn you about one thing. Don't be *too* eager to make your voice heard. I have seen many people like yourself who tried to set the world on fire. They were much too quick to push their own ideas and their own opinions. They made many of the older and more experienced members of Congress angry. And this ruined their careers in politics.

I urge you to try to understand the points of view of the other members. If they ask for your help and support, give it to them.

After a few years, your patience will be rewarded. As others learn to trust your judgment, you will gradually rise to a position of leadership. "To get along, go along"—that's a good motto. If you follow this advice, I am sure you will some day achieve great things.

Sincerely yours,

Della Barsten

Letter Number Two
December 12, 1884

Dear Bob:

I voted for you because I was impressed with your courage and your independence. You seem to be the type of person who stands up for what you believe.

In Congress, you will be under a lot of pressure to vote for laws that your party favors. It will be hard to oppose powerful party leaders.

Please, Bob, don't go along with them just because they tell you to. It's all right to listen to them. But use your own judgment. If you think they're wrong, then you should oppose them. Never mind if you're the only one in the whole House of Representatives who disagrees with them. You still have a duty to fight for what you believe.

Of course, if you're greatly outnumbered, you may lose your battle. But you must be strong enough to fight and keep on fighting. Eventually your voice will be heard.

Sincerely yours,

Winston Jones

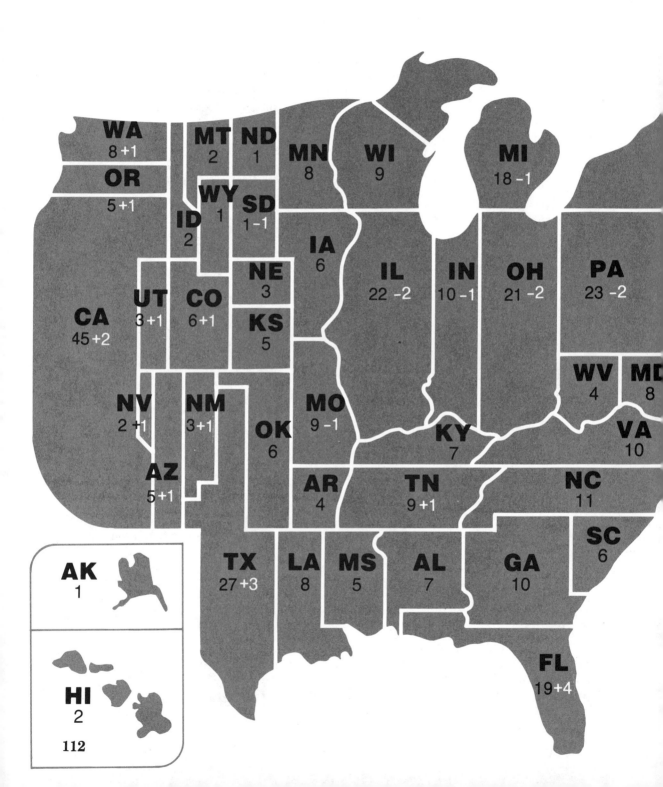

WA 8 +1

OR 5 +1

MT 2

ND 1

MN 8

WI 9

MI 18 −1

WY 1

ID 2

SD 1 −1

IA 6

IL 22 −2

IN 10 −1

OH 21 −2

PA 23 −2

UT 3 +1

CO 6 +1

NE 3

KS 5

CA 45 +2

NV 2 +1

NM 3 +1

OK 6

MO 9 −1

KY 7

WV 4

MD 8

VA 10

AZ 5 +1

AR 4

TN 9 +1

NC 11

SC 6

AK 1

TX 27 +3

LA 8

MS 5

AL 7

GA 10

HI 2

FL 19 +4

112

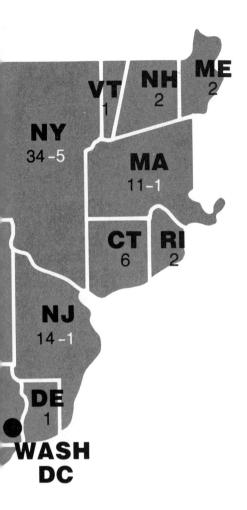

THE BIG STATES IN THE BIG HOUSE

Which 10 states send the greatest number of Representatives to the House? Which 10 states send the smallest number? This map gives you an easy way to find out. Just look for the biggest and smallest states. The boundaries of the biggest states have been stretched to show the size of their populations.

But populations constantly change. Every 10 years, the U.S *Census** Bureau reports changes in the population of each of the 50 states. If your state grows faster than other states, it will gain seats in the House of Representatives. If the Census Bureau reports a decrease in the population of your states, the state will lose Representatives.

The black numbers show the number of Representatives each state had after the 1980 census.

The white numbers show how many seats states gained or lost between 1970 and 1980. States without white numbers neither gained nor lost seats. Did your state's representation in the House change during those years? By how much?

The personal values of a Representative and Senator are constantly tested in Congress. This Action Project presents a real situation that tested Bob La-Follette. What would *you* have decided to do?

The year is 1917. Bob LaFollette is no longer a young man, and he is no longer in the House of Representatives. Instead, he has been elected to the Senate.

The question that now faces Senator LaFollette of Wisconsin is probably the most serious of his long career in politics.

Since August 1914, a terrible war has been fought in Europe. President Woodrow Wilson (at right) has tried to keep the United States out of the war. But now Germany has declared that it will sink all ships that attempt to trade with its wartime enemy, Britain. This includes American ships.

LaFollette still hopes that Germany's action will not lead to war. But throughout the United States, people are beginning to think that war is coming. Even President Wilson seems to be preparing for war. He has asked Congress to pass a bill that would give him power to place weapons aboard American merchant ships sailing to Britain.

Below are a number of questions that occur to LaFollette. Review these questions in your own mind. Then decide: If you were LaFollette, would you support the bill or oppose it? Write a paragraph explaining what you would do about the President's armed-ship bill.

1. If this bill passes, what do I think will happen? The United States will probably be drawn into war. The bill gives the President almost complete power to defend American merchant ships from attack. There will probably be shooting between German submarines and our ships. When that happens, we will go to war.

2. What do I think of this bill? I believe it is very dangerous. It gives the President too much power. And it will lead the United States into a war, which we should avoid at all costs.

3. What do other members of Congress think of this bill? Almost all of them are for it. They believe that this is a national emergency. They say that America's honor is on the line. America's sailors must be able to defend themselves. They feel very strongly about it. I cannot hope to change their minds.

4. If I am so greatly outnumbered, how can I hope to defeat this

bill? I can lead a *filibuster** on the Senate *floor.** The law requires Congress to end its *session** at noon on March 4. That's only 48 hours from now. If the bill hasn't been voted on by then, it is dead for this session.

With the help of a small group of Senators who feel as I do, we can prevent this bill from coming to a vote. We can take turns making speeches on the bill for 48 hours, day and night.

5. Do I risk anything by leading a filibuster? Yes, the risk is enormous. Many people would hate me for doing it. They would accuse me of treason against the nation. I would lose popularity everywhere, even in my home state. And I will probably also lose influence and respect here in the Senate.

6. What if I lead this filibuster and it is successful? Will this act keep the United States out of war? Probably not. The country seems to want war with Germany. If public opinion is strongly for war, I won't be able to stop it.

7. What should I do? Lead a filibuster — or allow the bill to go through? What did LaFollette decide to do? You can determine this for yourself, given one clue about LaFollette's personality. Throughout his life, he was the type of person who much preferred the advice offered in Letter Number Two. Other members of Congress, probably equally conscientious, tended to follow the advice in Letter Number One.

Judging from your answers to this Action Project, which type of person are you? Do you believe that on issues of importance you should stick to what you believe to be right, no matter what the risk? Do you believe that it is better to try to reach the best compromise you can on such issues? Or do you believe it is your duty to vote the way your constituents feel, regardless of your own views or the views of other members of Congress?

Woodrow Wilson

"THE LAST WORD"

by Fola and Belle LaFollette

After Senator LaFollette's death in 1925, his daughter and his wife wrote a book about his life. This section is adapted from their book. It describes Bob LaFollette (shown here after several years in the Senate) in the last minutes of his filibuster against the armed-ship bill.

At that point in the Senate debate,* the anger of the other Senators against LaFollette almost led to violence. Senators Hitchcock and Robinson, mentioned in this reading, were two of LaFollette's chief opponents.

Bob's son, Bob, Jr., was 22 at the time and working as his father's assistant.

Hitchcock again tried to get a vote at 11:30 o'clock. Bob then made the *point of order** that the request had not been presented correctly. Hitchcock ignored this and asked if there was an objection. Bob's voice rang out clearly, "Yes: I object now; and I will object again. And as often as the request is made until I have the opportunity to be heard."

Another Senator called him to order with the biting remark, "He is constantly violating the rules of the Senate."

Bob replied sharply: "So are you. You have not been recognized yet."

His son, Bob, Jr., standing over near the door, observed the tense scene with growing worry. He sent his father a penciled note: "Please, please, be calm . . . remember Mother. I expect you to make your protest. But there must be a limit to the lengths which you go. You cannot afford to get into a physical argument or be arrested for misconduct. You are extremely excited. Do not try to fight the Senate physically. I am almost crazy with strain."

Bob, Jr., himself, describes what he did next. "I rushed up to the Senate family gallery where a friend, Gilbert Roe, was sitting. I asked him for a suggestion on how to handle the situation. He said, 'Tell Bob the way to meet those fellows is to smile at them.' I went back to the Senate floor and sent him a note which gave this advice to Dad. He immediately smiled at me and from then on he followed Gilbert's advice."

The hour for ending the session drew near. Senator Robinson asked the Secretary to read the agreement calling for a vote at 11:45. Bob promptly objected. Hitchcock asked for a *roll call.** Bob objected and further delayed proceedings.

Only a few moments of the session remained. In a final angry blast, expressing the outraged temper of many Senators, Hitchcock said: "Twelve men in this Senate have defeated the will of 70 or 75 or possibly 80 men. They have defeated that will by carrying on one of the most hateful filibusters ever recorded in the history of any civilized country. Mr. President, I am using rather strong language and possibly I ought to apologize—"

Bob interrupted. "Oh, no; not at all. It is perfectly safe when no one has the right to reply."

A few moments later the Senate ended its session without having taken the vote.

(YOU HAVE THE LAST WORD)

What did "Fighting Bob" LaFollette accomplish? Only a month after he stopped the armed-ship bill, the United States went to war anyway. Knowing this, would you call LaFollette (a) a stubborn fool? (b) a brave man? (c) an impractical dreamer? (d) something else? Why?

"CHECKOUT"—8

Key terms

Congress	constituents	floor
Senate	appropriations	session
House of Representatives	census	point of order
district	apportion	roll call

Review

1. Give two reasons why Congress was created with two houses rather than one.

2. Identify the house referred to in each of these statements: **(a)** *It has 100 members.* **(b)** *Its members are elected for two-year terms.* **(c)** *It may have members who are 25 years old.*

3. The chapter describes the constituencies of Representative Cardiss Collins and Senator Orrin Hatch. Identify the constituency referred to in each of these statements: **(a)** *A majority of the constituents are black.* **(b)** *The constituency is in a small area of a state.* **(c)** *Almost a third of the constituents live outside cities.*

4. Explain the basis on which seats in the House of Representatives are apportioned among the states.

5. Name the action taken by Robert LaFollette in the Senate in 1917. Explain the purpose of this action.

Discussion

1. To serve in the House of Representatives, you must be at least 25 years old; in the Senate, you must be at least 30. Think about these requirements and the possible reasons for them. Then answer the following questions: *Should there be any minimum age restrictions? If so, what should they be? Should there be maximum age restrictions? If so, what should they be? If there should be age restrictions at either end of the spectrum, should they be the same for each legislative body?* Give reasons for your answers.

2. What other qualifications do you think that a member of Congress should have? What values? What personality traits? Why?

3. This chapter pointed out some of the differences between the House of Representatives and the Senate. Your class might discuss these differences — especially size, length of terms, and special powers — for the purpose of determining which of the two governing bodies most students would prefer to serve in.

4. As you learned in the previous unit on the Presidency, no one can be elected to the office of President more than twice. But there are no limits on the number of terms a person may serve in either the House or the Senate. Should there be? Why or why not? If you think there should be limits, what should they be?

5. If you have ever visited Washington, D.C. and Capitol Hill, you might describe for the rest of the class what you saw and learned, especially about Congress.

Activities

1. *The Congressional Directory* and *The World Almanac* are two useful sources of information about both houses of Congress. For example, do you know which Congressional district you live in? (Some students in your class may live in different Congressional districts.) There is a map in *The Congressional Directory* that will show you the districts in your state. Do you know who represents you in the House and in the Senate? Both of the books mentioned above (which you can probably find in your school or public library) will tell you. They will also tell you who the leaders are in both houses of Congress this year, which political party has the most members in Congress this year, and much more.

Interested students might form one or two committees to research and report to the rest of the class on this and other basic information about this year's Congress — especially about your own Senators and Representative(s).

2. A few interested students might write to each of your state's Senators and Representatives in the House re-

questing their photographs and biographical information for classroom display in the Gallery of Political Leaders. You might compare the biographical information they send with the information given in *The Congressional Directory*. Which seems more current, more personal, more useful?

3. Some of you might enjoy role-playing a TV interview—such as you see on *Meet the Press, Nightline,* or *60 Minutes.* One of you could play the role of a Senator or Representative being interviewed on an issue that is very much in the news at that time. Others could role-play the interviewers. All of you should prepare in advance by reading as much as you can find about the issue to be discussed. You should also be familiar with the way the interview programs named above are conducted.

Afterward other students could critique the performances.

4. Representative Cardiss Collins is one of the very few black women to serve in Congress. Most members of both houses have been white males. Interested students might want to research and report to the rest of the class on other minority-group members who have served in the House and Senate.

5. Making use of the most recent *World Almanac,* some students might draw a bar graph illustrating the number of U.S. Representatives each state sends to Washington. Other students might prefer to put the information on a map, similar to the one in this chapter.

9: AN ACT OF CONGRESS
(AND A LOOK AT BLOOD RIVER)

Imagine the rocky bed of a stream in the middle of a quiet wood. But instead of clear running water in this stream, there is the red blood and thick white fat of slaughtered animals. Such a stream did exist (see photo at left).

One fall day, a class of students from Manchester, New Hampshire, were taken to see it by their biology teacher, James Hall. Several students almost got sick at the sight and smell of it.

One of them said later: "I had heard about Blood River before. But to see it just freaked me out. We all wanted to do something about it. Have the owners arrested or something. But Mr. Hall said that wasn't the way to do it."

The people responsible for Blood River were the owners of a meat-packing plant that daily dumped its wastes into it. From there the waste flowed into the much larger Merrimack River. Other factories also dumped waste into the Merrimack. This made the Merrimack River one of the 10 dirtiest in the nation.

Mr. Hall's biology class spent the rest of the school year studying the causes of river pollution. They took pictures of Blood River to show the public what was happening. They tested the quality of the water at different points along the Merrimack River.

They then helped to get the case of Blood River tried in court. And they won their case. The judge fined the packing company for breaking a federal law against pollution—and he made the company stop polluting.

The money for this class project at West High School came from an office of the federal government. It paid for Mr. Hall's field trips and provided students with water-testing kits and camera equipment.

There have been many projects like this one all over the country. They have all depended on money provided by the Environmental Education Act.

How was this particular law created and passed by Congress? Dennis Brezina and Allen Overmyer tell how in their book, *Congress in Action: The Environmental Education Act.*

Introducing a bill in Congress. Each year, Senators and Representatives make many thousands of written proposals for new laws. These are called bills. Only a small number of the bills actually make it all the way through the long process of becoming a law.

On November 12, 1969, Representative John Brademas, a Democrat from Indiana, proposed a bill to support environmental education for young people. The clerk of the House stamped the proposal with a number—HR 14753.

One week later, on November 19, 1969, the same bill was proposed in the Senate by Senator Gaylord Nelson,

a Democrat from Wisconsin. It too was given a number—S 1525.

According to the Constitution, only three steps are needed for a bill to become law:

● A majority of the House of Representatives must vote for it.

● A majority of the Senate must vote for it.

● The President must then sign it.

This is all that the Constitution requires. Actually, the process of making laws is far more complicated. It involves much more than three short steps.

The diagram (page 123) shows everything that a bill must go through to become law. Think of the "Y" as a racetrack, with hurdles blocking the path of the runners at almost every point.

The "runners" in the race are those Representatives and Senators who believe in the importance of a bill. Their goal is to carry the bill over all the hurdles before the time comes for Congress to *adjourn**—end its session. It is both a race against time and a fight to defeat those who stand in the way of the bill's progress.

Who were the runners who carried the two bills through the finish line? How did they manage to jump each hurdle in their path?

How to move a bill through Congress. The chief runners were Representative Brademas and Senator Nelson. They planned their moves so that the two bills would be acted upon at the same time in each house of Congress. They knew that this would be faster than sending the bill through one house, and then the other house.

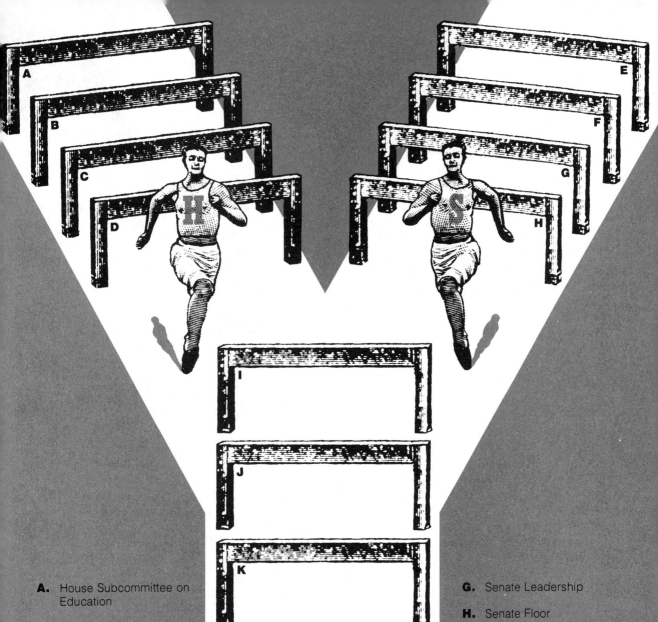

A. House Subcommittee on Education

B. House Committee on Labor and Education

C. House Rules Committee

D. House Floor

E. Senate Subcommittee on Education

F. Senate Committee on Labor and Public Welfare

G. Senate Leadership

H. Senate Floor

I. Conference Committee

J. House Rules Committee

K. House Floor

L. Senate Leadership

M. Senate Floor

N. White House

The sponsors of the two bills were also prepared for opposition to the bills. Representative Brademas and Senator Nelson were both Democrats. They feared that a Republican President, Richard Nixon, might oppose the bill. He could try to convince Republican members of Congress to vote against the measure. He could also tell important officials of the Executive Branch to go to Congress and argue against the proposed law.

Even so, Representative Brademas and Senator Nelson were hopeful. They believed their bills were so good and so popular that few members of Congress would dare to oppose them.

In 1969 the American people were becoming more and more concerned about pollution. A politician might think twice before opposing a law that would help America's young people learn about their environment.

This was the situation in late November 1969, when the two bills on environmental education started moving along the Y track. Each bill stated that the federal government would help set up environmental education programs for young people. A new agency of government would be created to give grants of money to worthy projects.

We can now follow these bills from start to finish. Eventually, as you'll see, the two bills became one law.

Subcommittee hurdles. In each house of Congress, bills are given to committees. The committees study the bills and may recommend changes. Different committees concentrate on different areas. Because HR 14753 dealt with education, it was given to

the House Committee on Labor and Education.

Since a committee cannot handle the many hundreds of bills that come to it, it divides itself into smaller groups called subcommittees. The House Committee on Labor and Education gave HR 14753 to a subcommittee led by none other than John Brademas himself.

Brademas now had to persuade other members of the subcommittee to approve his bill. To do this, he called to Washington a number of experts on education and the environment. For 13 days, these experts talked to the subcommittee about the need for educating young people about the environment.

Several high school students were also invited to give their opinions. Most of them thought environmental education was a good idea.

Meanwhile, Senate bill S 1525 was also being studied by the Senate

Subcommittee on Education.

It was up to each subcommittee to decide whether the bill was good enough to be recommended to the full committee. Each subcommittee could vote to drop the bill. But members of both subcommittees voted to recommend the bill to the full committee.

The two bills thus jumped cleanly over their first set of hurdles.

Committee hurdles. The bills had no trouble clearing the second set of hurdles. The House Committee on Labor and Education simply accepted the report of its subcommittee. The Senate Committee on Labor and Public Welfare did the same.

In the House, the next hurdle for a bill is normally the powerful Rules Committee. This committee decides when bills will be voted on by the full House membership. It also decides how much debate will be allowed before the vote. However, a special rule of procedure lets a few bills by-pass the Rules Committee on two days of each month. Because the Brademas bill was popular, it was passed on to the full House through this special rule.

In the Senate, the leadership, not a rules committee, decides when bills will be voted on. So now, both bills were on the floor ready to be voted on.

Floor hurdles. In political language, the *floor* means the large rooms of the House and Senate where members assemble to vote on bills.

The Senate leadership agreed to put Senator Nelson's bill on the top of the list of bills waiting for

Senate action. Once this hurdle was cleared, the bill passed in the Senate by a vote of 64 to 0.

In the House, there was a short debate on Representative Brademas' bill. Then the House members passed the bill by a vote of 289 to 28.

Both bills had cleared floor hurdles. But the Senate and House bills were not exactly alike. They had started out alike. But they had been changed by the two subcommittees in different ways. The differences were minor. But they now had to be ironed out at the center point of the Y track.

Conference hurdles. Special committees from both the House and the Senate met in a conference room. They talked about their differences until they had agreed on a compromise bill. It had some details from the Senate bill and some from the House bill. Instead of two bills, there was now only one.

Passing the House (a second time). Representative Brademas got the Rules Committee to let the House vote on the compromise bill without a delay. It reached the House floor October 13, 1970, and passed without a single "no" vote. The work of Representative Brademas was finished.

Passing the Senate (a second time). Once again, Senator Nelson got the Senate leadership to move his bill to the Senate floor quickly. And once again the bill passed the

Senate without a single "no" vote.

Passing the White House. The Environmental Education bill was now sent to the White House and placed on the President's desk. Would President Nixon sign his name to it? If so, the bill would become law.

If not, the President could send the bill back to Congress with a message stating his objections to it. Such action is called a Presidential *veto*. If the President vetoes a bill, the two houses of Congress have to take another vote on the bill. The bill then passes only if at least two thirds of the members of each house vote for it.

The President could also stop the Environmental Education bill by another means. He had received the bill only eight days before Congress was due to end its session.

The Constitution allows the President 10 full days to study a bill passed by Congress. After that, the bill automatically becomes law even if the President doesn't sign it. However, if Congress ends its session before the 10-day period is over, a bill may sit on a President's desk unsigned and not become law. Such action by the President is a *pocket veto*.*

President Nixon could have easily stopped the bill from becoming law. But on October 30, 1970, he signed his name to the law. The Environmental Education Act thus crossed the finish line. It was now a law of the land.

Three years later, in Manchester, New Hampshire, James Hall's biology class got their first look at the horrors of Blood River.

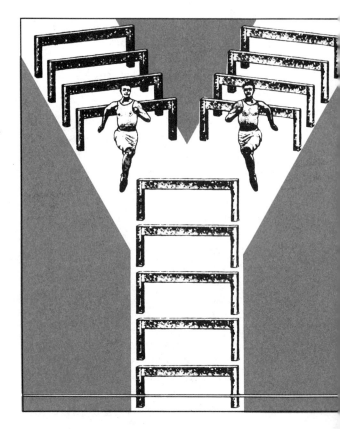

Here is a chance to test your understanding of how a bill becomes a law. Two student volunteers are needed for this Action Project. One should be a "Senator" and the other a "Representative."

These volunteers are the chief sponsors of HR 5101 and S 683, "A Bill to Create an Ice Cream Parlor." The bill proposes that your school spend $70,000 to build a wing onto the cafeteria for an ice cream parlor. It would be open during and after school hours.

For the purpose of this exercise, assume that there is no important opposition to this bill. However, the bill *can* be defeated if either sponsor makes just one mistake leading it through Congress.

Put the Y diagram on the chalkboard.

Below are the steps that the two bills must go through to become an act and then a law. The steps are out of order.

Without looking back in this chapter, the two sponsors of this bill should number each step on the board, using the numbers below. Others in the class should check that the steps are correctly labeled. If there is an error, two other sponsors should be selected. They must erase what's on the board and start again.

The Action Project ends when one team of sponsors successfully labels all 14 points on the Y diagram.

1. The Senate Subcommittee on Student Privileges holds a hearing on the bill.

2. The Conference Committee meets to draw up a new compromise bill.

3. The President signs the Student Lounge Act.

4. The House Rules Committee clears the bill for a final vote.

5. The House Committee on Buildings and Grounds receives a favorable report on the bill.

6. The Senate votes on the bill for the first time.

7. The Senate votes on the bill as previously passed by the House.

8. The House votes on the bill as changed by the Conference Committee.

9. The House Subcommittee on Student Affairs holds hearings on the bill.

10. The Senate Committee on Buildings and Grounds discusses the bill.

11. The Bill is debated for the first time on the floor of the House.

12. The House Rules Committee clears the bill the first time.

13. The Senate leadership puts the bill on top of the list.

14. The Senate leadership clears the bill a second time.

"THE LAST WORD"

by members of the House of Representatives

Speeches on the floor of the House and the Senate are recorded and printed in the Congressional Record. *These official proceedings of Congress fill several thick volumes every year. The following passage comes from one day of House debate. Some of the debaters on that afternoon of March 18, 1987 were:*

• Representative Kenneth Gray (Democrat—Illinois);

• Representative James Howard (Democrat—New Jersey);

• Representative Glenn Anderson (Democrat—California);

• Representative Bill Richardson (Democrat—New Mexico).

They were debating whether to pass a law to raise the national speed limit from 55 to 65 miles per hour. Representative Gray led the group in favor of passing the law. Representative Howard led the group that opposed passage. Each side was allotted 30 minutes which were "yielded" or given to those arguing its side.

As you read this shortened version, notice how the debate is controlled. Notice the polite way Representatives talk about each other.

The Speaker pro tempore: The Chair recognizes the gentleman from Illinois [Mr. Gray].

Mr. Gray: Mr. Speaker, I yield myself 1 minute.

Mr. Speaker, in 1974, our distinguished chairman and dear friend, the gentleman from New Jersey [Mr. Howard] offered a bill later adopted into law limiting the national speed limit to 55 miles per hour.

I want to compliment him, it was badly needed at the time, because we had an energy crisis; but like many other things, times change; it is an antiquated law and should be changed.

Mr. Howard: Mr. Speaker, I yield 3 minutes to the gentleman from California [Mr. Anderson], the chairman of our Subcommittee on Surface Transportation.

Mr. Anderson: Mr. Speaker, I rise in opposition to the resolution offered by my friend from Illinois.

Each of us in this chamber must recognize a basic truth, that raising the speed limit will increase the number of deaths and crippling injuries resulting from traffic accidents.

If there is to be a speed increase, it must be coupled with safety measures that a State would have to adopt to offset the deaths and injuries.

Mr. Gray: Mr. Speaker, I yield 1 minute to the gentleman from New Mexico [Mr. Richardson].

Mr. Richardson: Mr. Speaker, here are several reasons why we need to raise the speed limit.

First, hardly anyone is obeying the 55. Our cops should be chasing robbers and drug dealers, not those going 56 miles an hour.

Second, for rural and western states, it has been a big burden, losing money and infringing upon people's rights.

Third, circumstances have changed. There is no more [gas] shortage, and there have been many safety devices on automobiles to lessen the safety hazards.

Mr. Howard: Mr. Speaker, I yield 3 minutes to the gentleman from Florida [Mr. Lehman].

Mr. Lehman: Mr. Speaker, I rise in strong opposition to the amendment. When the limit was 65 or more, people also violated those limits. The difference was that then they were driving 70 to 75 instead of 60 miles per hour as they do now.

That difference is very important because, according to the National Safety Council, the chances of a person being killed in a crash doubles with each 10 miles per hour of speed over 55 miles per hour. If we vote to raise the speed limit, we are voting to kill and maim more people.

The vote was taken by electronic device, and there were—yeas 217, nays 206, not voting 10.

Mr. Gray's resolution passed the House.

(YOU HAVE THE LAST WORD)

Do you agree with the House's decision? Why or why not? Judging from the people arguing for and against this law, do party members always stick together? What differences in the states of these House members might explain their positions on this law?

Some students might want to debate this bill or the bill to create an ice cream parlor using the form of a House debate. Each side should be allotted a fixed amount of time, with the head proponents yielding portions of that time to members of their teams. One student should run the debate as the presiding officer. Speakers should refer to each other as distinguished gentlemen and gentlewomen.

"CHECKOUT"—9

Key terms

bill	veto	floor
adjourn	pocket veto	subcommittee
House Rules Committee		

Review

1. Name the act of Congress that enabled a class to visit Blood River.

2. Describe the three steps required by the Constitution for a bill to become law.

3. When a bill is introduced in the Senate or House of Representatives, what is the first hurdle it has to face? What is the last hurdle?

4. Describe the two ways in which a President can veto a bill. Explain how Congress can override the President's veto.

5. In the House debate in The Last Word, what were the roles of the two members who "yielded" the allotted time to the various speakers? What states did they represent?

Discussion

1. As this chapter pointed out, "Each year, Senators and Representatives make many thousands of written proposals for new laws." In a recent session of Congress, more than 22,000 bills were introduced. About 3,200 of these were passed, and 800 became laws. One Senator said: "We are losing control of what we are doing here ... there isn't enough time in the day to keep abreast of everything ... dealing with so many bills...."

Some people — especially business people — say that the federal government has gotten out of control, that there are so many laws and regulations and forms to fill out that they place a heavy burden on the average business person.

What do you think? Can you name examples of laws that seem unnecessary and annoying?

How might the proliferation of laws in Congress be cut down? Should there be a limit on the number of bills a member of Congress can introduce each year? Why or why not? What might be the result of such a limit? What might be the result of continuing without a limit?

2. Does it seem as if there are too many "hurdles" for a bill to get over in order to become a law? Should any of these steps be shortened or eliminated? Why or why not?

3. Bills passed by Congress often contain many different parts, sometimes dealing with widely different subjects. However, when Congress passes a bill, the President cannot veto parts of it and sign the rest. He must veto or sign the *whole* bill. Here's what can happen:

Say that most of the members of Congress want a new law. For example, they might want a law that says that the next members of Congress will be given a salary increase. They know that the President is against this new law. So they make it an amendment to a bill that they know the President wants to get passed — for example, a bill increasing revenue sharing for large cities.

Then, when the President gets the bill, he must sign or veto all of it — even though it has an amendment that he does not like.

Some people say that the President should be allowed to veto some items in a bill without having to veto the whole bill. Other people say that this would give the President too much control over Congressional legislation.

What do you think? Your class might hold a debate on the pros and cons of giving the President the power to veto parts of a bill. Then take a vote to see how the majority of the class feels on this issue.

Activities

1. You might write to your representatives in the House and the Senate, asking for copies of recent bills they have sponsored. The letters could also ask about the status of the bills. Have they been passed yet? Are they tied up in committees, hearings, etc.? When the information arrives, it could be displayed on the bulletin board.

2. Some students might want to research and report to the rest of the class on recent Presidential vetoes. What were the bills? What did the President say about why he was vetoing them? What happened on the next round of votes in Congress — were the bills passed by the necessary two-thirds vote of each house? If not, why not? What did the leaders of the House and Senate say about the President's actions?

3. Some students might look through recent issues of the *Congressional Record* for examples of debates and speeches that might interest members of the class. Students could then assume the roles of the various Senators or Representatives and read aloud some of the most interesting passages.

4. Your class might watch the televised proceedings of the House of Representatives. Afterward, you could discuss procedures, debating methods, and other events that you find interesting.

5. Most members of the Senate and House of Representatives maintain offices in their home states or districts. There may be one or more of these offices in or near your community. You might visit one of the offices to learn what is done there, what services are provided, etc. Or a staff member who works in one might speak to your class on the same topics.

HR 500
A bill to declare the United States
at war with Morocco.

HR 501
A bill to make the District of
Columbia a state.

HR 502
A bill to stop "unpatriotic" opinions from
appearing in newspapers and magazines.

HR 503
A bill to increase the penalty for smuggling
narcotics into the United States.

HR 504
A bill to place a sales tax on
soft drinks, coffee, beer, and wine.

HR 505
A bill to spend $10 billion for a new
antimissile missile.

10: HOW TO JUDGE A BILL

If you were in Congress and members introduced the following bills, which would you probably vote for? Which would you vote against?

HR 500. A bill to declare the United States at war with Morocco.

HR 501. A bill to make the District of Columbia a state, with a governor, a two-house legislature, and all the other privileges and responsibilities of a full-fledged state.

HR 502. A bill to stop "unpatriotic" opinions from appearing in newspapers and magazines.

HR 503. A bill to increase the penalty for smuggling narcotics into the United States.

HR 504. A bill to place a sales tax on soft drinks, coffee, beer, and wine.

HR 505. A bill to spend 10 billion dollars for a new antimissile missile.

Three ways to judge a bill. Hundreds of times a year, members of Congress must decide whether to vote for or against bills that other members have proposed. They must be able to decide whether each of these bills is good or bad. As an American citizen, you too should be able to make this decision.

This chapter describes three ways

of judging a bill. First, is the bill *constitutional**? That is, does it follow the principles of the Constitution? Second, is the bill needed? Will it be good for the country as a whole? Third, do the benefits it will provide for some people outweigh the harm it may cause to others?

1. When is a bill constitutional? How can you tell if a bill is allowed by the Constitution? The first thing to do is to look in the Constitution itself. As the highest law of the land, the Constitution gives Congress the power to make certain kinds of laws. But it also forbids Congress to make laws that might be harmful to the nation.

Here are two examples of laws that Congress is *not* allowed to make.

• Article I, Section 8, of the Constitution states: "The Congress shall have the power . . . to exercise exclusive legislation in all cases whatsoever, over such district (not exceeding 10 miles square) as may . . . become the seat of the government of the United States. . . ." Could Congress legally vote to allow the citizens of Washington, D.C., to elect their own "state" legislature?

• The First Amendment to the Constitution states: "Congress shall make no law respecting an establishment of religion, or prohibiting the free exercise thereof; or abridging the freedom of speech, or of the press. . . ." In other words, no law of Congress may interfere with your right to freedom of religion, freedom of speech, and freedom of the press.

Two of the six bills that you've looked at would violate the Constitution be-cause of the above two rules. Which ones are they? (Your teacher can give you the answer.)

The other four bills are allowed because of a list of 18 powers given to Congress by the Constitution. (See Article I, Section 8.) Four of these powers match up with the four constitutional bills you've looked at. These powers are listed here. Which of these powers matches up with which bill?

Taxing power. "The Congress shall have power to lay and collect taxes, duties, imposts, and *excises**. . . ." (Imposts and duties are taxes on goods imported from foreign countries. Congress can place a tax—duty—on motorcycles imported from Japan, for example. Excises are taxes on the sale, manufacture, or use of goods. For example, Congress has placed an excise tax on tobacco.)

Commerce power. "The Congress shall have power to *regulate** commerce with foreign nations, and among the several states. . . ."

War power. "The Congress shall have power to declare war. . . ."

Military power. "The Congress shall have power to raise and support armies. . . ."

Article I, Section 8, also gives Congress the power to issue paper money and to punish counterfeiters. Congress can borrow money. It has the power to build post offices and to create federal courts. It can give *patents** to inventors. It controls hunting and other activities on government land. It can make rules for giving American citizenship to *immigrants.** It can make laws concerning the state national guard, and it can control the city government of Washington, D.C.

Probably the most important power Congress has is listed in a section of the Constitution known as the *elastic clause*.* It's called this because its meaning can be stretched a long way. It gives Congress power "to make all laws which shall be necessary and proper" for carrying out its other powers. People in Congress sometimes disagree about what is "necessary" and what is "proper." But the elastic clause allows Congress to do many things that are not actually mentioned in the Constitution.

For example, the Constitution gives Congress the right to tax the American people. But it does not specifically give Congress the right to punish people

WHAT IS THE HEALTHIEST DRINK?

	Protein Grams	Carbohydrate (Sugar) Grams	Phosphorus Grams	Vitamin A Units	Vitamin B[1] Units
Orange juice (eight-ounce glass)	2	25	42	500	.2
Cow's milk (whole) (one pint)	16	24	465	780	.16
Cola drinks (sweetened) (12-ounce size)	0	38	0	0	0
Ginger ale (12-ounce size)	0	28	0	0	0
Root beer (12-ounce size)	0	35	0	0	0
Coffee, black	0	1	0	0	0

who break the tax laws. Tax laws would be worthless if there were no penalties for people who do not pay. So Congress has used its powers in the elastic clause to set penalties for people who do not pay their taxes.

2. When is a bill needed by the American public? Most bills introduced into Congress are allowed by the Constitution. But they are not all worth voting for. For example, would you have voted for HR 500, a bill that declares the United States to be at war with Morocco? The bill is legal since Congress has the power to declare war. But it's not needed if there is no reason to go to war with Morocco.

After judging that a bill is allowed

by the Constitution, you must decide whether it's needed. But how do you decide what the country needs? Isn't it a matter of opinion? Partly yes, partly no. Facts and careful thought also play an important part.

For example, take another look at HR 504, a bill to place a sales tax on soft drinks, coffee, beer, and wine. In your opinion, does the U.S. need a tax of this kind?

Anybody who likes soft drinks or coffee would probably say "no" to this question. But suppose you have just read two books on nutrition? In one book, you discover a chart that lists the food values of steak, milk, spinach, fish, eggs, orange juice, and most other foods and beverages.

In the table on the opposite page, compare the health benefits of milk and orange juice with the health benefits of coffee and soft drinks.

The second book talks about the terrible effects of gulping down too many sugar foods (such as soft drinks) and too much coffee. It says that people who make a habit of drinking such beverages may become nervous, depressed, tired, forgetful, confused, and cranky.

With this information, would you now vote for the tax proposed in HR 504? After all, a tax on soft drinks and coffee would raise their prices. People would probably buy them less often. And the American public might eat healthier foods as a result.

At least that's the argument that could be made in support of the bill. Other nutrition experts might disagree with the ideas you've read. But you can see the importance of basing your judgment of a bill on solid information, not just opinion.

3. Will the good effects of the bill outweigh the harm it might cause? Most bills in Congress, if passed into law, would affect different people in different ways. What seems good for some people may not be good for others. For example, nutrition experts may think that HR 504, the soft drink-coffee bill, is just what the country needs. But the owners of a soft drink company or a coffee factory might be ruined by it.

People most affected by certain bills may put pressure on members of Congress to vote one way or the other. Someone representing the nutrition experts may go to Washington to show how much the bill is needed. Someone representing the soft drink companies may tell a committee of Congress how terrible the bill is. This kind of organized effort to persuade lawmakers is called *lobbying*.*

Take one last look at the six bills on page 115. What groups in this country would be most opposed to a bill like HR 503? What groups would want such a bill? Ask yourself the same question about HR 505. Is there any bill which you think almost everyone in the country would oppose? Is there any bill which you think almost everyone in the country would favor?

There is something else a member of Congress must think about before deciding whether to support a bill: *How much will the bill cost?* A bill might offer benefits to many people but still involve spending so much money that it would do more harm than good.

You should now know three ways of judging whether a certain bill is "good" or "bad."

- Is it constitutional?
- Is it needed?
- Will the good it can do outweigh any harm it might cause?

Imagine that your class is the Senate Committee on Commerce, Science, and Transportation. It is a cold day in February 1987. The committee is holding a *public hearing** on two bills, S. 356 and S. 362. Because these two bills are similar, the committee is considering combining them into one bill.

In the committee room there are a number of people who are concerned about these bills. Senator Ernest Hollings, head of the Commerce Committee and chairman of the meeting, is also the sponsor of one of the bills. James Landry, who represents the airline companies, is also strongly in favor of the bills. Captain Richard Stone, head of the Air Line Pilots Association, is against the bills.

After listening to their arguments, the Committee must decide whether these bills are needed or not. The bills are about random drug testing for airline pilots and railroad engineers. This legislation was proposed in Congress soon after a train wreck killed 16 people. Initial investigations suggested the train crew was at fault. Traces of marijuana were found in the blood of an engineer and brakeman. The bills would require pilots and engineers to submit to unscheduled tests to determine if there were any drugs in their bodies.

This Action Project involves three steps and will test your skill as a lawmaker.

1. Read the Last Word. It is adapted from a February 20, 1987, hearing. It focuses only on the airline industry.

2. Decide whether to support S. 356 and S. 362. On a slip of paper, write "Pass" or "Reject." Be prepared to give reasons for your decision.

3. Count the ballots.

What would have happened to these bills if your class had been the Senate Commerce, Science, and Transportation Committee? (Your teacher can tell you what actually happened to this bill.)

"THE LAST WORD"

by U.S. Senators and others

You will be reading excerpts of the arguments of witnesses:
- *James Landry, Air Transport Association;*
- *Captain Richard Stone, Air Line Pilots Association;*
- *Garry Green, Air Line Pilots Association.*

Senator Ernest Hollings chairs the meeting. Senator John Breaux questions the witnesses against the bill.

Opening statement by the Chairman: The committee will come to order, please. Our hearing this morning will cover both of the random drug testing bills.

It is shameful that we in government need a tragic rail accident such as last month's Amtrak collision in Maryland to wake us up to the fact that such legislation is needed.

The tests performed after the tragedy showed that the engineer and the brakeman had been using marijuana.

The only way to ensure that drugs or alcohol will never be responsible for another accident like this is to require random drug and alcohol testing of transportation employees.

I know there will be constitutional objections. They do not sway me in the least. When there is a choice between a transportation employee's right to privacy or a passenger's right to safe travel, there's no question as to which is more important. We in government have a duty to provide for the safety of our citizens.

Mr. Landry: We hope that our testimony will lead this committee to support a federal air regulation which gives airline employers the tools they need to enforce company safety rules.

Almost all of our members support the use of random drug testing. We consider it the most effective way to stop drug abuse among employees.

Mr. Stone: It is important to understand that drugs thus far are not a serious problem among airline pilots. Based on accident reports compiled by the National Transportation Safety Board, there has not been a single U.S. scheduled airline accident due to alcohol or drug abuse by the pilots.

We don't believe in random testing where there is no reasonable suspicion. It is inefficient. It is also a threat to thousands of innocent individuals whose lives and careers will be tainted by possibly inaccurate test results. And it will be abused by employers to harass and rid themselves of so-called problem employees. I also

believe it violates the Fourth Amendment of the Constitution.

We have found that the way to drug and alcohol-free cockpits is through a good rehabilitation program coupled with a strong professional-standards program. Under our union program, a working pilot, whether he is at home or in the cockpit, is under constant observation by others who can and will report him, for they save his life. Random testing, which only looks at

and says, "Guess what, captain, I'm riding with you"; it's a random test. It's a random inspection of that particular pilot's ability to fly that plane.

Mr. Green: As the lawyer for the Air Line Pilots Association, I'd like to answer that question. What is at stake here is how much power we give our government to invade our homes and our bodies. I think the law has been quite clear that the police may not search us without cause. That rule has stopped investigations of much more serious threats to our safety than the drug test.

Senator Breaux: Mr. Green, the difference is very, very obvious. No pilot has to take a test unless he wants to fly; unless he wants to take into his hands the public safety of 200 passengers.

(YOU HAVE THE LAST WORD)

him once or twice a year, is nowhere near as good a detection device.

Senator Breaux: Mr. Stone, in your testimony, you talk about the unconstitutionality of these random tests. Why is it unconstitutional to have a random test when it's not unconstitutional to have required annual physical tests? You also have random FAA check rides, when an FAA [inspector] walks into the cockpit of an airplane

Before voting for or against S. 356 and S. 362, discuss with your classmates these questions: Is it constitutional? Do the facts lead you to believe that the bill is needed? What groups would benefit from the bill? What groups would be hurt by it? Would the good it can do outweigh the harm it might cause?

"CHECKOUT"—10

Key terms

constitutional
taxing power
commerce power
war power

military power
patents
elastic clause

public hearing
tariff
regulate

Review

1. Identify the Article and Section of the Constitution which lists most of the powers of Congress.

2. Which of the following powers are barred to Congress by the Constitution? (a) The power to regulate trade with foreign nations. (b) The power to declare war. (c) The power to ban public meetings.

3. Identify the clause of the Constitution that gives Congress more powers than are actually spelled out.

4. Describe three questions that should be asked in judging whether a bill should become law.

5. In 1987 the Senate Commerce Committee wanted to find out whether a bill to institute random drug testing of pilots and engineers was needed. What method did the committee use?

Discussion

1. In some cases, it is not readily clear whether or not a bill is constitutional. It may be passed by Congress, put into effect, and then ruled unconstitutional years later by the Supreme Court. Could, or should, something be done to try to prevent this from happening? For example, would it be a good idea to have members of the Supreme Court, or their staffs, rule on the constitutionality of every law passed by Congress *before* it was put into effect? What effect—if any—would such a procedure have on the separation of powers? Explain your answers.

2. If the class wrote to members of Congress and received samples of some bills (as suggested in the Checkout of Chapter 9), these bills could now be judged by the three standards presented in this chapter. First, sort out the bills which are too long and/or technical to be dealt with in class. Then handle the others in one of two ways:

(a) Each bill could be read aloud and then discussed by the class in terms of how it measures up to the standards. Or (b) the class could be divided into three committees, with each committee responsible for judging one aspect of all the bills. For example, one committee would read all of the bills to see if they are constitutional; the second committee would be responsible for judging if each bill is needed; and the third committee would try to decide if the good of each bill would outweigh any potential harm. Afterward, the three committees could discuss their findings with the rest of the class.

3. This chapter discussed three ways to judge a bill. Which of the three seems most important to you? Why? Do these three standards cover everything that should be asked about a bill? What other standards — if any — might be useful?

Activities

1. The class might enjoy playing the following bill-judging game:

Students could form two (or more) teams. Each team should read and discuss Article I, Sections 8 and 9, and the first 10 amendments to the Constitution. Then each team should prepare eight or more proposed bills. Some of the bills should be constitutional; others — intentionally — should *not* be. When each team has prepared its bills, one team could start the game by reading aloud one of its bills. The other team could then have 30 seconds to decide if the bill would be constitutional. (Those answering could have their texts open to the Constitution.)

Then the second team could read aloud one of its proposed bills, and the first team would then have to decide within the time limit if that bill would be constitutional.

The teams could take turns reading aloud and deciding until all bills had been dealt with. Then, with the teacher serving as referee, the class could consult the Constitution to determine which team scored the most points. (A team might be awarded one point for each unconstitutional bill it slipped by the opposing team and two points for each bill which it decided correctly as the judging team.)

2. Some students might research and report to the rest of the class examples of laws passed by Congress that were later ruled unconstitutional. They might prepare answers to some of these questions:

When was the law passed? When was it ruled unconstitutional? By whom and why was the law brought to the attention of the Supreme Court? What, if anything, have been — or will be — the results of the law being overturned?

3. Some of you might study carefully the list of 18 powers given to Congress by the Constitution in Article I, Section 8. Then you could try to find at least one example of a law passed by Congress that falls under each of those powers. If possible, newspaper or magazine articles about each example could be brought to class for discussion and displayed on the bulletin board under the heading of the appropriate power.

4. Many different groups in our society have committees that act as "watchdogs" to judge proposals of new bills in Congress. A representative of one or two such groups might be invited to speak to the class about how they judge bills. Examples of groups that might be invited to send speakers are: the League of Women Voters, the American Conservative Union, Common Cause, the Chamber of Commerce, the American Legion, the American Civil Liberties Union.

11: POWER IN CONGRESS

Two Senators are talking in an office in Washington, D.C. One of them is about 40 years old. The other man has snowy white hair. He's about 65 years old.

"Well, Jim," the older man says, "I can see how much this bill means to you. And, except for a few points, I don't see any problem with it. I'll do my best for your bill when it comes before my committee. Now we may have to make a few changes in it. But nothing big. So I don't see any real problems, do you?"

"Not with your help, Eric," Jim replies. "I really do appreciate this. I'll be glad to return the favor later, when I can."

"That's fine. Fine. I'm sure we'll be seeing a lot of each other," says Eric.

"I certainly hope so. Maybe you'll come over to my home sometime for dinner. My family would love to meet you."

"Sounds good to me. Thanks for stopping by."

Someone who knows how Congress works would tell you that one of these Senators has more power and influence than the other. Perhaps, from the talk, you too can tell. Who is more powerful—Jim or Eric? What makes you think so?

The scene illustrates two basic principles about the way members of Congress work together and influence each other. These principles are *logrolling** and *seniority.**

Logrolling or "trading favors."
Logrolling is a common practice in Congress. The term goes back to the days when people on the frontier built their own cabins out of wooden logs. To get the job done, a frontier family would ask their neighbors to help roll the heavy logs into place. In return, the family would be expected to help its neighbors when they needed it.

Members of Congress help each other in much the same way. For example, Jim was asking Eric to help move his bill through a committee. It was probably a bill that interested Jim, but not Eric. Later, Eric will call upon Jim to vote for a bill that Eric has a special interest in.

Senior members get on the "best" committees.
Because of Eric's age, it seems likely that he has spent more years in the Senate than Jim. If so, he has greater seniority (years of service). This almost certainly means that he has greater power. It gives him the privilege of being placed on one of the "best" committees.

Power in Congress depends partly on what committee a member belongs to. All Senators and Representatives are members of committees. But some committees are more powerful (and, therefore, "better") than others.

Some of the most powerful committees are those that work with money bills — bills for raising taxes and spending government money. A member of the House Appropriations Committee, for example, has a voice in deciding how billions of dollars of government money shall be spent.

Some members of Congress consider certain committees unimportant. Usually these are committees that deal with bills that do not involve the interests of most Americans.

The committees of Congress usually decide whether a bill gets passed or not. This is because there are too many bills for every member of Congress to study carefully. Therefore, Congress relies upon the work and judgment of its various committees.

If House and Senate committees approve a bill, the chances are Congress will vote to pass it.

Most bills that come to a committee, however, are never approved. Committees can reject or simply ignore bills that most members do not like.

The head of the committee is the *chairperson.** He or she has more power than the other committee members to decide which bills shall be given attention and which bills shall be ignored. Therefore, some of the most powerful members of Congress are the chairpersons of committees.

Because of his seniority, the Senator we've been calling Eric might be the chairperson of a Senate committee. But it's not a sure thing anymore—as it was 20 years ago. In recent years, the importance of seniority has been challenged by younger members of Congress. But in most cases, a senior member of Congress can expect to be chairperson of a committee if he or she is a member of the majority party.

146

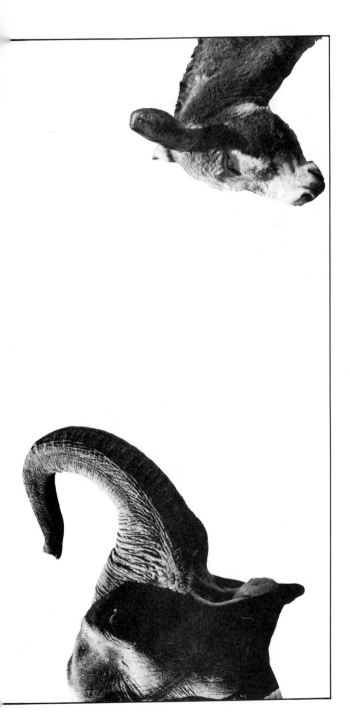

Majority party rules the House.

Visiting Eric in his office, Jim was probably very much aware of Eric's seniority and power.

Throughout the conversation, Jim might have been thinking: "So this is the great Eric Maxwell, chairman of the Senate Committee on Foreign Relations. He's not such a bad guy. And we're both Democrats. We seem to understand each other pretty well. Maybe, in another two years, I can get on his committee."

Jim is very aware that both he and Eric belong to the same political party. For members of Congress, their party is a key part of their identity and power. With very rare exceptions, Congress consists of Republicans and Democrats. A Democrat usually seeks help from a fellow Democrat. And a Republican works mainly with fellow Republicans. Republicans and Democrats may joke with each other and even be friends. But they are still rivals —rivals for power.

To have power in Congress, you may need more than seniority and a place on a powerful committee, though both are important. It is also important to belong to the party that controls the most seats.

In the Senate, for example, there may be 55 Democrats and 45 Republicans. This makes the Democrats the majority party. It gives them the power to control all Senate committees. Most of the members of each committee will be Democrats. All committee chairpersons will be Democrats.

While the Democrats are in power, Republicans will not control a single committee. You may be 80 years old and

Edward Geller
has served 14 years as a Democratic Senator from Rhode Island, seven years on the Banking Committee.

Judith Adams
has served 22 years as a Republican Senator from Kansas, 12 years on the Banking Committee.

have served 30 years as a Senator. But if you belong to the minority party, you will not be a committee chairperson.

However, it is always possible for a minority party in one Congress to become the majority party in the next Congress.

Every two years all members of the House of Representatives and one third of the members of the Senate must face the voters in an election.

After the election, there is a new Congress (even though two thirds of the Senate remain the same). Instead of 55 Democrats and 45 Republicans in the Senate there may be 55 Republicans and 45 Democrats. If this happens, our imaginary Senator Eric Maxwell must give up his position as chairperson of a committee. The person who replaces him probably will be the Republican with the most seniority on the committee.

You now know enough about power in Congress to work on the following problem:

Imagine that the four people above are U.S. Senators serving on the Senate Banking Committee. The Democrats have 52 seats in the Senate. The Republicans have 48. Only one of the four people will become chairperson of the Banking Committee. Who is it most likely to be?

Suppose that an election is held and the Republicans now hold more seats than the Democrats. Who will most likely be the chairperson? (Your teacher has the answer.)

Case study: Mr. Sam vs. Judge Smith. Having power is one thing.

Eileen Brady
has served nine years as a Democratic Senator from North Carolina, all of them on the Banking Committee.

Joseph Fernandez
has served 32 years as a Republican Senator from New Mexico, 28 years on the Banking Committee.

Knowing what to do with it is another. Often the goals of one powerful politician may clash with the goals of another powerful leader. There may then be a contest or tug-of-war that tests the power of each opponent.

A struggle of this kind occurred in January 1961. The struggle concerned two bills that the President, John Kennedy, wanted Congress to pass. One bill proposed a higher minimum wage for workers. The second bill concerned medical care for the aged. Both of these bills could be blocked by a former judge from the state of Virginia, Representative Howard Smith.

As chairman of the House Rules Committee, Judge Smith (as he was called) had enormous power. Any bill that he disliked could be killed in his committee. And Judge Smith especially disliked the President's minimum wage and medicare bills.

The only way to get the two bills through Congress was to challenge Judge Smith's power over the Rules Committee. President Kennedy called upon an old friend, Sam Rayburn, to lead the fight.

Mr. Sam, as he was nicknamed, held a position in the House even more powerful than the Rules Committee chairman. Mr. Sam was Speaker of the House. So he had the power to lead and control debates on the House floor.

At the beginning of every session of Congress, each house may make changes in its rules for doing business. Now Mr. Sam, the Speaker, proposed to change the size of the Rules Committee—from 12 members to 15 mem-

Sam Rayburn

bers. Two of the three new members would be supporters of President Kennedy. Their votes in favor of Kennedy's bills would be just enough to defeat Judge Smith's supporters. But first, the members of the House would have to vote "aye" or "no" on Mr. Sam's proposed change in the rules.

To prepare for the big vote, Mr. Sam invited Democratic Representatives to see him in his office. He called others on the phone. He reminded them of favors that he had done for them in the past. Now, said Mr. Sam, it was time for his friends to repay their old debts.

Meanwhile, Judge Smith was fighting to keep his power. He too called Democrats who owed him a favor. He also won the support of many Republicans who opposed Kennedy's program.

On January 31, 1961, every seat in the House was occupied. The galleries were packed with spectators and reporters. The Speaker (above) banged his gavel.

Mr. Sam's proposal was read aloud: "Resolved: That during the 87th Congress the Committee on Rules shall be composed of 15 members."

The clerk of the House then read off

a list of names. As their names were called, the Representatives stood and shouted out either "aye" or "no." At the end of this vote, the result was announced. There were 217 aye votes and 212 no votes.

The Speaker and the President had won this crucial test of their power by only five votes. Judge Smith (below), a powerful chairman of a powerful committee, had lost much of his power to block the President's program.

In this contest between Judge Smith and Mr. Sam, you see how power is used in Congress. The chairperson of a powerful committee can often decide whether a bill gets passed or not. The only way to overcome this person's power is to weaken his or her control over the committee. This usually requires a change in the rules of the House or the Senate.

But a change in rules is hard to get. It takes a powerful politician to lead and win such a fight. Thus a fight over rules may be more important than the floor debate about a particular bill.

Howard Smith

Imagine that you are a new Senator in the U.S. Congress. At the beginning of the session, you must let the leaders of your party know what committees you are interested in joining.

Although Senators normally have numerous committee assignments, let's say you will be assigned to only one of the committees listed below. Which would be your first choice?

Agriculture, Nutrition, and Forestry. Recent legislation reviewed by this committee concerned: **(a)** nutrition labeling for food products; **(b)** use of agricultural waste as an energy source; **(c)** soil conservation programs; **(d)** budget requirements for the U.S. Forest Service.

Appropriations. This committee has recently reviewed legislation to: **(a)** provide money for the defense budget; **(b)** deny money for the Air Force to develop a long range transport plane;

(c) provide various aid packages to foreign countries.

Armed Services. This committee has recently reviewed legislation on: **(a)** changes in the military pay structure to make it more attractive to young people; **(b)** strategic policy and combat readiness; **(c)** the impact of technology on new weapons systems.

Commerce, Science, and Transportation. This committee has recently reviewed bills on: **(a)** a national policy for the cable television industry; **(b)** recall for hazardous toys; **(c)** regulation for inner-city bus companies; **(d)** air bag requirements in passenger cars.

Foreign Relations. Issues and bills recently reviewed by this committee include: **(a)** treaty to create a nuclear-free zone in Latin America; **(b)** nomination for assistant secretary of state; **(c)** peacekeeping forces for the Middle East; **(d)** maritime boundary dispute with Canada.

To complete this Action Project, follow these steps:

1. Write your first choice of a committee on a slip of paper. On another slip of paper write the name of the committee that is least important to you.

2. Have someone collect and count the choices and announce the results.

3. Finally, answer this multiple-choice question: Which is probably the most powerful committee? **(a)** Agriculture, Nutrition, and Forestry; **(b)** Appropriations; **(c)** Armed Services; **(d)** Commerce, Science, and Transportation; **(e)** Foreign Relations.

"THE LAST WORD"

Congresswoman Bella Abzug (at right) served in Congress (1971-76) from a district in New York City. She strongly distrusted the American military and wanted to take away some of its power. Therefore, she announced that she wanted to become a member of the House Armed Services Committee.

But this was one of the most powerful committees in Congress. Members usually do not get on that committee until they have been in Congress for some time. The section below is adapted from a diary Abzug kept at the time.

January 22, 1971. The first time I mentioned that I wanted a seat on the Armed Services Committee was at a dinner for the New York Congressional *delegation** a few weeks ago. Everybody seemed to approve, except for John Rooney [a powerful Representative from New York who had been in Congress for 27 years].

"Agriculture for you," he told me. "You start at the bottom. You stay at the bottom."

"John," I said. "I can't believe you would be so mean to a member of this delegation."

"Like I said," he went on. "You start at the bottom, you stay at the bottom."

The tradition down here is that new members, like myself, take what they get. They don't make a lot of noise; they don't ask for anything unreasonable.

January 23. One of the basic reasons that I'm claiming a right to a seat on the Armed Services Committee is that I'm a woman. A woman hasn't served on it in 22 years. I can't tell you how outrageous that is. Do you realize that there are 42,000 women in the military? Do you realize that about half the civilian employees of the Defense Department are women?

January 29. I saw Ed Hebert. [Hebert was chairman of the Armed Services Committee.] I went up to him, put my hand on his shoulder, and said, "Ed, look at how all this looks to the country. Let's face it. You would show great understanding if you put me on your committee. Certainly, if you think you're right, you can take someone on who disagrees with you."

"You know it's not up to me, Bella," he said. "I have no objection to your being on the committee, but it's up to the Committee on Committees to put you there." [Each political party in Congress has its own Committee on Committees. Its job is to decide which party members should be assigned to which committees of Congress.]

January 30. The news came late yesterday from Hugh Carey, on the Committee on Committees. He called and said, "Bella, I'm sorry, but you didn't make it. You got some votes, but not enough. A lot of people said there were already two Democrats and two Republicans from New York on the committee. They didn't feel it was right to put any more New Yorkers on."

"What do you mean? These guys are great at making exceptions when the exceptions suit *them*. Let them make an exception and put me on the committee."

"Bella, you know they're not going to do it. Will you consider any other committees?"

"Banking and Currency, because it deals with housing. Or Government Operations—maybe," I said. "So you'd better get back in there and get me on one of them. This excuse for not getting on Armed Services is baloney."

An hour or so later, Carey called back.

"You got Government Operations," he said, "and you ought to be happy. It's very rare for a freshman to get on it."

"That's a lot of baloney," I said. "You're not fooling me."

(YOU HAVE THE LAST WORD)

Why do you think Bella Abzug failed to get on the Armed Services Committee:
(**a**) Because she was not qualified?
(**b**) Because there were already too many New Yorkers on the committee?
(**c**) Because she was a woman?
(**d**) Because she was a new member of Congress? (**e**) Some other reason?
Be prepared to explain your answer.

Bella Abzug

"CHECKOUT"—11

Key Terms
logrolling   chairperson   minority party
seniority   majority party   delegation

Review

1. Define *logrolling* and *seniority* (in their political senses).

2. Describe how seniority can lead to more power in Congress.

3. Explain how party membership affects power in Congressional committees.

4. A power struggle took place in Congress in January 1961. Explain the cause of the struggle. Identify the two front-line "fighters" in the struggle. Who won?

5. What committee did Bella Abzug want to join when she was elected to the House of Representatives? Was it a powerful committee? Was her request granted?

Discussion

1. What is *power* (in the sense used in the chapter)? Does it depend on a person's character? A person's position? Both? On anything else? Give examples of people not in government who have different kinds of power. What does their power depend on?

2. Give examples of logrolling — trading favors — in everyday life. Do people ever refuse to return a particular favor? Do you think this hap-

pens among members of Congress? Should it happen? Would you say logrolling is the ideal way to legislate — or just a *practical* way? Do you think those Senators and Representatives who practice logrolling get more good legislation passed than those who don't? Do you think they get more bad legislation passed? Give reasons for your answers.

3. In recent years, younger members of the House have challenged the seniority rule. In one or two cases, they were able to elect committee chairpersons who did not have the most seniority. What do you think of such challenges? What are the advantages of the seniority rule? What are the disadvantages?

4. What method or methods should be used to choose committee members? Your class might brainstorm this question for a few minutes, writing all the methods suggested on the chalkboard. Then, after discussion of all of them — including seniority — try to agree on one that seems best.

5. Does the majority party have too much power in Congress? Look back at the case study of Mr. Sam v. Judge Smith. Did one of them belong to the majority party and one to the minority party? Or did they both belong to the same party? How do you know? Does this case change your view of Congressional power in any way? If so, how?

6. Do you think Bella Abzug would have had more success in getting on the House Armed Services Committee if she had tried a different approach? Or would the result have been the same? Imagine that you are a newly elected member of the House. How would you try to get the committee assignment of your choice?

7. Suppose a member of Congress, having served on a committee for a few years, wants to switch to another committee. What might be the disadvantages of this move? What might be the advantages?

Activities

1. Using *The Congressional Directory*, your class could find answers to the following questions about your Senators and Representatives: *How many years has each been in Congress? What committee assignments do they have? Are any of them chairpersons of committees?*

2. Your class might role-play a committee hearing. Six or eight students could be members of the committee. Each should pick a constituency to represent: farmers, business people, urban workers, retired people, young people, ethnic minorities, working women, or any other large group of his or her choice. (Of course, many of the groups overlap, but that is what happens with real constituencies.) The chairperson could be appointed (by the teacher, representing the party leaders) or chosen by some other method. The committee could debate a bill proposed by the rest of the class. Students not on the committee might testify in favor of—or against—the bill. Committee members, in voting on the bill, should remember that their constituencies will expect them to judge how the bill will affect them. A simple majority can amend the bill —and can decide whether to recommend or disapprove it.

3. Imagine a meeting between Bella Abzug and Howard Smith in which they discuss House traditions and procedures. What advice do you think Judge Smith might offer? How do you think Bella Abzug might respond?

4. Some students might research the ways in which the House or Senate can get a bill to the floor for consideration, even though the committee considering it wants to keep it bottled up.

5. Students might work in teams of two or more, each team to research and prepare a talk or a written report for the class on one of these topics: **(a)** The ages of current committee chairpersons in Congress compared with the ages of leading corporation executives. **(b)** Recent efforts in Congress to change the way committee chairpersons are chosen. **(c)** How the power of the Speaker of the House has changed in the last 100 years. **(d)** Famous—or infamous—examples of logrolling.

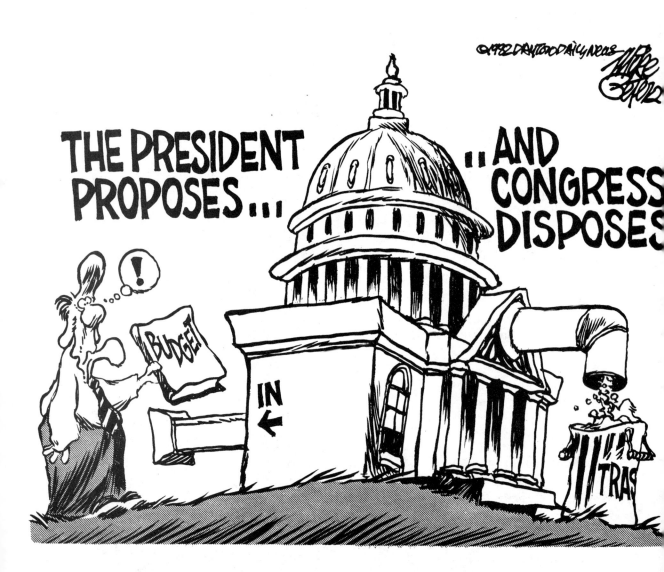

12: DOES CONGRESS DO ITS JOB?

A cartoonist meets with a group of newspaper editors. They are talking about the trouble the President will have getting his new budget through Congress.

The next day's paper will carry an editorial about the budget. What the editors would like is a cartoon to sum it all up.

Back at his drawing board, the cartoonist remembers a quote from a Representative who says the House will probably tear the budget to shreds. "That's exactly what Congress has been doing with everything lately," he thinks.

With swift strokes of his pencil he draws the cartoon shown on the opposite page. The next day, thousands of readers of the Dayton *Daily News* will smile at the cartoon. Few of them will wonder if the criticism is fair.

Cartoonist Mike Peters has used his sense of humor to draw attention to a serious topic of debate in our democracy. Is Congress doing its job? Is it too slow? Is it democratic? Finally, is Congress honest?

This chapter will deal with these questions. You will look at three political cartoons. Each makes a different criticism of Congress. You must decide if the criticism is fair or not.

To help you decide, there is an im-

aginary debate with each cartoon. First a "critic" explains the cartoonist's point of view. Then a "member of Congress" defends Congress on each point.

DEBATE 1
Is Congress too slow?

Critic. This country needs a legislative body that can act quickly and decisively. We live in a modern world, and Congress still acts like it is the 18th century.

The talk is endless, and rarely to the point. A foreign visitor to Wash-

ington once remarked, "Congress is so strange. A man gets up to speak and says nothing. Nobody listens—and then everybody disagrees."

He had a point. Nobody listens because members are too busy pushing their own points of view.

There was a time when political parties held members together on an issue. Today, Congress is full of mavericks. Members are just as likely to be influenced by single-issue special interest groups as they are by party leaders.

Another reason Congress is so slow is that the members get so much "help." It is the most heavily staffed

158

legislature in the world. Do you know that Congress employs 31,000 people? I can't imagine it wouldn't work better if members only had a few aides. The British House of Commons gets by with only 1000 employees, and it has 650 members to Congress's 535.

The rules of Congress don't help make things efficient. Before a bill ever comes to a vote it goes through a real maze of House and Senate committees.

Also, members can hold up bills by tacking on amendment after amendment. Very often these amendments have nothing at all to do with the subject of the bill.

Member of Congress. Whoever said democracy was supposed to be efficient? I'm far more concerned with operating fairly than operating quickly.

It's not that members are expressing their own selfish points of view. They represent real voters with real opinions—and the power to make themselves heard. It is true that single issue groups have gotten into the act in recent years. They lobby us about everything from animal rights to airline safety. I guess they felt the Democrats and the Republicans were not listening to them. A lot of members owe their election to single-issue groups, so naturally they pay attention to them.

Party politics still play an important role in Congress. Their rivalry is important in making sure all sides get heard on a bill. But I suppose you'd say that slows things down, too.

As for our huge staffs, Congress needs all the help it can get these days. We are faced with complex problems that often require complex solutions. For example, economic decisions now have world-wide impact. And science and technology move so quickly, no member can keep up without technical help. We can't ask members to make decisions about the future of human genetics unless they understand the scientific and ethical questions involved, for example.

Also, there is no comparing our legislature to that of Great Britain. That nation has less than a quarter of our population. Geographically, it would fit into one of our medium-sized states. Congress represents an increasingly diverse population—spread from Florida to Alaska—with many different needs. Americans look to their Representatives and Senators for all kinds of help. We, in turn, look to our staffs to guide us.

As for all our committees, we review them regularly to make sure each one is necessary. There are also rules limiting the number of subcommittees a committee can form. If a bill has to go through many subcommittees and committees, it's because different parts of it require their attention.

I know that amendments are sometimes added to a bill to stall its progress. But that's not always the case. The 99th Congress passed 664 laws. Many of these were huge *omnibus bills** with many amendments. Without those amendments, we would have accomplished far less.

All I can say to those who think we

move too slowly is: If Congress moved any faster, more people would be unhappy than they are now.

DEBATE 2
Is Congress undemocratic?

Critic. The cartoon shows the public interest knocked flat by the filibuster. To me, Congress should be doing its

best to serve the public interest.

A large majority of Senators may favor a certain law. But the majority won't get to vote on that law because Senate rules allow members to talk and talk. A handful of Senators can tie up a bill until the majority gives up.

In the past, the filibuster was only used for very important issues. Now it's used often, and for minor issues. It's gotten to the point where just the threat of a filibuster is enough to kill a bill. To me this is undemocratic. It goes against the principle that the majority rules.

The power held by committee heads is also undemocratic. They can control what bills will be considered and in what order. Why should a few members of Congress hold so much of the power? Many Americans are hurt by this system, without even realizing it. For example, the woman who represents me in the House heads no committees. She has very little power compared to the Representative in the next district who heads several committees. So I have less power than a voter in the next district.

Member of Congress. The rules of Congress are very democratic.

We Americans believe in the importance of free speech. Why shouldn't Senators be allowed to speak as long as they wish? The nation's founders wanted the Senate to be more deliberate than the House. The filibuster protects the minority against unjust laws. So it is really a safeguard of democracy.

2

"The winner and still heavyweight champion of the U.S. Senate. . . ."

FILIBUSTER

PUBLIC INTEREST

"...So, how much did you bribe them to get on this committee?..."

Furthermore, the Senate *can* control a debate if 60 Senators vote for what we call *cloture**. This is a rule which sets a time limit on debate.

As for the power of committee heads, power is more decentralized, or spread out, than ever before. In the past, the member with the longest service on a committee automatically became its head and could serve until he or she left Congress.

Today, most committee heads are elected at party caucuses by secret ballot. If the members who head committees act unfairly, they can be replaced by their party members.

Now that the people you elect to Congress have a better chance of being in positions of power, be sure you elect people who have good leadership qualities. Then you will get your share of the power.

DEBATE 3
Is Congress honest?

Critic. I know this sounds really negative, but I think pay-offs account for a lot of legislation getting through Congress. I read about wealthy foreigners buying members of Congress as easily as beads in a bazaar.

The cartoon is accurate. It shows that even members of the committee that's supposed to police Congress are accustomed to giving and taking bribes. If the very people who make the laws break them, why should anyone obey them?

And to think we give these people special privileges. For example, the Constitution allows Congress to make laws that set its own salaries. Congress has voted for a number of pay raises. In 1987 members of Congress earned $89,500. That's four times as much as they earned 25 years before.

In addition, members get many other benefits. Some of them rarely buy a stamp or pay a telephone bill. The Constitution grants them what is called a *franking privilege*—free use of the mails for official business only. But I wonder how many members also use the franking privileges to send Christmas cards to friends, free of charge.

I also wonder how much of the taxpayer's money is wasted because members are out campaigning for reelection when they should be working on the public business. Representatives in the House face an election every two years. Many of them never stop campaigning.

I wouldn't mind paying my Representative a big salary if I knew that he or she was always on the job, studying bills. Instead, Representatives may spend half their time hustling for my vote.

Member of Congress. I have three quick points to make.

First. You're right. In recent years a number of Congressmen have been convicted of accepting outside money for performing official duties. But the number is small—only 16 in the last 10 years. The same can be said of members taking advantage of special privileges. Most of us are scrupulously honest.

Second. A salary of $89,500 may sound like a lot of money. But much of it has to be spent on politics and government. I have to do a lot of entertaining, for example, at my own expense. I have to go deeply into debt every two years to get the money I need to run for reelection. In fact, it's a real financial sacrifice for me to be in Congress. I could make much more money as a private lawyer or as a business executive.

Third. Campaigning for office is a fact of political life. How else are you going to have free elections? Meeting the voters back home is one of the important duties of a politician. In a democracy, there is no other way. If I don't campaign and my opponent back home does, I'm not going to be reelected.

ACTION PROJECT

You have now seen the criticisms of three cartoonists. You have heard members of Congress reply to the cartoonists' charges. Who presented the more convincing arguments?

Tear a sheet of paper into three pieces or ballots. Review the arguments in each of the three debates. Then, on each of your ballots, vote on whether Congress is doing its job as well as it should.

Count the ballots in your class and announce the results.

If you think the cartoonist was unfair in any of the arguments, you might try to think of a cartoon that would give a fairer picture of Congress. Perhaps you might enjoy drawing such a cartoon. Don't worry about making it beautiful—just get your idea across.

"THE LAST WORD"

by Robert Dole

Between 1986 and 1987, U.S. Senator Robert Dole of Kansas played a central role in the Senate as Republican majority leader. In 1987 elections, the Democrats took control of the Senate, and Senator Dole became minority leader of the 100th Congress. In this interview with Maura Christopher of Update Magazine *Senator Dole revealed his ideas about the role of the Senate, and a number of issues facing it.*

Update: What strategy will the Republicans take in their new Senate role as the minority party?

Dole: The Democrats are going to find out very quickly that bills are going to be *bipartisan** or they are not going to pass. In the Senate, it is not enough to have a majority, you've got to be able to end the debate and stop filibusters.

    We've worked with the Democrats on a number of things during the past six years. We'll need that same cooperation. There will be times when the Democrats or the Republicans want to make a political point. On those occasions, we won't agree. But that's not always bad—it just means we have different views.

Update: What are the top issues facing the 100th Congress?

Dole: The Democrats must face up to the same problems that we did—the deficit, trade, defense, aid to the *contras* in Nicaragua. At least I hope they will face up to them. Plus, they will face the kinds of issues that we deal with on an annual basis: How much should we spend on programs such as Medicare and Social Security?

But the biggest issue of all is the federal deficit. How do we reduce the rate of growth of federal spending? Whether you are a Democrat or a Republican, that is a big, big challenge. If we don't address that problem, it's going to have a very negative impact on the people who are leaving high school and college.

Update: Senator Patrick Leahy (a Democrat from Vermont) says the Democrats will be tougher in fighting to lower the federal budget deficit than the Republicans were.

Dole: I don't agree at all. They might be tougher in their rhetoric, but the ones who make the toughest speeches sometimes are hard to find when you have a tough vote.

Update: What are the chances of a tax increase by the new Congress?

Dole: If you're talking about other revenue enhancements or closing loopholes, that can happen, but only with the President's consent.

Update: Will the Iranian arms scandal cause Congress to push for more control of foreign policy?

Dole: The Congress probably meddles too much in foreign policy now. I don't believe you can have 535 Secretaries of State in Congress or 535 Presidents. The President has the constitutional authority to make foreign policy. Congress should not be excluded, but when a head of state visits this country, he sees the President, because the President is the one who makes the decisions.

(YOU HAVE THE LAST WORD)

There were 55 Democrats and 45 Republicans in the 100th Congress. What does Senator Dole mean when he says "the Democrats are going to find out very quickly that bills are going to be bipartisan or they are not going to pass"? Do you think this will help Congress act more efficiently? More democratically?

Senator Dole describes the federal deficit as "the biggest issue of all." Imagine the Democrats supporting a bill for a big tax hike designed to reduce the deficit. What might happen to the bill? Do you think a long debate in Congress over such a bill is a good thing? A bad thing? A little of both?

"CHECKOUT"—12

Key terms

filibuster   franking privilege
cloture   omnibus bill

Review

1. Choose the best word to complete this sentence: *Cartoons often criticize Congress by making it look* (uninteresting, ridiculous, overserious, horrific).

2. Identify three common criticisms of Congress.

3. State one argument for and one against members of Congress having large staffs.

4. What is the salary of a member of Congress?

5. Name two changes in the rules of Congress that made it possible for more members to have a chance of getting committee chairmanships.

Discussion

1. In Chapter 9 you read about Senator Robert Lafollette as he led a fili-buster against the armed ship bill. (See pages 114–117 to refresh your memory.) Imagine how he would respond to each of the cartoons in this chapter. Would he think they were fair? Do you think they are fair? Do you think political cartoons *should* be fair?

2. The Congress of 1947–48 passed 905 laws. The Congress of 1985–86 passed only 664. Does this mean that the 1947–48 Congress accomplished more? Might the "size" of the bills make any difference? How?

3. The political party organization in the home state once provided the main link between a member of Congress and his or her constituents. Some say that television has changed all this. Through T V, members of Congress, especially those trying to

get reelected, can reach their voters directly. Do you agree? Why or why not? Would this affect the importance of the party? How?

4. Do you believe that a filibuster is undemocratic? Explain your answer.

5. House members must run for reelection every two years. Some people say that this is too often—that, because of such frequent elections, members spend too much time worrying about the next election and not enough about what is good for the people they represent. Others say that *because* House members run every two years, they try harder to represent the interests of their district so that they will be reelected.

Senators run every six years. Some people say this is not often enough, that it takes too long to get rid of a poor Senator. Others say that it gives a Senator time to do a good job—without having to worry so much about reelection.

Discuss the pros and cons of each time period. Then try to reach a class consensus on how often Representatives and Senators should be required to run for reelection.

6. In 1981 seven members of Congress were convicted after accepting bribes from FBI agents disguised as wealthy Arabs. Do you think this is a good way for the government to keep Congress honest? Consider such facts as: this type of operation is extremely costly; those who were accused argued that such methods constituted entrapment, or luring them into doing something they wouldn't ordinarily do.

Activities

1. You might look through newspapers and magazines for other cartoons about Congress. Clip or copy them for the class bulletin board.

2. Imagine that you have just been elected to the House as the Representative of your local district. Make a list of items that will have to be added to your budget (one example, a place to live in Washington). Be prepared to defend yourself against a TV interviewer who believes that members of Congress get too much money. Alternatively, you might play the TV interviewer. Prepare a list of probing questions to ask a member of Congress about his or her income.

3. Using the figure given in the chapter, compute the average staff size for a member of Congress. Then find out the size of the staff of one of your representatives in Congress. You can get this information by contacting your Senator's or Representative's office. It might also be interesting to ask for a job description for each staff member.

4. You might read one of the books in the bibliography at the end of this unit and prepare a short report on it.

5. In recent years, many people have had a negative attitude toward politicians, including members of Congress. To balance this view, your class might, for one week, look for and clip or copy newspaper stories and magazine articles that tell of positive achievements by members of Congress. You could discuss the more significant stories and articles in class.

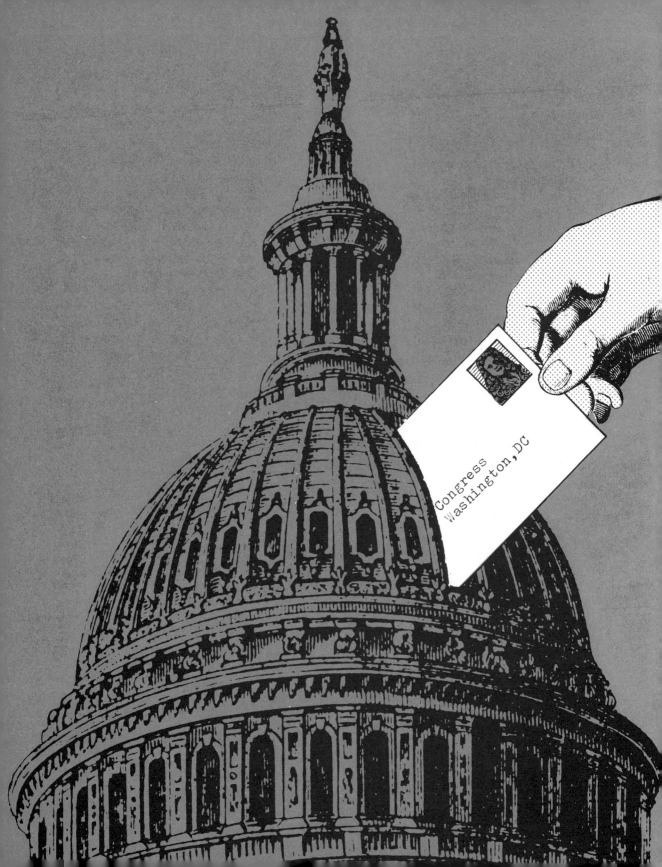

Congress
Washington, DC

13: HOW TO INFLUENCE CONGRESS

You're represented in Congress by three people. Two Senators represent you in the Senate. One Representative speaks for you in the House. How do you get their attention? How do you get them to listen to your thoughts, opinions, and problems?

It's really not difficult. The best way to do it is to write to them in Washington, D.C. The first step is to look up their names. Any librarian can give you this information. In the Last Word, you'll find helpful tips on how to write such a letter.

Letters to and from Congress.
Write briefly about any public issue that interests you. Pollution. Crime. Capital punishment. Drugs. Gun control. Schools. Elections. War. Consumer problems. Jobs. No matter what subject you choose, you can expect to receive a letter back.

Members of Congress usually get thousands of letters a week. These letters are on many different subjects.

Obviously, nobody can personally answer thousands of letters a week. Therefore, most of the replies are form

169

letters. Senators or Representatives or someone on their staffs who knows their views will first compose letters on subjects that might concern their constituents. Then these form letters are entered into a computer and stored.

Suppose you write a letter to a member of Congress about gun control. If you say you're in favor of gun control, a staff worker chooses one kind of letter from the computer file. If you say you're against it, the staff member chooses a different reply.

Why should you send a letter if it might be answered by a form letter? Two reasons. First, members of Congress need to know what people are thinking. They like to believe they are in touch with citizens back home. Therefore, they spend many hours a week reading their mail. They don't always have time to compose a personal reply. But your opinion is read and it does enter into their thinking.

Second, the return letter from Washington can be very helpful. It will tell you what your member of Congress is trying to do about a certain problem. You'll be better informed about him or her. And your Congress member will be better informed about you. In other words, you both gain from the exchange of letters.

It's even possible for a member of Congress to help you with personal problems. All members employ a staff to answer a citizen's request for special services and information.

Suppose you are interested in a career in the armed forces. Or you want to know if the government can help you find a job in industry. Your representative's staff may be able to help you. They're trained to take care of individual problems.

Keeping in touch with the voters. Members of Congress keep in touch with the voters in many different ways. In addition to all the mail, they get many phone calls from citizens who need help. Tourists in Washington want to meet the person who represents them. Much time is spent greeting families, school groups, church groups, scout troops, and other visitors to the nation's capital. Finally, civic groups expect a Representative to speak at their dinners, meetings, conventions, and parties.

One Congressman summed up a week of his life as follows:

"Addressed students of three high schools visiting the Capitol. Addressed veterans' groups from two counties, and civil-defense officials of seven states. Attended meeting of 13th District Community Council. Attended a church picnic, two bull roasts, and the dedication of a school. Went to a Democratic club dinner, a political cocktail party, and dinner for a visiting Indiana businessman."

All this activity may seem like a waste of time, but is it? After all, how can politicians and voters understand each other unless they meet and talk together? How can a member of Congress know what the voters are thinking unless he or she makes an effort to speak to them? Members of Congress thus work hard at the job of pleasing the voters back home.

The problem of campaign expenses.

To be elected and reelected to Congress costs money as well as time. A lot of money. It costs a lot for the campaign ads on TV and radio, for the buttons and bumper stickers, and for travel and hotels.

Some members of Congress need far less publicity than others. Because they are already well-known to the voters, they may have to spend only a few thousand dollars on their campaigns. But most politicians are not so fortunate. For them, an election campaign can be very costly.

Where do candidates get the money they need to pay for their campaigns? Concerned citizens pay for some of it by contributing to their candidate's campaign chest. But this isn't enough.

To pay the big bills of campaigning, a candidate needs more money than he or she could get from the contributions of "average" citizens. Therefore, the candidate often depends, for contributions, on the people who have the most to win or lose from the laws that Congress passes.

Lobbies and pressure groups.

Organizations such as business corporations and labor unions are very much interested in what laws are passed. Every labor union in the country wants laws that support the worker. Every grocery, liquor store, clothing store, barber shop, church, beauty parlor, truck farm, dairy farm, and TV station is touched by one law or another.

Name almost any organization—the Girl Scouts of America, the National Football League, General Motors Corporation, the Sierra Club. You have very likely named an organization that needs to influence Congress.

When organizations join together to support or oppose legislation, they are sometimes called *pressure groups** because they put pressure on Congress to satisfy their needs. One kind of pressure is money pressure. Organizations can raise campaign money for Representatives and Senators who are friendly to their cause. They can also refuse to give money to someone who votes the "wrong" way.

Another way to put pressure on Congress is to hire a lobbyist. A lobbyist is someone who tries to influence the passage of laws. There are many hundreds of lobbyists in Washington.

Lobbyists for different organizations visit the House and Senate constantly. They keep their employer informed about what's going on in Washington. And they try to persuade members of Congress to vote a certain way on bills that affect their employer.

Lobbyists try to make themselves useful to members of Congress. For example, here's how one lobbyist became friends with a Congressman:

"An assistant to a Congressman called me the other day and said the Congressman wanted to poll the voters in his area on how they felt about various issues. He said they were short of money for the poll and needed another $250.

"My firm has plants in more than 100 communities, and one of them is in this Congressman's district. I called the manager of that plant and told him about the poll. About a week later, I ran into the assistant, and he said: 'I don't know who you called, but it certainly did the trick. We got the $250 in a few days.'"

Do lobbyists have too much influence?

Was it right for the Congressman to seek a favor from this lobbyist? After all, the lobbyist is being paid to influence laws in his *company's* favor—not the country's favor. If a friend of yours helped you to get $250, would you feel obliged to help him or her at some later time? Lobbyists, of course, are hoping that Congress-people will at least feel more friendly toward them and their companies.

Some people believe that lobbyists have too much influence. There is concern about the huge sums of money that powerful pressure groups contribute to the campaigns of members of Congress.

Lobbyists today are more closely controlled than they used to be. A law now requires them to fill out a form that gives their names, their salaries, the organizations they represent, and the money they spend

on lobbying.

Even so, lobbyists can do many things which raise questions. They can give Senators and Representatives small personal gifts. They can take the members of Congress to dinner at the finest restaurants in Washington.

Are members of Congress "softened up" by a lobbyist's personal favors? Most members admit that this can happen. But they claim that it doesn't happen very often. Instead, they say that there is only one good way that a lobbyist can influence them: Lobbyists sometimes change a member's vote by presenting a strong argument.

Often there isn't time for members of Congress to study all the details of every bill. They may be unaware of a weakness in a bill unless a lobbyist points it out. It is this part of a lobbyist's job that some members of Congress find useful.

The laws do not allow a company or a union to contribute to a candidate in its own name. But both companies and unions can use their own money to set up separate *political action committees** or PAC's. These committees raise money for their favorite political candidates by asking for contributions from employees or union members.

You may say that people need not contribute to those funds if they do not want to. But it isn't always so simple.

Pretend for a moment that you are a salesman for company X. You know that your boss likes your work and you think that you might soon be promoted to sales manager. With the promotion will come a nice salary boost.

In walks the boss one day. "Hey Joe," says he, "how'd you like to contribute $100 to our political fund? We've got to make sure that Smith gets elected. He's a friend of the company and his opponent Jones is not."

What can you do? If you say no, you might lose a few nights' sleep worrying about that promotion. Or you might not get the promotion at all.

Or pretend you are a member of a union. You make a contribution to your union's political action commit-

tee. The union convention endorses Smith. You favor Jones. Nevertheless, the union committee will probably contribute your share of the political action money to Smith's campaign.

Attempts to limit the power of money. In 1974 Congress passed a law about campaign spending. The law says that:
- No individual may contribute more than $1,000 *directly* to the election campaign of one candidate. If the individual wants to contribute to more than one campaign, he or she is limited to a total of $25,000 a year.
- No business or union political action committee may contribute more than $5,000 to the election campaign of one candidate. But such committees can contribute to as many candidates' campaigns as they wish.
- All campaign contributions of more than $100, and expenditures of more than $10, must be made public.
- A special commission, independent of the President and Congress, will enforce the terms of the law.

The law has allowed the public to see who is making big campaign contributions. But big spenders have found ways around the law. For example, if people want to give more than the limit to a candidate, they can run a newspaper or television ad for this person. This is not considered a contribution to the *candidate's* campaign. These people are running *their own* campaign.

The problem is that campaign costs are rising. This makes the big contributors more important than ever.

ACTION PROJECT

Imagine that one of Colorado's Representatives in the House is a person named Shirley Strong. She is a member of the House Special Subcommittee on Gun Control.

Representative Strong has been under pressure recently to decide whether to support or oppose a bill on gun control. The bill was written by a pressure group called the National Council to Ban Handguns (NCBH) and introduced by a Representative who shared the group's views.

If passed into law, this bill would make it illegal for anyone except a police officer to carry a pistol or a handgun.

Another pressure group, the National Rifle Association (NRA) is strongly opposed to this bill. The NRA contributed $750 to Representative Strong's campaign in the last election.

Until now, Representative Strong has been opposed to all forms of gun control. She herself enjoys target-shooting. But the Congresswoman is also a politician. What the voters think about this issue is important to her.

She therefore asks her staff to prepare a brief report, giving various arguments for and against gun control. The first page of the staff's report lists these arguments. As you read, try to decide whose arguments are stronger.

A handgun firing class offered for women by Macoupin County, Illinois in 1981. The training was for self-defense against criminals.

175

STAFF REPORT ON GUN CONTROL

Part I
What are the major arguments of the NCBH and the NRA?

NCBH arguments for the bill:

1. Guns in the home are a constant danger to those who possess them. They often lead to fatal accidents and murders. Besides, the bill does not prevent hunters from owning rifles for sporting purposes.

2. The Supreme Court has ruled that Congress does have the right to pass gun-control laws. The Second Amendment to the Constitution, said the Court, gives people the right to establish *militias*.* That does not mean that all individuals have the constitutional right to own a gun.

3. The ownership of handguns is a poor protection against robbery, rape, and other violent crimes. An experienced criminal can shoot you before you shoot him or her.

NRA arguments against the bill:

1. Despite what the Supreme Court has said, the bill takes away a citizen's "right to bear arms" as guaranteed in the Second Amendment to the Constitution. Every citizen has a right to own a gun for his or her self-defense.

2. Criminals will always be able to get handguns in illegal ways. Knowing that citizens are now defenseless will only make criminals bolder.

3. If this bill is passed, it may lead to laws which will ban rifles and other sporting equipment.

Part II
How do voters in your district feel about this bill?

The second page of the staff's report summarizes the mail Representative Strong has been receiving on the gun-control issue. Ask yourself: Does the majority seem to be for or against the bill? Does the majority of letter-writers agree or disagree with your own opinion of the bill?

	Mail Favoring Bill	Mail Opposing Bill
March	523	211
April	611	422
May	422	500
Total	**1,556**	**1,133**
Percentage	**58**%	**42**%

Now assume you're Congresswoman Strong. Will you vote for or against the gun-control bill in your committee meeting this afternoon? Write your decision on a piece of paper. Which influenced you more: Part I of the staff report listing arguments, or Part II listing public opinion?

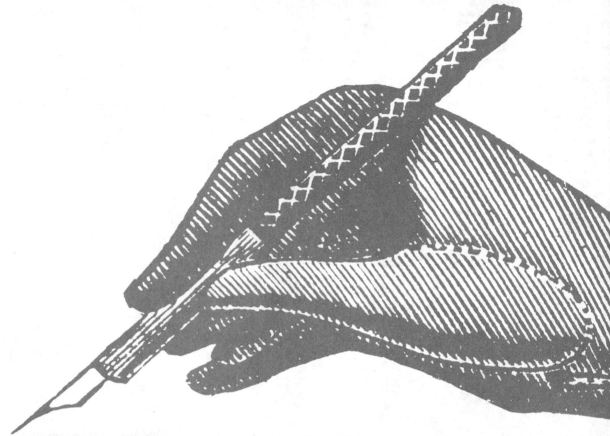

"THE LAST WORD"

by Jim Wright

Suppose you want to get in touch with your Representative. How do you go about it? Here are seven tips adapted from You and Your Congressman, *a book by Speaker of the House Jim Wright of Texas.*

1. A letter is better than a telegram or a phone call. It requires more effort in the first place and therefore shows greater sincerity.

2. Write your Representative at the office—never at home. A member of Congress has little time at home and may resent your contacting him or her there. Besides, if your Representative forgets to bring your letter to the office, it may take weeks for it to be given proper consideration. The *worst* thing to do is to telephone long distance to your Representative's home.

The best place to write a member of the House is at his or her Washington office. Call your Representative's district office to get the address.

3. Try to keep your letter short. Remember how many letters your Representative gets. There's a better chance that your letter will be read personally by your Representative if it is short and sincere. But a long letter running

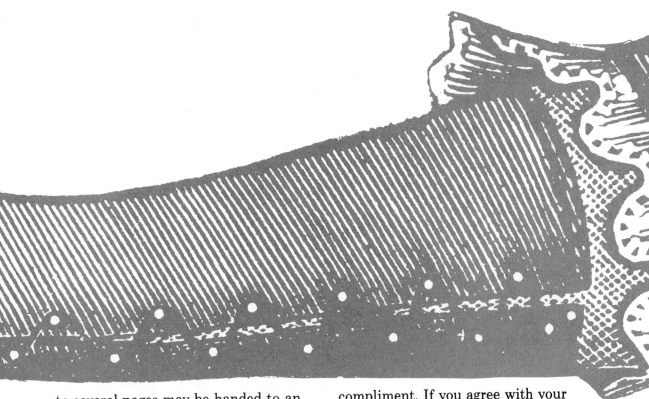

to several pages may be handed to an assistant to summarize.

4. Be fair with your subject matter. Don't exaggerate your point of view. Bear in mind that you are writing to a person who is used to hearing all sides and who knows at least something about the issues at stake.

5. Be reasonable in what you expect. Don't threaten or use ugly language. Don't promise political help at the next election in exchange for a vote on a certain bill. (Your Representative will resent either, just as you would.)

6. Don't repeat *slogans** to prove your point. Your Representative has probably heard them all. Don't try to be cute. Just write in your own words and try to express your thoughts as best you can.

7. Remember that everybody loves a compliment. If you agree with your Representative, it isn't a bad idea to say so. It's just human nature to value the opinions of those who agree with us at least part of the time.

(YOU HAVE THE LAST WORD)

Write a note to your Representative or one of your Senators.

You may either **(a)** state an opinion, **(b)** ask for information, **(c)** send a clipping from your local newspaper about a problem that interests you, or **(d)** ask to be placed on the mailing list for the Representative's or Senator's newsletter. Look up names and addresses in the library.

"CHECKOUT"—13

Key terms

pressure groups	contributors	form letter
lobbyist	campaign spending	political action committee

Review

1. How do individual citizens usually make their views known to their representatives in Congress?

2. Members of Congress often attend picnics, dinners, conventions, and other meetings with citizens' groups. In what way can this be considered a Congress member's work?

3. Describe two ways organizations can influence members of Congress.

4. How did a law of 1974 try to limit the influence of money on Congress?

5. Describe two steps that a member of Congress is likely to take in deciding how to vote on a bill.

Discussion

1. Should members of Congress pay more attention to the views of large contributors than to the views of small contributors or to the views of constituents who did not contribute any money to a Congress member's election campaign? What are some reasons people might have for contributing to an election campaign of a member of Congress? Some people give equal amounts to both the Republican and the Democratic candidates for a Congressional seat. Why do you think they do this?

2. Should members of Congress receive campaign contributions from groups that want certain laws passed? Should a candidate accept such contributions when he or she does *not* intend to vote for those laws? What would you do?

3. A 1974 law set limits on campaign contributions. Do you think these limits are fair? Should there be a limit on how much a candidate can spend on a campaign? What are the advantages of such a limit? What are the disadvantages?

4. Imagine you are a member of Congress about to vote on an energy conservation bill. You feel that it is right to vote for the bill, and that the advantages of the bill far outweigh the disadvantages. However, mail from your constituents is running 4 to 1 against the bill. What would you do? Why?

5. Do you think that a Congressional staff should spend time doing services for constituents? Why?

6. Have you ever visited a member of Congress in Washington, or met him or her in your community? If you have, you might tell the class about your experience.

7. From 1979 to 1986, the amount a Senator could earn from outside income (mainly speaking engagements) was increased more than four

times, from $8,625 to $35,800 a year. Those favoring such increases have argued that only independently wealthy people could afford to serve in Congress without substantial outside income. Those opposed have said that salaries and expense accounts were adequate. Even if they weren't, they argued, there is the risk that people seeking favors will set up speaking engagements with high fees for Senators in order to influence them. What do you think? If you were a Senator, how would you have voted on proposals to increase the amount of outside income you could earn? Why?

Activities

1. You might compose a form letter, on a subject which interests you, that a member of Congress might send to a constituent. You might compare your letter with the letters of others in the class.

2. You might pretend that you are a member of Congress running for re-election. In your campaign speeches, you want to show what you have done to serve the needs of your constituents. Make a list of six (imaginary) activities. Be as specific as possible, giving the names of the groups or individuals helped, and stating how they were helped.

3. You might enjoy pretending that you are a lobbyist in Washington. You could choose the company or group you represent (Multinational Oil, Automobile Drivers' Union, Pizza Makers of America, etc.). Then you could write a report to your employers de-

scribing the work you have been doing for the past week and the progress you have made. Or you could role-play the report to the class. You might have some fun with the report and boast about your achievements.

4. You might choose a topic that interests you—perhaps one on which you already have a strong opinion. You could write a letter to one of your representatives in Congress, expressing your opinion, and following the guidelines given in The Last Word. You might also enjoy writing a letter—*not* to be mailed—which ignores these guidelines. Then exchange your letters with those of another student. Read his or hers as if you were the member of Congress. How would you react to each of them? Which one would be more likely to influence you? Why?

5. In the early '70's, Congress passed laws providing for government financing for Presidential elections. Some funding came from people who made donations as part of their income tax returns. In 1988 more than $50 million was made available to Presidential candidates from these funds.

Some students might research the following question and report their findings to the class. *Why did Congress establish government financing of Presidential campaigns—but not for Congressional campaigns?* Afterwards, the class might discuss whether Congressional campaigns ought to be government financed.

6. Your representatives probably issue newsletters. See if the class can be put on the mailing lists.

TEN GOOD BOOKS ABOUT CONGRESS

Man of the House—The Life and Political Memoirs of Speaker Tip O'Neill

by Tip O'Neill and William Novak
Tip O'Neill served as Speaker of the House of Representatives for ten years, and what exciting years they were. Read about his perception of Watergate and why he broke with President Lyndon Johnson on Vietnam. Random House, New York, 1987.

Hard Right: The Rise of Jesse Helms

by Ernest B. Furgurson

How do you get to be a Senator after you've been a TV commentator? Jesse Helms from North Carolina tells you how he became a political leader of the far right. W.W. Norton, New York, 1986.

How Congress Works

All you ever wanted to know and more about how Congress works: Who leads the party? Who heads the committees? How are laws made? Learn it all in this comprehensive book. Congressional Quarterly, Washington, DC, 1983.

The Washington Lobby

Read about the history of lobbying, from its beginnings in colonial times through the growth of special interest groups in Washington in the 1970s and 80s. There are case studies of specific lobby interests and an index. Congressional Quarterly, Washington, DC, 1982.

Congress
by Harold Coy

Would you like to spend a day with your representative in Congress? Find out how you can in this book. And bone up on life in Congress—the struggle to get elected, the role of lobbyists and pressure groups—so you can talk to your representative like an insider. Julian Messner, New York, 1980.

The New Congress
by Stephen Goode

There were problems that led to the reforms and changes in Congress in the 1970s. Here you'll find what they were and how they were solved. Chapters include such topics as the House and Senate in practice, the Watergate affair, and lobbying. This book has a good bibliography and index. Julian Messner, New York, 1980.

Came the Revolution: Argument in the Reagan Era
by Daniel Patrick Moynihan

Get the inside track on how this popular Senator from New York State feels about the 80s in politics. Moynihan covers the years between Inauguration Day, 1981 and the Iran-Contra scandal. Harcourt Brace Jovanovich, San Diego, CA, 1988.

Profiles in Courage
by John F. Kennedy

Eight stories about U.S. Senators who dared to be different. Take Senator Hart Benton of Missouri, who once said, "Mr. President, sir . . . I never quarrel, sir. But sometimes I fight, sir; and whenever I fight, sir, a funeral follows, sir." Harper & Row, New York, 1983.

Advise and Consent
by Allen Drury

Here's a look at game playing at its best. This time it's the game of politics. See how it's played—in the United States Senate. Drury's novel is based on his sixteen years as a Washington reporter. Avon Books, New York, 1981.

Politics in America: Members of Congress in Washington and at Home
Alan Ehrenhalt, ed.

If you're curious as to who your members of Congress are, what they do in Congress, what they did before election, where they went to school, even about their families, you can find it in this book. This is a great reference book: it has lots of information organized in an easy-to-access fashion. Congressional Quarterly, Inc., Washington, DC, 1983.

UNIT III: THE U.S. COURTS

14: JOHN DOE IN A U.S. COURT

You've probably seen the "wanted" signs, the mug shots, and the fingerprints on your post office bulletin board. But where do they fit into the U.S. system of government?

They all have to do with the third branch of government created by the Constitution—the federal *judiciary*.*

What is a federal case? The Constitution describes the Judicial Branch in a very few words. (See Article III of the Constitution.) It mentions a "Supreme Court" and "inferior courts." It doesn't say how many judges there shall be on any court. It doesn't even say how many courts there shall be. It leaves these matters for Congress to decide.

Article III says that people accused of breaking a federal law have a right to trial by jury. And it lists the kinds of cases that may be brought to U.S. courts for trial. Federal courts, it says, shall handle cases involving certain types of people. Such people include:

- ambassadors from foreign governments;
- ship crews and passengers involved in incidents at sea;
- immigrants to the U.S. who are trying to keep from being *deported*.*

187

- officials and employees of the U.S. government charged with official misconduct;
- officials of a state government who complain about the actions of the U.S. government;
- citizens of one state who claim to be harmed by citizens of another state;
- tourists from foreign countries;
- people who have suffered injury while on property belonging to the U.S. government;
- citizens who complain of being unjustly treated by the U.S. government and U.S. laws.

There are many types of people left off this list. What happens, for example, if a neighbor's car rams into the side of your car? Your insurance company would take the case to a state court, not a federal court.

There are two kinds of courts in this country: **(a)** those run by the U.S. government and **(b)** those run by the state governments. The U.S. government usually lets the state courts settle problems such as car accidents that occur within state boundaries. However, if your car is hit by the car of a Japanese tourist, the case goes to federal court.

The most important part of Article III has not yet been mentioned. It reads: "The judicial power shall extend to all cases . . . arising under the Constitution, the laws of the United States, and treaties made . . . under their authority." This is the clause that allows the U.S. government to arrest John Doe and other persons suspected of breaking federal laws.

Seven steps in the system of justice. Why do we need courts of any kind? What is their purpose? We need them mainly because people often hurt each other in a number of ways—injuring their bodies, their minds, their property, and their reputations. And there needs to be a fair way to decide who did what to whom—and what shall be done about it.

The series of drawings here shows how the U.S. system of justice works. It shows what happens when a federal law is broken.

1. First, there is the law itself. All U.S. laws, as passed by Congress, are contained in a set of thick books called the *U.S. Code** (abbreviated "USC"). These books sit on every lawyer's bookshelf as surely as a dictionary sits on an English teacher's desk.

In one of these books, you will find an act of Congress passed in 1909. It reads:

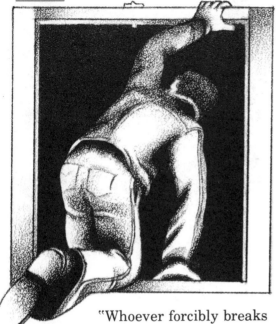

"Whoever forcibly breaks into or attempts to break into any post office, or any building used in whole or in part as a post office with intent to commit in such post office, or building or part thereof, so used, any *larceny** . . . shall be fined not more than $1,000 or imprisoned not more than five years, or both."

2. Someone breaks into a post office late at night in a town near Pittsburgh, Pennsylvania. Call this the *offense.**

3. The burglary is discovered the next morning and the search begins for the lawbreaker.

The Federal Bureau of Investigation (FBI) does most of the detective work for the U.S. government. But the U.S. Postal Service has its own agents and inspectors. The postal inspector for the Pittsburgh area finds clues that lead to the arrest of John Doe, an unemployed steelworker.

4. Is there enough evidence to hold John Doe for trial? This is a question for a federal *grand jury.** The clerk in the U.S. court in Pittsburgh asks 23 citizens to act as a grand jury in this case.

A U.S. district attorney then tries to persuade this jury that the government has enough evidence against John Doe to put him on trial. The district attorney does not work for a judge or for the Judicial Branch. Instead, he or she is employed by the Justice Department of the Executive Branch.

Suppose, in this case, the U.S. district attorney wins the argument. A majority of the grand jury agree that the evidence against John Doe is strong enough. Doe now stands accused or *indicted** for breaking a federal law. But he has not yet been proven guilty of breaking the law.

4

5

5. The accused person has a right to trial by a jury of 12 fellow citizens. Or he can be tried by a judge without a jury. John Doe and his lawyer agree that he will probably have a better chance of being found not guilty in a jury trial. So the trial is held.

Again the U.S. district attorney questions witnesses, presents evidence, and argues the case against John Doe. His case must be even stronger now than during the indictment stage. At that time, he had to convince the grand jurors only that the "weight of evidence" seemed to run against Doe. Now, in the trial stage, he must try to prove that Doe is guilty "beyond a reasonable doubt."

Again, the district attorney wins the case. The jury decides that Doe is guilty of the burglary.

6. The judge announces the penalty —three years in jail with a chance of *parole** in 18 months. This is where most cases stop. But in the case of John Doe, his lawyer decides to go one step farther.

7. The lawyer tells John Doe: "That was an unfair trial. I think the judge was wrong in some of the instructions he gave to the jury. I'm going to *appeal** your case to a higher court. And we'll win next time, I promise you."

The lawyer argues the appeal before three judges who sit on a higher court —one of 13 courts called the U.S. Courts of Appeal (or *Circuit Courts**). He loses again and takes the case to the U.S. Supreme Court in Washington, D.C.

But before learning the rest of the story, you should realize that while many cases in the federal courts

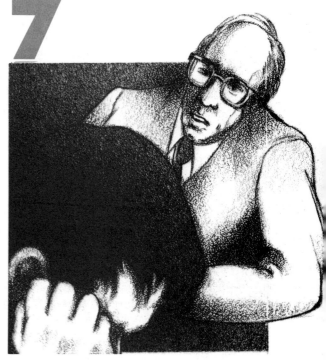

are like John Doe's, many more cases are *not* like his.

The difference between criminal cases and civil cases. The burglary of a post office is a crime. It is a purposeful attempt to break the written laws of society. You may be sent to jail for committing a crime. You cannot be sent to jail in something called a "civil case."

A civil case may begin simply by your shouting at a friend in the presence of other people, "You're a liar!" Your friend may then *sue* you for hurting his or her reputation.

Another civil case might begin if you're late paying back a bank loan. To recover the money, the bank's lawyers may take you to court.

There are usually fewer steps in a civil case than in a criminal case.

There is no arrest in a civil case and no indictment by a grand jury. There is, however, a trial by either a judge alone, or by a judge and a jury. Witnesses are called; evidence is presented.

In a civil case, there is no verdict of guilty or not guilty. Instead, there is a verdict in favor of the *plaintiff** or the *defendant.**

There is neither a prison sentence nor a fine if the verdict goes against the defendant. Instead, the defendant is usually required to pay money to the plaintiff for the damages (harm) done.

For calling your friend a liar, the court may order you to pay several thousand dollars, several hundred dollars, or nothing at all. If you're unhappy with the settlement, you may appeal the case to a higher court.

Of course, there are easier and less costly ways to settle conflicts than going to court over them. A simple apology often soothes hurt feelings. But there are times when people have trouble agreeing about who owes what to whom. In some cases, simple courtesy and politeness do not help much. Then, people ask their lawyers to take their problems to court.

In the federal courts, civil cases outnumber criminal cases by more than two to one. The number of civil cases is so large the courts cannot keep up with them. In 1987 lawyers brought 238,982 civil disputes into the district courts. Only eight percent came to trial in the same year. The others had to wait for another year or two to be settled.

The federal judges in the appeals courts have an even more difficult task keeping up with all the work.

John Doe and the appeals courts.

The U.S. court system has three levels. In the lowest level are the district courts. Next are the U.S. Courts of Appeals, or U.S. Circuit Courts. Finally at the top is the U.S. Supreme Court.

Most cases begin and end in the district courts. These are located throughout the country in different zones or districts. For example, John Doe was accused of breaking into a post office in a town outside Pittsburgh. His trial therefore took place in the federal district court in Pittsburgh.

There is another district court in the middle of Pennsylvania and a third district court for eastern Pennsylvania. A fourth district court serves all of Delaware and a fifth serves all of New Jersey.

These five district courts belong to one judicial group or "circuit." The work of the federal judges in the district courts may be overruled by another group of judges—the "circuit judges." These are the judges of the U.S. Circuit Courts.

These more powerful circuit judges travel around the five districts in their charge. They may either accept or reject a lawyer's appeal to give a case a second hearing. On a single day, a group of three circuit judges may hear the appeal of John Doe's lawyer from Pittsburgh and another appeal about a civil case in Delaware. For each case, they decide whether the district court judge was right or wrong.

But the judgment of circuit judges may also be appealed to an even higher court. The United States Supreme Court is known as the last court of appeal. It has the power to overrule the decisions of all 94 district courts in the country and all 13 appeals courts. You'll be learning more about this most powerful court in the next chapter.

The United States Supreme Court is also at the top of the state court system. Just as in the federal court system, cases tried in the state courts can be appealed through several levels. Cases not resolved in the highest level of the state court system can be appealed to the U.S. Supreme Court.

The John Doe story could of course end either happily or unhappily for him. Do you think Doe's lawyer should win or lose his appeal?

A journey to the courthouse for judges, lawyers and clients.

Which of the U.S. Circuit courts serves your area? How many states are served by your U.S. Circuit Court? What are the names of the federal judges in your district?

This map and *The World Almanac* give you the answers. The map shows the areas served by 11 of the U.S. Circuit Courts plus Washington, D.C. which has its own Circuit Court. The Federal Circuit, not shown on the map, handles special cases nationwide.

Below the map is a listing of U.S. judges. It is part of the complete list printed every year in *The World Almanac*.

From the map and *The World Almanac* you can discover how the U.S. court system is organized. Take the 10-question quiz below. All statements can be proved either true or false by studying the two sources. (Write your answers on a separate piece of paper.)

Answer true or false:

1. Your state has only one federal district court.

2. All states have at least one fed-eral district court.

3. The numbers on the map stand for different circuit courts.

4. The District of Columbia is the smallest area served by a U.S. Circuit Court.

5. Suppose a federal district court in Dallas, Texas, sentences Doris Jones to five years in jail for breaking a federal liquor law. To appeal the case, a lawyer would have to present it to the Seventh U.S. Circuit Court.

6. The Ninth Circuit Court hears appeals from district courts in Wyoming, Montana, and Idaho.

7. Every district has the same number of judges.

8. There seem to be very few fe-male judges in the U.S. court system.

9. It's possible for the same judge to serve in two different districts.

10. William Brevard Hand is the Chief Judge for the Southern District of Alabama.

After completing the quiz, ask yourself whether you agree or disagree with the following three statements about the U.S. courts. Write either "A" for agree or "D" for disagree. Be prepared to explain your opinion.

1. There should be many more women judges in the U.S. courts.

2. New York State with a population of 17.8 million has only one more district court than Alabama with a population of only 4 million. This is unfair to the citizens of New York.

3. Federal district court and circuit court judges should be paid more than members of Congress because the judges' jobs are more important.

U.S. CIRCUIT AND DISTRICT COURTS

Your state may have more than one district. If so, the letters within your state tell whether you live in the North, South, East, West, Middle, or Central District.

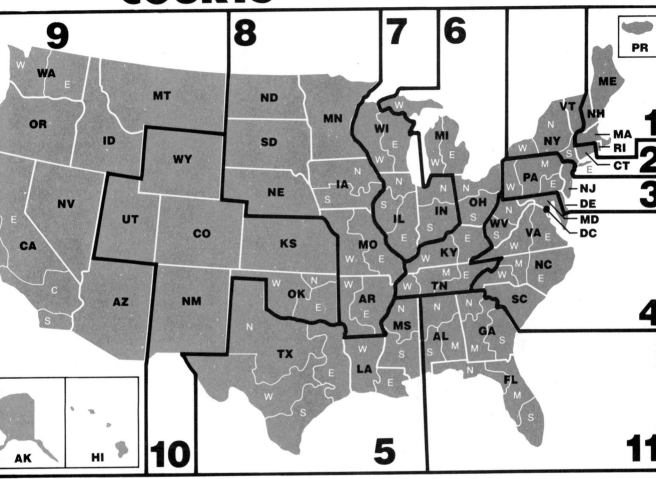

From the 1988 World Almanac: U.S. District Courts
(Salaries, $89,500. CJ means Chief Judge)

Alabama—Northern:
Sam C. Pointer, Jr., CJ
James Hughes Hancock
J. Foy Guin, Jr.
Robert B. Propst
E. B. Haltom, Jr.
U. W. Clemon
William M. Acker, Jr.

Middle:
Truman M. Hobbs, CJ
Robert E. Varner
Myron H. Thompson
Joel F. Dubina

Southern:
William Brevard Hand, CJ
Emmett R. Cox
Alex T. Howard, Jr.

Alaska:
James M. Fitzgerald, CJ
H. Russel Holland

Arizona:
Richard M. Bilby, CJ
Vlademar A. Cordova
Charles L. Hardy
Alfredo C. Marquez
Earl H. Carroll
William D. Browning

Paul G. Rosenblat
Robert C. Bloomfield
Roger G. Strand

Arkansas—Eastern:
Garnett Thomas Eisele, CJ
Elsijane Trimble Roy
William Ray Overton
Henry Woods
George Howard, Jr.

Western:
H. Franklin Waters, CJ
Elsijane Trimble Roy
George Howard, Jr.
Morris S. Arnold

195

"THE LAST WORD"

by Marvin Frankel

Should a person convicted of a crime be sent to jail? Or should this person be given another chance to live in society? That is one of the questions that federal judges must answer every day.

One judge's opinion is given here. The writer is Marvin Frankel, a former judge for a U.S. district court in New York City. He says in this adaptation of an article that judges sometimes are known as either "soft sentencers" or "hard sentencers." Which kind of judge is Marvin Frankel?

Judges are reminded every day that the "typical" criminal is a young male. Roughly eight of every 10 crimes are the work of a man or boy 14 to 29 years old. Therefore, federal judges often face someone who probably has many years of his life to be lived—or taken away. It may be better to put such a person on *probation** than sentence him to a long jail term.

I am not saying that a young defendant always gets probation—not at all. Most of the people sent to prison are young. I mention youth only because they are involved in so many cases faced regularly by judges.

I sent an older man to prison the other day. Why did I do this instead of putting him on probation?

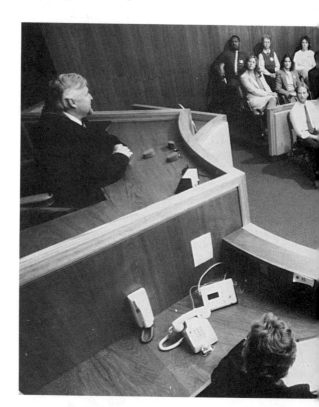

The fact was that this man sold narcotics for profit though he was not addicted. He had lived to be 50 without learning better. It also was important to me that he seemed to be lying when he explained his action. It seemed likely that he would return to his criminal ways, if released soon to the streets.

Compare this to the case of another narcotics seller. This youth was now on methadone, a cure for addiction. He seemed to be serious about breaking the drug habit. Also he was finally ready to work at a legitimate job. His loyal young wife was expecting their child.

This defendant struck me as a fair probation risk. Risk is always with us in this business. Of course the probationer is supervised and later maybe imprisoned if he misbehaves.

The defendant on probation, if he deserves the opportunity, supports himself and his family. It costs something to supervise his activities. But if he were sent to prison, instead, it would cost us much more. In fact, to keep one prisoner every year costs the price of a college education—plus welfare for his family.

Of course judges make mistakes. Defendants betray that trust and go wrong. But a mistake in the other direction may be worse. For suppose you send someone to prison who could have made it on probation. You then have condemned this person to live as an enemy behind walls, at terrible expense all around.

(YOU HAVE THE LAST WORD)

If you were a judge on a federal court, would you probably be a "hard sentencer" or a "soft sentencer"? Would you give a lighter sentence to (a) a 19-year-old youth who robbed a bank but has no previous criminal record or (b) a 40-year-old counterfeiter who has twice been in jail?

"CHECKOUT"—14

Review

1. What kinds of federal courts are mentioned in the Constitution? What three main kinds exist today? Which is the highest of these courts?

2. Which of these cases would *not* be tried in a federal court? **(a)** A passenger on a cruise ship in the mid-Atlantic is accused of robbing other passengers. **(b)** A Treasury Department worker is badly injured when a gold bar falls on his foot. **(c)** A driver runs into and injures a woman in front of a post office.

3. Fill in the gaps in the following sentences. *John Doe is entitled to a trial by _____ . The prosecutor must try to prove that Doe is guilty beyond a _____ .*

4. Is the story of John Doe an example of a criminal or a civil case? Which of the following are civil cases? **(a)** A person is months late in paying back a bank loan. **(b)** A bank is robbed. **(c)** One person publicly accuses another of being a cheat and a liar.

5. When an accused person is found guilty of a crime, who does the sentencing? In The Last Word, what two kinds of sentences are compared and discussed?

Discussion

1. What does it mean when people say, "Don't make a federal case of it"? Most serious crimes — such as murder and armed robbery — are tried in state courts. In what ways are federal cases sometimes more important? Can you give examples of federal cases that have had widespread or long-term effects?

2. Many critics of our legal system are concerned over the wide variations in sentences given by judges for the same crime. A person convicted of armed robbery in one court may get 20 years. In another court, someone convicted of the same crime may get only two years. Do you think this is right?

Are there circumstances which might justify differences in sentences for the same crime? If so, what are they? Or do you think everyone convicted of the same crime should get the same sentence? Why or why not?

Activities

1. Your class might wish to hold a trial of the John Doe case. The key roles are John Doe, the judge, the prosecutor (a lawyer from the U.S. District Attorney's office), the defense counsel, members of the jury, and witnesses. One of the witnesses for the prosecution would be the postal inspector for the Pittsburgh area. A friend of John Doe's could be one of the witnesses for the defense, perhaps to give him an alibi. The trial procedure would be as follows:

(a) Prosecutor states case against Doe to jury (one-minute speech).

(b) Prosecutor calls his or her witnesses and asks questions to bring out the evidence.

(c) Defense counsel cross-examines (questions) the prosecution witnesses, trying to throw doubt on their testimony.

(d) Defense counsel states case for Doe to jury.

(e) Defense counsel questions his or her witnesses to bring out evidence favoring Doe. He or she may call Doe himself as a witness, but does not have to.

(f) Prosecutor cross-examines defense witnesses.

(g) Prosecutor sums up case against Doe (one minute).

(h) Defense counsel sums up Doe's defense.

(i) Prosecutor makes final statement to jury.

(j) Judge instructs jury to decide whether there is reasonable doubt about Doe's guilt.

(k) Jury discusses and votes. (A verdict of guilty must be unanimous.)

(l) Jury announces its verdict.

If the verdict is guilty, the class might discuss whether the sentencing should be "hard" or "soft."

2. Some of you might wish to study an actual federal case from its beginning to the final Supreme Court decision. One interesting choice would be *Brown v. Board of Education*, which led to the decision that segregation in public schools is unlawful. Students could consult the card catalog in the school or public library for books on the case they choose. You could report your findings to the class for discussion.

3. Before there were courts and juries in England (where our judicial system had its birth) people accused of crime were tried by ordeal. An *ordeal* was a kind of test in which the odds were somewhat loaded against the accused. In what was called the *ordeal by fire,* an accused person's clothing was covered with wax, and he or she was made to walk through a blazing fire. The theory was that God would protect an innocent person from the flames. If the accused was burned, he or she was guilty.

Some students might read about other kinds of ordeals in a good encyclopedia and report on them to the class.

4. A local attorney might be invited to speak to your class about the U.S. court system and his or her experiences with it.

5. If it can be arranged, your class might visit a federal courtroom and observe a trial in progress.

15: WHO SHALL JUDGE?

In 1948 Harry Truman criss-crossed the country by train in what looked like a hopeless campaign for re-election as President. Polls showed that he didn't have a chance. His "whistlestops" were drawing small, lukewarm crowds.

One morning, his train pulled into the farming community of Dexter, Iowa. Instead of a small, listless group, an enthusiastic crowd greeted the President. Among those on the platform was a lawyer named Carroll Switzer. Truman had never met Switzer before, and after this brief meeting he moved on with his campaign.

The polls turned out to be wrong, and Truman won the election. A few months later, a vacancy occurred on an Iowa District Court. The President brushed aside names suggested to him. The assistant to an Iowa Senator recalled what happened:

"Every time the Iowa judgeship came up, Truman would hear of no one but Switzer. Truman would say, 'That Switzer backed me when everyone else was running away, and by God, I'm going to see that he gets a judgeship.'"

The President appoints (if you're lucky). Carroll Switzer got the chance to wear the black robes of a federal judge because he happened to meet and impress a President. Luck can play an even larger part in winning one of the rare Supreme Court seats.

A few months after her appointment to the Supreme Court, the first woman Supreme Court justice, Sandra Day O'Connor, commented:

"While there are many supposed criteria for the selection of a justice, [the nomination] is probably a classic example of being the right person in the right spot at the right time. Stated simply, you must be lucky."

Justice O'Connor did have the right legal background, such as experience on an Arizona state court. But her luck included the fact that great pressure had built up to name a woman to the highest court. In addition:

• She was the right age (51). Most Supreme Court *nominees** are in their 40's or early 50's. Presidents want their choices to serve on the court for many years. So they rarely choose older people.

• She was a judicial conservative, the kind of judge Reagan wanted. Only a person who favored *judicial restraint** had any hope of being named by President Reagan. Judicial restraint is a judge's willingness to accept the laws of Congress and of state legislatures whenever possible.

• A good friend and law school classmate already sat on the Supreme Court. Justice William Rehnquist spoke up for her nomination.

On the bench for life? To protect the independence of the judicial branch, judges of the District Courts, Courts of Appeals, and the Supreme Court keep their jobs during "good behavior." The phrase is in Article III of the Constitution. In effect, they serve until they die or choose to retire. They cannot be forced to retire even if they become disabled. (Judges of lesser federal courts, such as customs courts, serve specific terms.)

Federal judges can be removed only by the rare and difficult process of *impeachment.** Only 11 federal judges have ever been impeached, and only five of those were actually removed.

The Constitution gives federal judges another protection. Their compensation, or pay, "shall not be diminished during their continuance in office."

The judiciary has been called the weakest of the three branches. Yet lifetime appointments give federal judges great independence. Judges may serve 30 or more years, handing down rulings on laws of the land.

Who can become a federal judge? The Constitution sets no rules at all. In practice, however, a person needs a law degree. Other qualifications have become customary over the years.

• **Legal competence.** The Justice Department checks the legal qualifications and ability of those the President might appoint. For instance, suppose a state court judge is being considered for a Circuit Court of Appeals. The background check shows that half of the judge's decisions have been reversed by higher courts. The judge probably would not get a recommendation.

The American Bar Association, the attorneys' "union," also checks out the nominee. A 14-member Committee on Federal Judiciary talks to people who have worked with candidates, and studies their legal experience.

The President may ignore these findings. You can see from the chart on page 205 that nominations do not necessarily go to someone ranked "exceptionally well-qualified" or "well-qualified."

● **Political party.** Presidents are not in the business of rewarding people in the opposing party. Federal judgeships are an important part of the *patronage** a President can hand out. Only about 6 per cent of those named to District or Circuit Courts have not belonged to the President's party. Surprisingly, about 15 per cent of Supreme Court choices belonged to the other party.

● **Residence and geographical balance.** Federal District Court judges must live in the district they serve. There is no residency rule for Circuit Courts. Yet by custom, at least one appeals judge is picked from each state in the Circuit.

To satisfy people from all parts of the country, Presidents try to see that all regions are represented on the Supreme Court. Lincoln, for instance, had a vacancy to fill, and insisted that it go to someone from west of the Mississippi River.

● **Religion, race, and sex.** When a vacancy occurred on the Supreme Court in 1932, other justices, legal scholars, and Senators urged President Herbert Hoover to choose Benjamin Cardozo of New York. But there was a problem. Cardozo was Jewish, and the so-called "Jewish seat" on the court was already filled. Over the years a tradition had developed that one seat on the Supreme Court went to a Roman Catholic and one to a Jewish justice. When justices holding those seats died or retired, Presidents usually named someone of the same religion.

This tradition did not allow for two Jewish justices. Nor did it allow for women, blacks, or other minorities.

But the informal rules can be changed. Cardozo did get the nomination and, much later, so did a black and a woman justice.

Thurgood Marshall was the first and, by 1988, the only black justice. When his seat becomes vacant, the President will almost certainly name another black. Since the choice of Justice O'Connor, there is probably a "woman's seat" as well.

Do you think these informal rules are fair? Are there any other rules you think should be added?

The Senate confirms (sometimes). After a person is nominated to the federal bench, the Senate must confirm—or reject—the nomination. Before the Senate takes its vote, however, the Senate Judiciary Committee screens the nominee.

For District Court judges, the committee traditionally consults the Senators from the state where the vacancy occurs. Carroll Switzer would not have become a district judge if an Iowa Senator had objected. Only if the state's Senators approve does the nomination go forward. (This custom does not hold for the higher courts.)

If committee members have doubts about a candidate, they may delay the start of hearings. By stalling, they give those who oppose the candidate time to organize. Robert Bork, one of the most controversial candidates for the Supreme Court, was nominated on July 1, 1987. The Judiciary Committee did not begin its hearings until mid-September. Not surprisingly, it voted against nomination—and so did the Senate.

ACTION PROJECT

The year is 1983, part way through President Ronald Reagan's first term in office. So far, he has appointed 68 District Court judges.

Minority groups and womens' legal organizations are complaining that the President picks only white males for federal courts. They point out that the previous President, Jimmy Carter, made a special effort to name female, black, and Hispanic judges.

A legal journal has just published the table on page 205.

First, imagine that you are a member of the President's staff. You must prepare briefing notes for a press conference he is about to hold. You want to supply some answers to criticisms he faces about judicial appointments. You begin to make notes.

1. Carter wasn't typical. What facts can you give the President to show that President Carter's choices were not typical of most Presidents? What percentage of female District Court judges did he name? What percentage of blacks and Hispanics? How did these figures compare with the percentages named by earlier Presidents?

2. What about professional abilities? What facts can you give the President when critics say his choices aren't always the best in the legal profession? Which President appointed the fewest judges rated "exceptionally well qualified"?

Now imagine that you are a Republican Senator. There's a vacancy on a federal District Court in your state, and you plan to suggest someone to President Reagan, a Republican. Which of the following do you choose? Who is your second choice?

• A white male lawyer who is a partner in a top law firm, and a big contributor to your political campaigns. A prominent Republican.

• A male state court judge whose parents were Mexican farm workers. A Democrat, highly regarded by other judges.

• A black female law professor who backed your opponent in the last Republican primary election. An outstanding legal scholar.

• A male criminal lawyer who helped you win the last election by appearing at your side in black neighborhoods. One of the few well-known black Republicans in the state.

Is the choice difficult to make? What factors are most important to you?

Now suppose you are the President, about to fill the District Court vacancy just described. The Senator has sent all four names to you as candidates for the vacant judgeship.

What other information might you ask for? Which candidate would you choose?

WHAT KIND OF JUDGES DO PRESIDENTS CHOOSE?

An analysis of District Court judges appointed by five recent Presidents

President	Johnson	Nixon	Ford	Carter	Reagan (to 1983)
Number appointed	122	179	52	202	68
Political party	%	%	%	%	%
Democratic	94.3	7.2	21.2	94.1	2.9
Republican	5.7	92.8	78.8	4.5	97.1
Religion					
Protestant	58.2	73.2	73.1	60.4	63.2
Catholic	31.1	18.4	17.3	27.2	30.9
Jewish	10.7	8.4	9.6	12.4	5.9
Ethnic group					
White	93.4	95.5	88.5	78.7	95.6
Black	4.1	3.4	5.8	13.9	—
Hispanic	2.5	1.1	1.9	6.9	2.9
Asian	—	—	3.9	0.5	1.5
Sex					
Male	98.4	99.4	98.1	85.6	95.6
Female	1.6	0.6	1.9	14.4	4.4
American Bar Association ratings					
Exceptionally well qualified	7.4	4.8	—	4.0	1.5
Well qualified	40.9	40.4	46.1	47.0	47.1
Qualified	49.2	54.8	53.8	47.5	51.5
Not qualified	2.5	—	—	1.5	—

Source: Sheldon Goldman, "Reagan's Judicial Appointments at Mid-Term: Shaping the Bench in His Own Image," *Judicature*, March 1983.

U.S. SUPREMEME COU

ROTHCO

BORO / THE PHOENIX GAZETTE '87

"THE LAST WORD"

by Justices of the Supreme Court

Justices of the Supreme Court are appointed by the President. If they are confirmed by the Senate they are sworn into office. Do they decide cases as the President had hoped? No, not usually. Presidents try to "pack" the Supreme Court by choosing justices who share their political views. (The cartoon imagines how one President —Ronald Reagan—would have liked to pack the court.) But people often change once they are on the Supreme Court.

"Nothing is more striking in the history of the Court than the manner in which the hopes of those who expected a judge to follow the political views of the President appointing him are disappointed," wrote Charles Warren, a historian of the Court.

Here are a few examples:

Theodore Roosevelt and Oliver Wendell Holmes, Jr.:

Justice Holmes, whom Roosevelt had appointed, voted to strike down some of the President's anti-trust legislation. Roosevelt exploded:

"I could carve out of a banana a judge with more backbone than that!"

Later, when a supporter of the President urged Justice Holmes to approve laws the President had suggested, Holmes replied coolly:

"What you want is favor, not justice."

Harry Truman and Tom Clark

"Packing the Supreme Court simply can't be done," said President Truman in a 1959 speech. "I've tried and it won't work. . . . Whenever you put a man on the Supreme Court he ceases to be your friend. I'm sure of that."

In the book *Plain Speaking: An Oral Biography of Harry S Truman,* the former President did indeed speak more plainly. "Tom Clark was my biggest mistake," he said. "No question about it. That . . . fool from Texas that I first made Attorney General and then put on the Supreme Court. I don't know what got into me. He was no . . . good as Attorney General, and on the Supreme Court . . . it doesn't seem possible, but he's been even worse. He hasn't made one right decision that I can think of. . . ."

Dwight Eisenhower and Earl Warren

After he had left the White House, President Eisenhower was asked if he had made any mistakes as President.

"Yes, two, and they are both sitting on the Supreme Court," snapped Ike. He referred to his appointment of Chief Justice Earl Warren and Justice William J. Brennan, Jr. Both men had quite conservative records when they were appointed. Yet the Warren Court became one of the most activist in the nation's history. One of its early decisions was *Brown v. Board of Education* (1954), which made racial segregation illegal.

Justice Warren once remarked that he did not see "how a man could be on the court and not change his views substantially over a period of years . . . for change you must if you are to do your duty on the Supreme Court."

(YOU HAVE THE LAST WORD)

"We are under a Constitution," remarked Charles Evans Hughes, "but the Constitution is what the justices say it is." What kind of person do you think should have the last word on the Constitution? If you could choose a justice of the Supreme Court, what personal qualities and experience would you look for? What clues might you look for to see how that person might change after becoming a justice?

"CHECKOUT"—15

Key terms

nominees
judicial conservative
judicial restraint
"good behavior"

impeachment
compensation
American Bar Association

patronage
Senate Judiciary Committee
activist

Review

1. Describe three factors that influence the selection of a justice of the U.S. Supreme Court.

2. Explain what is meant by "judicial restraint."

3. List the steps by which a person becomes a federal District Court judge.

4. How long do federal judges serve (at the District Court level and above)? How can they be removed from office?

5. Explain how just one Senator can kill the nomination of a District Court judge.

Discussion

1. What qualities do you think are most important for a judge to have? List the character traits and skills that you think a judge should possess. Does our system of choosing federal judges ensure that the kind of person you have described will sit on the federal benches? Why or why not?

2. Suppose you were a young lawyer whose career goal is to become a federal judge. Are there any actions you could take to increase your chances of being nominated? If so, what actions? If not, why not?

3. When he became chairman of the Senate Judiciary Committee in 1979, Sen. Edward Kennedy of Massachusetts said: "The federal courts must become more representative of the people of this nation. Congress and the Administration must work together to insure that more women and more members of minority groups are appointed to the federal bench. A judicial branch in which only 5 per cent of the judges are women and only 2 per cent are black is unacceptable." Do you agree or disagree? What pressure could the Judiciary Committee bring on the President to name more women and minorities?

4. The Supreme Court started out with six justices and at one time had as many as ten. Since 1869, however, its membership has remained at nine. Do you think the court would function better with fewer justices? More justices? Or should it remain with nine? Explain your answer.

5. Many state judges serve for spe-

cific terms, and must stand for re-election to keep their jobs. Suggestions have been made to amend the Constitution to set terms for federal judges. To continue on the bench, they would have to be reappointed by the President and confirmed again by the Senate. Supporters argue that specific terms would be a way to get rid of disabled or incompetent judges. What would be the advantages of this suggestion? The disadvantages? Would such a change strengthen or weaken the judicial branch?

Activities

1. Legal scholars and historians were asked to grade justices of the Supreme Court from A ("great") to E ("failure"). Those with the most votes as "great" justices were John Marshall, Louis Brandeis, Oliver Wendell Holmes, and Hugo Black. You might do some research about one of these justices (in biographies, encyclopedias, and books on the Supreme Court) to see what was said of him when he was nominated as a justice. Was there opposition? On what grounds? Once on the court, did he hand down the type of opinions the President who appointed him expected?

2. Your class might wish to hold mock confirmation hearings on a nominee for the Supreme Court.

(a) One person would act as the nominee. This person should prepare notes on his or her background, trying to provide answers for the kinds of questions the committee will ask.

(b) One person should be the chairman of the Senate Judiciary Committee, who will be a member of the majority party in the Senate. This student will chair the hearings.

(c) One person will be the ranking Senator of the minority party. Note that if the nominee is a Democrat, Democratic Senators are more likely to support confirmation, just as Republicans are more likely to back a Republican.

(d) Other students can serve as Senators and committee staff.

When all are ready, the chairman should call the hearings to order, and announce the ground rules. After all committee members have questioned the nominee, the committee should vote on whether to confirm or reject the nomination.

3. The class might break into groups to prepare oral reports on people who were nominated by the President to the Supreme Court but not confirmed by the Senate. Reports could be presented in the format of a TV documentary.

Use the *Readers' Guide,* copies of *Congressional Quarterly,* and other library resources to prepare your reports. Subjects could include: Harrold Carswell (1970), Robert Bork (1987), Donald Ginsburg (1987).

4. You might want to read a book about choosing Supreme Court justices, and prepare a written book report. Most books on the Supreme Court have chapters or whole sections on choosing justices. One lively and well-written account is *Justices and Presidents: A Political History of Appointments to the Supreme Court,* by Henry J. Abraham (Oxford University Press, 1985).

16: THE NINE MOST POWERFUL JUDGES

The picture at the left shows the Supreme Court of the United States as it looked in 1940. Notice the apparent ages of the nine men in the picture and the robes that they wear.

The bearded man in the center of the picture is the Chief Justice, Charles Evans Hughes. The Chief Justice is the central and most powerful person in the Judicial Branch of the United States government.

Who are the two men who are shown by arrows in the picture? The man with white hair standing in the back row is Justice Felix Frankfurter. The other man, seated in the lower right-hand corner of the picture, is Justice Hugo Black.

In their black robes, these two people may look very much alike. But the robes say nothing about the true character of these men.

The story of two judges. When Felix Frankfurter was born, no one could have guessed that he would ever be an American judge. He was born in Austria and could not speak a word of English when he came to the U.S. at the age of 12. He grew up in a neighborhood in New York City where many people like himself spoke only German.

He once was asked about his early life in school. This is the way he remembered it:

"I was pitched into a class. I was in a daze. English, of course, was a great barrier. We had a teacher, a middle-aged Irish woman, named Miss Hogan. She was one of my greatest helpers in life because she was a lady of the old school. She believed in corporal punishment. She saw this enthusiastic kid who by that time had picked up some English. So she told the boys that if anybody was caught speaking German with me, she would punish him. She would give gentle uppercuts to the boys."

That was how Felix Frankfurter got his start in life and learned to speak English better than most American-born citizens.

While Felix Frankfurter (below) adjusted to life in an American city, Hugo Black (at right) was growing up in a totally different world. He was born on a farm in Alabama and later grew up in a town of 500 people. Black spent his early youth picking cotton, studying books, and working in a newspaper office.

His mother and older brother wanted him to be a doctor. Instead he went to law school and set up his first law office over his father's grocery store. Black went into politics and rose quickly. He served two terms in the United States Senate. In 1937 President Franklin D. Roosevelt named him to the Supreme Court.

Frankfurter took a different path to the court. He also became a lawyer.

Felix Frankfurter

Hugo Black

But instead of politics, he went into teaching. He taught law at the Harvard Law School. In 1939 he was also named by President Franklin Roosevelt to the Supreme Court.

When they were young men in their early twenties, Black and Frankfurter studied the Constitution in law school. As lawyers, they argued about certain words and phrases in the Constitution hundreds of times. A justice on the Supreme Court is expected to have a firm knowledge of the law—and especially the Constitution. That is one chief qualification for serving on the highest court in the land.

Death by a vote of 5–4. Supreme Court justices often disagree about the cases that come before them.

A 1947 case is a good example. It was the case of a 15-year-old boy who faced going to the electric chair for a second time. The boy, Willie Francis, had confessed to the crime of murdering a man in Louisiana.

The state of Louisiana had tried once to execute him for this crime. But something had gone wrong with the electric chair. The electric current had been strong enough to cause Willie pain—but not death.

Willie's lawyer appealed the case to the Supreme Court. He argued that the Eighth Amendment of the Constitution protected citizens against "cruel and unusual punishments." Wasn't it cruel and unusual, the lawyer asked, for a person to suffer in the electric chair, not just once, but twice?

Most of the judges on the Supreme Court disliked the idea of capital punishment. But as judges, they were trained to put personal feelings aside. They tried to think only of the words in the Constitution.

Five of the nine justices thought the "cruel and unusual" phrase in the Constitution did not protect Willie Francis from execution. The four other justices disagreed. The Supreme Court makes its decisions by a majority vote. Thus, Willie Francis lost his case—and his life—by a vote of 5–4.

Role of the Supreme Court. The Supreme Court has a special role to play in the United States system of government. The Constitution gives it the power to check, if necessary, the actions of the President and Congress.

It can tell a President that his actions are not allowed by the Constitution. It can tell Congress that a law it passed violated the U.S. Constitution and is, therefore, no longer a law. It can also tell the government of a state that one of its laws breaks a rule in the Constitution.

The Supreme Court is the final judge in all cases involving laws of Congress, and the highest law of all — the Constitution.

The Supreme Court, however, is far from all-powerful. Its power is limited by the other two branches of government. The President nominates* justices to the court. The Senate must vote its approval of the nominations. The whole Congress also has great power over the lower courts in the federal system.* District and appeals courts are created by acts of Congress. These courts may be abolished if Congress wishes it.

The Supreme Court is like a referee on a football field. The Congress, the President, the state police, and other government officials are the players. Some can pass laws, and others can enforce laws. But all exercise power within certain boundaries. These boundaries are set by the Constitution. As the "referee" in the U.S. system of government, it is the Supreme Court's job to say when the government officials step out-of-bounds.

How the justices make decisions. The decisions of the Supreme Court are made inside a white marble courthouse in Washington, D.C. Here the nine justices receive about 5,000 requests for hearings each year. Of these the Court will agree to hear fewer than 150. If the Court decides not to hear the case, the ruling of the lower court stands.

Those cases which they agree to hear are given a date for argument.

On the morning of that day, the lawyers and spectators enter a large courtroom. When an officer of the Court bangs his gavel, the people in the courtroom stand. The nine justices walk through a red curtain and stand beside nine tall, black-leather chairs. The Chief Justice takes the middle and tallest chair. "Oyez! Oyez! Oyez!" shouts the marshal of the Court. (It's an old Court expression meaning "hear ye.") "God save the United States and this Honorable Court."

The justices take their seats. The lawyers step forward and explain their case. The justices listen from their high seats and often interrupt to ask the lawyers questions. Several cases may be argued in one day. Finally, in the late afternoon, the Chief Justice bangs his gavel, rises from his seat, and leads the other justices through the red curtain out of the courtroom.

The justices may take several days to study a case. Then they meet around a large table in a locked and guarded room. From their table, they may occasionally look up to see a painting on the wall.

It is a portrait of a man dressed in an old-fashioned, high-collared coat. This man is John Marshall (at right), one of the greatest Chief Justices in American history. More than anyone else, he helped the Supreme Court develop its power and importance.

Before Marshall became Chief Justice, the Supreme Court had not yet challenged an act of Congress. The Constitution did not clearly give the Court power to judge laws passed by Congress. Therefore the Court wasn't even sure it had this power.

But Marshall made a daring move. In a famous court case in 1803, *Marbury v. Madison,* he wrote the Court's opinion which declared a law passed by Congress to be unconstitutional.

This decision gave the Supreme Court its power of *judicial review.** Ever since, the highest court has used

John Marshall

the power to review the nation's laws and judge whether they were allowed under the Constitution. It has also reviewed the actions of the President.

The Constitution does not allow Congress or state legislatures to pass laws that "abridge the freedom of speech." Freedom of speech is protected in the United States, and no lawmaking body may interfere with that freedom. Right? Usually. But there may be limits, even to free speech.

No freedom, even one specifically mentioned in the Constitution, is absolute. People convicted of serious crimes lose the right to vote. Some religions encourage a man to have several wives. But that practice is forbidden in the United States, even though the Constitution says that there shall be no laws that prohibit the "free exercise" of religion. Even words themselves may pose a "clear and present danger" to the well-being of the country.

When are mere words so dangerous that Congress (or a state legislature) may limit the freedom of speech?

THE SUPREME COURT, 1980

REHNQUIST

WHITE

How has the Supreme Court changed since 1980? Which of these justices are still on the Court today? Look it up in *The World Almanac*.

That is the sort of difficult question that the Supreme Court justices must often answer.

Here's an example. The justices sat around the conference table in their locked room, trying to decide what to do about a man from Chicago named Terminiello. The year was 1949.

It seems that Mr. Terminiello had given a speech to an audience in a hall in Chicago, attacking all sorts of people. A crowd had collected outside the hall to protest. Terminiello had called the crowd "a surging, howling mob." At other points in his speech, he called those who disagreed with him "slimy scum," "snakes," "bedbugs," and the like. The crowd outside screamed back: "Fascists! Hitlers!" Windows were broken, a few people were injured, and Terminiello was arrested. For what? All he did was talk. But by talking, he broke the law.

This Chicago law outlawed speech that "stirs the public to anger, invites dispute, [or] brings about a condition of unrest." But maybe this law was unconstitutional.

Justice William Douglas said that the Chicago law went against the First Amendment. He said that freedom of speech is important *because* it invites dispute. It allows people to raise tough questions, questions which should be answered in a democracy. Just because people get angry or annoyed at something that is said, Justice Douglas went on, does not mean that it should not be said.

Justice Robert Jackson felt differently. Yes, he agreed, Terminiello had not said anything illegal. But because of the crowd and the anger around him, his speech was dangerous to the peace and order of the community. Therefore it was not protected by the First Amendment. There is a point, said Justice Jackson, beyond which a person may not provoke a crowd.

Finally the Court voted. Each justice, including the Chief Justice, had one vote. Five agreed with one opinion, four with the other. One of the justices in the majority was then asked to write a long essay explaining the legal reasons for the majority's decision. Another justice announced that he would write a *dissenting opinion.** This was an essay telling why he disagreed with the Court's decision.

How do you think the Court ruled in *Terminiello v. Chicago?* (Your teacher can tell you the Supreme Court's decision.)

What if Terminiello had been a Republican campaigning for office among bad-tempered Democrats? What if he

BLACKMUN   POWELL   STEVENS

BRENNAN   BURGER   STEWART   MARSHALL

had been a Communist? Consider these and other important questions that might occur to you. Which is more important—protecting free speech, or the peace and order of the community? Where do you draw the line?

If you had been on the Court in 1949, would you have voted to allow the Chicago law to stand or would you have voted to rule it unconstitutional?

The role of the Chief Justice.

The nine justices of the Supreme Court are equals, with one vote each. Yet the Chief Justice is first among the equals. A strong "chief" has great influence on the Supreme Court and the entire legal system.

When John Marshall died after 34 years as chief, the Liberty Bell tolled in mourning, and promptly cracked. Some said his shoes would be impossible to fill, for he had dominated the court. So have a few other "chiefs," notably Charles Evans Hughes (1930–1941) and Earl Warren (1953–1969).

How is the Chief Justice able to in-fluence the other Supreme Court justices? The chief has several advantages. When the justices meet to choose cases to review or to decide on cases they have accepted, the Chief Justice chairs the meeting and sets the agenda. When the justices confer on cases, the Chief Justice speaks first and can set the tone of the conference.

The chief keeps an eye on the clock. Hughes allowed about three and a half minutes of conferences for petitions to the court to review cases. He had studied them ahead of time, and had clear recommendations.

"Brethren," he would say when he thought they had talked enough, "the only way to settle this is vote. So let us do just that—now."

By speaking first when the 1954 *desegregation** cases came up, Earl Warren clearly signaled that he wanted to overturn an 1896 decision allowing separate schools for blacks and whites. Warren also insisted that the desegregation cases be decided unanimously to give the full weight of the Supreme Court to the rulings.

Here are two rulings of the Supreme Court at different times in history. Both involve cases of racial segregation.

In one case, a black citizen, Homer A. Plessy, protested a state law that kept him out of a railroad car marked "for whites only." Plessy lost the case.

The Supreme Court's decision in the *Plessy* case established racial segregation as constitutional. But in 1954, with *Brown v. Board of Education,* the Supreme Court changed its opinion. Why?

ONE TOWN, TWO SCHOOLS

Two photos taken on the same day in 1949 in West Memphis, Arkansas: Below, left, a classroom in the new all-white high school; below, the room in the African Methodist Church that served as the elementary school for black students.

1896: The justices rule that railway cars may be "separate but equal."

[*Justice Henry Brown writes the opinion of the Court.*]

The question before this Court is whether a certain law of Louisiana is constitutional. This law provides for separate railway cars for whites and for blacks.

The plaintiff [Plessy] argues that a law of this kind treats members of the Negro race as if they were inferior. But the Court cannot agree with this. We think that if a Negro feels inferior because of the separate railway cars it is not because of anything found in the law itself. It may seem so only because the Negro race chooses to see it that way.

The plaintiff also argues that social prejudice may be overcome by law. It is argued that a Negro cannot enjoy equal rights unless the law forces the two races to live and work together. We, the majority of the Court, cannot accept this argument. The two races will become social equals only as the result of their natural desires.

1954: The justices rule that schools cannot be "separate but equal."

[*Justice Earl Warren writes the opinion of the Court.*]

In this case, children of the Negro race seek to be admitted to the public school of their community. They wish to be admitted on the same basis as whites. But they have been denied admission to schools attended by white children. Their lawyer argues that this segregation deprives them of a right guaranteed in the 14th Amendment to the Constitution. It is the right to *equal protection of the laws.**

In approaching this problem, we [the Court] cannot turn the clock back to 1896 when *Plessy v. Ferguson* was written. Instead, we must think of public education as it is today.

We come then to the question. What is the result of segregating children in public schools, solely on the basis of race? Does it deprive Negro children of equal opportunities for education? The majority of this Court believes that it does.

Separating one group of children from another leads to a feeling of inferiority. This feeling may permanently affect their hearts and minds. We quote from the opinion of a lower court:

"The policy of separating the races is usually understood to make the Negro group feel inferior. This feeling of inferiority affects the desire of a child to learn."

We know more today about human psychology than this Court knew in 1896. For this reason, we may now reject some of the language of *Plessy v. Ferguson.* We rule instead that schools separated on the basis of race cannot be equal. They are clearly unequal. Therefore we hold that the plaintiffs have been deprived of the equal protection of the laws guaranteed by the 14th Amendment.

The court's rulings in both the *Plessy* and the *Brown* cases were based on the 14th Amendment of the Constitution. This reads: "No state shall . . . deny to any person within its jurisdiction the equal protection of the laws."

Why do you think the Supreme Court changed its mind about the meaning of those words? Do you respect the court more because it sometimes changes its mind about the law? How would you feel if the court changed its rulings several times a year?

Now imagine that you are a Supreme Court justice. The court is reviewing two cases that involve the 14th Amendment:

In one case, a group of 16-year-old students argue that they are denied equal protection because they are not allowed to vote.

The other case involves contracts—binding agreements to do or pay for something. In all states, minors are free to break any contracts they may sign. Some adult citizens argue that they are denied equal protection because they are not allowed to break contracts.

How would you interpret the 14th Amendment in each case? Why?

"THE LAST WORD"

by Bob Woodward and Scott Armstrong

In 1954 the Supreme Court ruled in Brown v. Board of Education *that separate schools for blacks and whites were unconstitutional. Schools were told to desegregate "with all deliberate speed."*

How fast is that? Many state and local governments found reasons for delay. Appeals for more time dragged through the courts. Fifteen years after the Supreme Court's ruling, many places in the South still had all-white and all-black schools.

In 1969 a lower court granted a delay to several Mississippi school districts. The case was appealed to the Supreme Court, which accepted it. The federal Justice Department said that there were practical difficulties against immediate desegregation. Some justices believed that a short delay should be granted. Others felt that the time for any delay was long past. How did they deal with the problem?

The scenes below are adapted from the book The Brethren, *by Bob Woodward and Scott Armstrong.*

The Cast
Warren Burger, the new Chief Justice.
Hugo Black, 83-year-old Supreme Court justice, from Alabama.
Thurgood Marshall, great-grandson of a slave, the court's only black justice. In 1954, as a lawyer for the National Association for the Advancement of Colored People (NAACP), he had argued *Brown v. Board of Education* before the court.
Jerris Leonard, spokesperson for the Justice Department.
Jack Greenberg, lawyer for the NAACP.
Louis Obendorfer, former law clerk of Justice Black, speaking for a group of lawyers.

John Harlan, Supreme Court justice. His grandfather, John Marshall Harlan, was the only Supreme Court justice who dissented from the ruling in *Plessy v. Ferguson.*

SCENE ONE: *The Supreme Court Courtroom, October 23, 1969*

Greenberg: Mr. Chief Justice, and may it please the court, there has been enough stalling and enough lawlessness by Southern school officials. This court's rulings are not being obeyed.

The sorriest part of the story lies in the stalling by some Mississippi District Courts. They have delayed. They have refused to proceed. They have taken advantage of every loophole to stall. This court should declare that integrated schools are the rule now, today. This court should order immediate desegregation.

Leonard: Mr. Chief Justice, and may it please the court, the Justice Department sees many practical problems here. The department does not have enough lawyers to press these cases.

Oberdorfer: Mr. Chief Justice, and

may it please the court, I speak for a group of attorneys who oppose any more delay. If the Justice Department cannot provide lawyers, we will do so at no cost to open these schools to black—

Black *(interrupting):* The thing to do is to say that the dual system of black and white schools is over, and that it is to go into effect now. Do you agree?

Oberdorfer: I agree with that, without knowing exactly what "now" is.

Black: I mean when we issue an order. *(Pause)* If we do. *(Laughter from courtroom audience)*

Leonard: The situation is very complicated.

Black: What's complicated?

Leonard: What I'm pleading with this court is not to do something hasty.

Black: Could anything be hasty with all the years gone by since our order?

Burger: If there had been no appeal . . . Can you assure me that the desegregation plans would have been submitted on December 1?

Leonard: Yes.

Black: Too many plans and not enough action. *(Laughter from courtroom audience)*

SCENE TWO: *Justices' Conference room, October 24, 1969*

Burger: We have suggested giving the Mississippi schools five weeks to draw new desegregation plans.

Black: Five weeks is not the issue. Five weeks is a symbol. The court must not give any sign that it is willing to accept further delay. The law calls for one single school system for blacks and whites. We should issue an order rejecting "all deliberate speed." If anyone writes otherwise, I dissent.

Harlan: I agree that we should put an end to the delays. But we also have to recognize reality. We cannot suddenly tell school districts to desegregate overnight.

Marshall: This court must stand united on this matter. We cannot have it look as if the court is backing down on desegregation. Let's give them until January, when a new semester begins.

(YOU HAVE THE LAST WORD)

Even if the school districts ended their stalling it would still take some time for them to set up integrated schools. Should the Supreme Court make a realistic ruling that allowed for this further delay? Or should it make a symbolic ruling that called for immediate desegregation? Were there any other choices that the court might make?

Suppose you were one of the justices. What would you have decided in this case? Why? (Your teacher can tell you what the court finally decided.)

"CHECKOUT"—16

Key terms

nominate
federal system
judicial review
Chief Justice

majority opinion
dissenting opinion
desegregation

separate but equal
equal protection
all deliberate speed

Review

1. Name the two justices described at the beginning of the chapter. What did their backgrounds have in common?

2. Must all nine justices agree before the Supreme Court can issue a ruling? Or is a simple majority enough? Give an example to support your answer.

3. Explain the power that the Supreme Court has over the President, Congress, and state governments.

4. Justices often have widely differing opinions on a case. What determines the decision of the Court as a whole? Describe two cases in which the Supreme Court reached opposite decisions (at different times).

5. All nine justices of the Supreme Court have the same voting power. But the Chief Justice performs certain tasks that enable him or her to influ-

ence the court's choice of cases and its rulings. Describe two of those tasks.

Discussion

1. The Supreme Court is compared to a football referee. In what ways does the Court act like a referee? In what ways does it act differently? To what else might you compare the role of the Court?

2. Does the Constitution set down any qualifications for Supreme Court justices? (See Article III, Section 1.) Judging from the chapter, what qualifications do you think they should have?

3. Supreme Court justices are appointed for life. The President and members of Congress have to consider the next election if they make unpopular decisions, but the nine justices do

not. What are the advantages of this system? What are the disadvantages? Do you think it is right for the justices to be "above the fray"? Do you think there should be a mandatory retirement age for justices? If so, what age? Explain your answers.

4. Sometimes the Supreme Court has changed or reversed an earlier decision. Do you think this shows a weakness in the Court—or a willingness to adjust the Constitution to changing times and conditions? If so, is this willingness a good—or bad—way to interpret the Constitution? Give reasons for your answers.

5. Suppose you are a Senator considering a nominee for the Supreme Court. What are the three most important questions *you* would ask about the nominee and his or her background?

6. Some years ago the attorney of an accused murderer sued a newspaper reporter for refusing to hand over background information on the case. The attorney argued that the information was necessary for his client's defense. The reporter argued that much of the information was confidential. This was a conflict between two constitutional rights. The Sixth Amendment guarantees a fair trial to the accused murderer. The First Amendment guarantees freedom of the press to the reporter. The state courts decided that the First Amendment had to give way to the Sixth. The Supreme Court refused to review the case. Suppose the Court had decided to review it. What further information do you think they would want before reaching

a decision? What questions would *you* ask if you were trying to make this decision?

7. In the book *Justices and Presidents,* Henry J. Abraham writes that Supreme Court justices "are well aware of two important facts of life: they do not have the power to enforce their decisions, for the purse is in the hands of the legislature and the sword in those of the executive. . . ." What is meant by "the purse" and "the sword"? How might the two important facts influence the justices' decisions?

Activities

1. You might choose one of the present Supreme Court justices. Using encyclopedias, a biography, or a dictionary of biography, you could research the justice's life. Then write a brief profile for the class.

2. You might look up some recent Supreme Court decisions. (You can find these in such sources as newspapers, news magazines, *Facts on File,* and *Congressional Quarterly.*) You could study one of the cases and make notes of the constitutional issue(s) involved and the main arguments on each side. You might then report on the case to the class.

3. How did John Marshall manage to assert the power of the Supreme Court in *Marbury v. Madison?* Some of you, using a good encyclopedia, might research the history of the Supreme Court and report to the class your findings on that question—as well as other interesting and pertinent information about the Supreme Court.

17: TAKING A CASE THROUGH THE COURTS

In May 1983 a high school principal objected to two articles planned for the school newspaper. He ordered them removed before the paper was printed. His action triggered a dispute that went all the way to the Supreme Court.

More than 320,000 cases enter the federal District Courts each year. In 1983, one of them was brought by three members of the *Spectrum* staff at Hazelwood East, a school in a St. Louis, Missouri, suburb. *Spectrum* is produced by the Journalism II class at the school under the supervision of a teacher.

The problem began when principal Robert Reynolds (photo) read page proofs of two articles. One consisted of interviews with three Hazelwood students who had become pregnant. The other described the effect of parents' divorce on teenagers.

The articles used fake names, but Reynolds thought the people described were easy to identify. He also said some of the material was not suitable for younger students.

Leslie Smart, Cathy Kulhmeier, and Lee Ann Tippett-West of the *Spectrum* staff sued the school. By the time a Supreme Court ruling had been made four and a half years later, the students had graduated from high school and were seniors in college.

What makes an issue a "federal case"? When is a case important enough for the Supreme Court to consider? For answers, track the *Hazelwood* newspaper case through the fed-

From left: Cathy Kuhlmeier, Leslie Smart and Lee Ann Tippett-West.

eral court system.

The main issue was whether the principal had violated students' First Amendment rights to free expression by censoring a school newspaper. The school district argued that *Spectrum* was part of the curriculum, and therefore not a public forum protected by the First Amendment. Who was right?

First step: District Court. Each year about 15 percent of the 320,000 cases that reach the District Courts are criminal. The other 85 per cent, like the *Hazelwood* case, are civil disputes.

The Hazelwood students took their case first to the U.S. Court for the Eastern District of Missouri. It was a federal case because they charged that their First Amendment rights had been violated. The students asked for an *injunction** (a court order preventing something) that would protect the *Spectrum* staff against censorship.

Judge John Nangle ruled that *Spectrum* was not a public forum, and that Principal Reynolds had the right to censor articles. The case would have ended there, but the students appealed the decision to a higher court.

Second step: Appeals Court. The *Hazelwood* case went next to the Court of Appeals for Missouri. Appeals courts have two main functions:

1. To correct any errors made by District Courts. A federal Court of Appeals does not hear new facts in a case. No new testimony by witnesses is introduced. The Appeals Court examines only whether the lower court

decision was correctly made.

2. To identify cases worthy of Supreme Court review. In writing their opinions, Courts of Appeals judges sometimes hint pointedly that they think the highest court should settle certain questions as a guide for lower courts.

Nearly 30,000 cases reach the 13 Courts of Appeals every year. For most disputes, these courts have the last word and make a final decision.

The Missouri Court of Appeals held that the District Court was wrong on *Hazelwood,* and reversed the lower court's ruling. The Appeals Court said the school newspaper was not just a "part of the school adopted curriculum" but also a public forum. As a public forum, *Spectrum* was protected by the First Amendment.

The Missouri Circuit Court gave as *precedent** the Supreme Court's 1969 ruling in *Tinker v. Des Moines Independent School District.* (A precedent is a previous decision that can be followed.) In the *Tinker* case, a principal had suspended three students who wore black armbands to school in protest against the war in Vietnam. In deciding for the students, the Supreme Court said that students in public schools do not "shed their constitutional rights to freedom of speech or expression at the schoolhouse gate."

At this point, the students had won. However, the Hazelwood School District appealed the Court of Appeals decision to the Supreme Court.

Will the Supreme Court accept the case? People often threaten to take a case "all the way to the Supreme Court." Filing an appeal is easy, but getting it heard is not. Each year more than 5,000 *petitions,** or appeals, reach the Supreme Court.

The number of cases the court can act upon is limited by the time the justices have to read, review, discuss, decide, and write opinions. The justices choose which cases to put on the court *docket*. A docket is the schedule of cases to be heard by a court.

About 100 petitions come up for review each week. These are first screened by the Chief Justice with the help of the law clerks who work for other justices. Only about one third of the petitions survive this screening. Thus the Chief Justice plays an important role in deciding what cases will be reviewed.

The surviving cases are put on a "Discuss List." Every Friday morning the nine justices meet to discuss the list and choose which cases they will review. For a case to be placed on the Supreme Court docket, at least four Justices must agree to "grant cert."

This is legal slang for granting a writ of *certiorari* (sur-shuh-RAIR-ee), a Latin term that means "to make more certain." The writ orders a lower court to send up a complete record of the case for review.

By long tradition, the Supreme Court follows a rule of judicial self-restraint in choosing cases. The court restrains itself, or holds itself back, from taking certain kinds of cases. (The Action Project on page 230 lists some of the court's guidelines for rejecting cases.) As a result, fewer than 150 of the 5,000 cases appealed each year end up on the justices' docket.

Why, then, does the court take a case like *Hazelwood?* First, there must be a federal matter involved. Here it was First Amendment protections. Second, there must be some uncertainty about interpreting the Constitution. In this case, a Court of Appeals had interpreted the First Amendment differently from a District Court. Other courts needed to know whether the Supreme Court would let this interpretation stand.

The court divides. In January 1988 a sharply divided court issued a 5–3 ruling on *Hazelwood*. The court held that public school officials do have broad power to censor school newspapers and other "school-sponsored . . . activities" such as plays.

What reasons did the majority give for this decision? Why did the minority disagree? The Last Word on page 232 cites the views of justices for and against the ruling.

229

ACTION PROJECT

Do teachers have the right to search student purses and lockers? Or do such searches violate student rights? Is this the kind of issue the Supreme Court should decide? Here is an actual case that raised those questions.

A teacher at Piscataway High School in New Jersey suspected a student of smoking in the washroom. The student denied that she had been smoking. A vice principal then asked her to open her purse. In it were cigarettes and rolling papers. The vice principal connected rolling papers with marijuana, and therefore searched the purse. Inside were marijuana, a pipe, and a list of students who owed money to the girl.

School officials turned the evidence over to the police, who brought charges against the girl as a delinquent. She was identified in the records only as T.L.O.

At the delinquency hearing, T.L.O.'s lawyer asked to have the evidence thrown out. The lawyer argued that it had been seized in violation of the Fourth Amendment, which bans unreasonable searches and seizures. The judge disagreed, declared T.L.O. a delinquent, and sentenced her to a year's probation.

She appealed through state courts. The New Jersey Supreme Court ruled that the search of her purse violated T.L.O.'s Fourth Amendment rights.

The school asked for a review by the U.S. Supreme Court. The school's lawyers argued that teachers must be allowed to keep discipline. To do this, they said, teachers must be able to search student's purses and lockers.

Would the Supreme Court take the case? Federal courts work under rules of judicial restraint. These prevent judges from handling many cases, and limit the rulings they give on many cases they do handle. The rules have been worked out over many years. As listed by Robert A. Carp and Ronald Stidham in *The Federal Courts*, the rules include:

• There must be a real dispute.

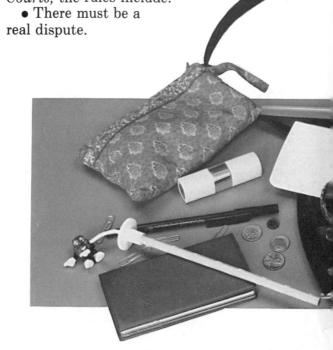

Someone must have been wronged or have a personal stake in the case. Thus the Supreme Court will not hear a complaint against a law that has not yet wronged anyone.

• An appeal to the Supreme Court must be based on the Constitution. The plaintiff, or person bringing the case, must cite part of the Constitution that he or she believes has been violated.

• The Supreme Court rules on questions of law, not fact. The court doesn't decide if the facts presented in the lower courts were wrong. For instance, justices do not determine if witnesses lied. Their duty, Chief Justice John Marshall noted, is "to say what the law is."

• Other remedies must be exhausted. Plaintiffs have to work their way up the ladder of justice—such as government agencies or lower courts—before going to the Supreme Court.

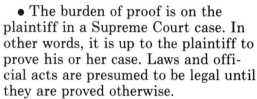

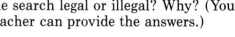

• The burden of proof is on the plaintiff in a Supreme Court case. In other words, it is up to the plaintiff to prove his or her case. Laws and official acts are presumed to be legal until they are proved otherwise.

• The Supreme Court is not bound by precedents. Lower courts must decide cases on the basis of precedents from earlier rulings. But the Supreme Court can break new ground.

"If the Supreme Court were totally bound by . . . its prior rulings, it would have very little flexibility," write Carp and Stidham. "By occasionally allowing itself the freedom to overrule a past decision or to turn a blind eye toward a precedent . . . the Supreme Court carves out for itself a corner of safety to which it can retreat if need be."

How do these rules apply to the *T.L.O.* case? Would any of them prevent the Court from hearing an appeal on *T.L.O.*? Why or why not?

In one or two sentences, identify the main issue or issues in the *T.L.O.* case. Next, make two lists. Label one list "Reasons why the Supreme Court should review *New Jersey v. T.L.O.*" Label the other list "Reasons why the Court should *not* review *New Jersey vs. T.L.O.*"

After discussing the issues and sharpening arguments on both lists, the class might vote as if students were justices. Does the Supreme Court "grant cert" and review the *T.L.O.* case?

If so, how does the court rule? Was the search legal or illegal? Why? (Your teacher can provide the answers.)

"THE LAST WORD"

adapted from Justices Byron White and William Brennan, Jr.

In deciding the Hazelwood *case, five justices voted with the majority, and three disagreed. Justice Byron White wrote the majority opinion on* Hazelwood. *Justice William J. Brennan, Jr., wrote the* dissenting,* *or disagreeing, opinion. Here are some key parts of their opinions. Words and phrases in quotation marks are from earlier court decisions, and are cited by the justices as precedents. The most important precedent was* Tinker v. Des Moines Independent Community School District *(see page 228).*

Justice Byron White, for the majority:

We deal first with the question whether the school newspaper *Spectrum* may be considered a forum for public expression. School facilities may be considered public forums only if school authorities have opened these facilities "for indiscriminate [uncontrolled] uses by the general public."

The question raised in *Tinker*—whether the First Amendment requires a school to *tolerate* particular student speech—is different from the question whether the First Amendment requires a school to *promote* particular student speech. The former question involves a student's personal expression that happens to occur on the school premises. The latter question concerns school-sponsored publications and other activities that might seem to have the approval of the school. These activities may fairly be described as part of the school curriculum.

Educators are entitled to exercise greater control over this second form of student expression. They may do

against censorship of any student expression that neither disrupts classwork nor invades the rights of others.

In *Tinker,* this court struck the balance. We held that official censorship of student expression is unconstitutional unless the speech "materially disrupts classwork or involves substantial disorder or invasion of the rights of others."

The mere fact of school sponsorship does not license such thought control in the high school.

Instead of "teaching children to respect the diversity of ideas that is fundamental to the American system," the court today "teaches youth to discount important principles of our government as mere platitudes [empty words]." The young men and women of Hazelwood East expected a civics lesson, but not the one the court teaches them today.

this to ensure that students learn whatever lessons the activity is designed to teach, that readers or listeners are not exposed to material above their level of maturity, and that the views of the individual speaker are not attributed to the school.

A school must be able to set high standards for the student speech that it sponsors, and it may refuse to publish student speech that does not meet these standards.

The basis in *Tinker* for deciding when a school may punish student expression need not also be the basis for deciding when a school may refuse to lend its name and resources to student expression. We hold that educators do not offend the First Amendment by exercising editorial control over student speech in school-sponsored activities that are related to educational concerns.

Justice William Brennan, Jr., dissenting:

In my view the school violated the First Amendment's prohibitions

(YOU HAVE THE LAST WORD)

Suppose you were an undecided Justice who has just heard the *Hazelwood* case argued. Two draft opinions are being circulated, one by Justice White, one by Justice Brennan. Which of the opinions do you decide to join? Or do you want to suggest yet a third opinion? How would you have decided the *Hazelwood* case?

"CHECKOUT"—17

Key terms

case	docket	judicial self-restraint
injunction	petition	dissenting
precedent	*certiorari*	

Review

1. Briefly describe the facts of the *Hazelwood* case.

2. List the three courts in which the *Hazelwood* case was heard. In which court did the first trial take place?

3. Identify the constitutional issues in the *Hazelwood* case.

4. How does the First Amendment affect what is said in a public forum? On what grounds did the Supreme Court determine that schools were not normally public forums?

5. What are the two main functions of the 13 Courts of Appeals?

6. Describe the two steps by which cases are placed on the Supreme Court docket.

7. In your own words, list three rules of "judicial self-restraint."

Discussion

1. "We were trying to make a change with the school paper and not just write about the school proms, football games and piddly stuff," said Cathy Kuhlmeier of the articles in *Spectrum*. What kinds of articles should a student newspaper print? Are students old enough to use good judgment on when an article might be harmful to someone? Explain your reasoning.

2. In his dissent, Justice Brennan warned that the *Hazelwood* decision would turn public schools into "enclaves of totalitarianism . . . that strangle the free mind at its source." What did he mean? Do you agree or disagree? Why?

3. Suppose the East Hazelwood students had decided to produce their own newspaper at home. In it, they published the same articles that the principal had censored in *Spectrum*. The student editors then started to distribute the newspaper, free of charge, to their fellow students at school. The principal stopped the distribution. Once again the student editors sued the school, and once again the case finally reached the Supreme Court. Do you think the court would make the same ruling this time? Why, or why not?

4. In the *Hazelwood* case there was a split decision, five justices against three. (One seat was vacant at the time.) Many decisions have resulted from a 5–4 vote. Do you think any distinction should be made between decisions resulting from narrow majorities and those resulting from wide majorities? For example, should the Supreme Court be required to review a narrow decision after a set time, such as two years? Or is it best to remain with a simple majority decision, whatever the vote?

5. The Courts of Appeals and the Supreme Court do not look into the facts of a case. Their job is to state what the law is. Does this rule make sense, or should higher courts also consider the facts? Why, or why not?

6. One rule of judicial self-restraint is that the Supreme Court does not give advisory opinions. In other words, the court will not hear a complaint that is made simply to test whether a law is constitutional. The law must touch off a real dispute or alleged wrong before the court will make a decision about it. What do you think is the reason for this rule? Do you agree with it?

Activities

1. You might want to find out more about the *Hazelwood* case. Excerpts from the court's ruling appeared in the January 14, 1988, issues of most newspapers, and in national news magazines of the 25th. Get copies of the opinions, then read and discuss in class key arguments from both sides.

2. You might role-play a search and seizure skit for the class. Five or more students would play the following roles: a student whose locker is searched, a teacher, a principal, and bystanders. After the skit, the class can debate whether the search and seizure violated the student's Fourth Amendment rights. When is a search "unreasonable"? Under what circumstances can school officials search a student's belongings?

3. What has the Supreme Court ruled on the rights of teenagers? The following cases involve the rights of minors. Use almanacs, newspaper and magazine indexes, and books on law to find how the Court has ruled on one or more of the following:
- The rights of accused minors (*In re Gault,* 1967)
- Students and free speech (*Tinker v. Des Moines,* 1968)
- Student suspensions (*Goss v. Lopez,* 1975)
- Physical punishment (*Ingram v. Wright,* 1977)

4. You might imagine that you are the editor of your school newspaper at the time the *Hazelwood* case was decided. Write an editorial on the decision, and how it affects school newspapers, yearbooks, and plays.

5. You might invite the editor of a local newspaper to talk to the class about any limits on free speech that affect the press in general. The class might prepare a list of specific questions about **(a)** the constitutional limits on free speech and **(b)** any self-imposed limits based on moral, commercial, and other considerations.

EIGHT GOOD BOOKS ABOUT THE U.S. COURTS

Free Speech, Free Press, and the Law

by Jethro K. Lieberman

Fifty controversial cases decided by the Supreme Court show how the First Amendment protects freedom of speech and freedom of the press. The final chapter lets you be the judge. Which way would you rule? Why? The answers the Supreme Court justices gave are there, too. A good test for prospective judges. Lothrop, Lee & Shepard, New York, 1980.

The Brethren: Inside the Supreme Court

by Bob Woodward and Scott Armstrong

"In San Clemente, California, President Nixon picked up his phone . . . Alexander Haig, Chief of Staff, told him the Supreme Court decision [on the Watergate tapes] had just come down. Nixon contemplated not complying if he lost. He had counted on . . . at least one dissent.

'Unanimous?' Nixon guessed.

'Unanimous,' Haig said. 'There is no

air in it at all.'

Seventeen days later, he resigned." Read about the justices who made that decision, up close and personal. Avon Books, New York, 1980.

Justice Sandra Day O'Connor
by Judith Bentley
A wonderful biography of the former Arizona State Senator and judge, who, in 1981, became the first woman ever appointed a justice of the Supreme Court. Julian Messner, New York, 1983.

The Controversial Court: Supreme Court Influences on American Life
by Stephen Goode
Find yourself confusing Earl Warren with Warren Burger? Both were Chief Justices of the Supreme Court just past the middle of the twentieth century, the decisions of their courts had great impact upon American life, and they share one name. There the similarities end.

Read about the striking difference between Earl Warren's active, liberal court and Warren Burger's 11 years of judicial modesty, and you'll never confuse them again. Julian Messner, New York, 1982.

Unlikely Heroes
by Jack Bass
The story of the southern judges of the Fifth Circuit who translated the Supreme Court's *Brown* decision into a revolution for equality. Simon and Schuster, New York, 1981.

The Supreme Court
by Lawrence Baum
Learn how the Supreme Court works from the inside out. You will find out how a case reaches the court, how the court makes decisions, and how to research a specific case. There is even a list of the Supreme Court nominations from 1789 on. Congressional Quarterly Inc., Washington, DC, 1985.

The Constitution: That Delicate Balance
by Fred W. Friendly and Martha J.H. Elliot
Each chapter explores landmark cases that shaped the Constitution, from *Barron's Wharf* through *Bakke*. Great stories as well as great history. Random House, New York, 1984.

The Defense Never Rests
by F. Lee Bailey
Are the trials in a real courtroom anything like the trials on TV? Sometimes —but the real cases are more interesting, especially when told by F. Lee Bailey, a very clever lawyer. The book tells about four murder cases, one of which goes all the way to the Supreme Court. Unlike the lawyers on TV, Bailey wins some and loses some. New American Library, New York, undated.

THE CONSTITUTION OF THE UNITED STATES

Preamble. We, the people of the United States, in order to form a more perfect Union, establish justice, insure domestic tranquility, provide for the common defence, promote the general welfare, and secure the blessings of liberty to ourselves and our posterity, do ordain and establish this Constitution for the United States of America.

Article I.

Section 1. All legislative powers herein granted, shall be vested in a Congress of the United States, which shall consist of a Senate and House of Representatives.

Section 2. The House of Representatives shall be composed of members chosen every second year by the people of the several States; and the electors in each State shall have the qualifications requisite for electors of the most numerous branch of the State Legislature.

No person shall be a Representative who shall not have attained the age of twenty-five years, and been seven years a citizen of the United States, and who shall not, when elected, be an inhabitant of that State in which he shall be chosen.

Representatives and direct taxes[1] shall be apportioned among the several States which may

be included within this Union, according to their respective numbers, which shall be determined by adding to the whole number of free persons, including those bound to service for a term of years, and excluding Indians not taxed, three fifths of all other persons. The actual enumeration shall be made within three years after the first meeting of the Congress of the United States, and within every subsequent term of ten years, in such manner as they shall by law direct. The number of Representatives shall not exceed one for every thirty thousand, but each State shall have at least one Representative, and until such enumeration shall be made, the State of New Hampshire shall be entitled to choose three, Massachusetts eight, Rhode Island and Providence Plantations one, Connecticut five, New York six, New Jersey four, Pennsylvania eight, Delaware one, Maryland six, Virginia ten, North Carolina five, South Carolina five, and Georgia three.

When vacancies happen in the representation from any State, the Executive authority thereof shall issue writs of election to fill such vacancies.

The House of Representatives shall choose their Speaker and other officers; and shall have the sole power of impeachment.

Section 3. The Senate of the United States shall be composed of two Senators from each State, chosen by the legislature thereof, for six years; and each Senator shall have one vote.

---

[1] Those parts of the U.S. Constitution which are no longer applicable or which have been changed by amendments are marked through with color lines.

~~Immediately after they shall be assembled, in consequence of the first election, they shall be divided equally as may be into three classes. The seats of the Senators of the first class shall be vacated at the expiration of the second year, of the second class at the expiration of the fourth year, and of the third class at the expiration of the sixth year,~~ so that one third may be chosen every second year; ~~and if vacancies happen by resignation, or otherwise, during the recess of the legislature of any State, the Executive thereof may make temporary appointments until the next meeting of the legislature, which shall then fill such vacancies.~~

No person shall be a Senator who shall not have attained the age of thirty years, and been nine years a citizen of the United States, and who shall not, when elected, be an inhabitant of that State for which he shall be chosen.

The Vice-President of the United States shall be President of the Senate, but shall have no vote, unless they be equally divided.

The Senate shall choose their other officers, and also a President *Pro Tempore,* in the absence of the Vice-President, or when he shall exercise the office of President of the United States.

The Senate shall have the sole power to try all impeachments. When sitting for that purpose, they shall be on oath or affirmation. When the President of the United States is tried, the Chief Justice shall preside: and no person shall be convicted without the concurrence of two thirds of the members present.

Judgment in cases of impeachment shall not extend further than to removal from office, and disqualification to hold and enjoy any office of honour, trust or profit, under the United States; but the party convicted shall nevertheless be liable and subject to indictment, trial, judgment, and punishment according to law.

Section 4. The times, places and manner of holding elections for Senators and Representatives, shall be prescribed in each State by the legislature thereof; but the Congress may at any time by law make or alter such regulations, except as to the places of choosing Senators.

The Congress shall assemble at least once in every year, ~~and such meeting shall be on the first Monday in December~~, unless they shall by law appoint a different day.

Section 5. Each House shall be the judge of the elections, returns, and qualifications of its own members, and a majority of each shall constitute a quorum to do business; but a smaller number may adjourn from day to day, and may be authorized to compel the attendance of absent members, in such manner, and under such penalties, as each House may provide.

Each House may determine the rules of its proceedings, punish its members for disorderly behaviour, and, with the concurrence of two thirds, expel a member.

Each House shall keep a journal of its proceedings, and from time to time publish the same, excepting such parts as may, in their judgment, require secrecy; and the yeas and nays of the members of either House on any question, shall, at the desire of one fifth of those present, be entered on the journal.

Neither House, during the session of Congress, shall, without the consent of the other, adjourn for more than three days, nor to any other place than that in which the two Houses shall be sitting.

Section 6. The Senators and Representatives shall receive a compensation for their services, to be ascertained by law, and paid out of the Treasury of the United States. They shall, in all cases, except treason, felony, and breach of the peace, be privileged from arrest during their attendance at the session of their respective Houses, and in going to, and returning from, the same; and for any speech or debate in either House, they shall not be questioned in any other place.

No Senator or Representative shall, during the time for which he was elected, be appointed to any civil office under the authority of the United States, which shall have been created, or the emoluments whereof shall have been increased during such time; and no person holding any office under the United States, shall be a member of either House during his continuance in office.

Section 7. All bills for raising revenue shall originate in the House of Representatives; but the Senate may propose or concur with amendments as on other bills.

Every bill which shall have passed the House of Representatives and the Senate, shall, before it becomes a law, be presented to the President of the United States; if he approves he shall sign it, but if not he shall return it, with his objections, to that House in which it shall have originated, who shall enter the objections at large on their journal, and proceed to reconsider it. If after such reconsideration two thirds of that House agree to pass the bill, it shall be sent, together with the objections, to the other House, by which it shall likewise be reconsidered, and if approved by two thirds of that House, it shall become a law. But in all cases the votes of both Houses shall be determined by yeas and nays, and the names of the persons voting for and against the bill shall be entered on the journal of each House respectively. If any bill shall not be returned by the President within ten days (Sundays excepted) after it shall have been presented to him, the same shall be a law in like manner as if he had signed it, unless the Congress by their adjournment prevent its return, in which case it shall not be a law.

Every order, resolution, or vote, to which the concurrence of the Senate and House of Representatives may be necessary (except on a question of adjournment), shall be presented to the President of the United States; and before the same shall take effect, shall be approved by him, or being disapproved by him, shall be repassed by two thirds of the Senate and House of Representatives, according to the rules and limitations prescribed in the case of a bill.

Section 8. The Congress shall have power

To lay and collect taxes, duties, imposts and excises, to pay the debts, and provide for the common defence and general welfare of the United States; but all duties, imposts, and excises shall be uniform throughout the United States:

To borrow money on the credit of the United States:

To regulate commerce with foreign nations, and among the several States, and with the Indian tribes:

To establish an uniform rule of naturalization, and uniform laws on the subject of bankruptcies throughout the United States:

To coin money, regulate the value thereof, and of foreign coin, and fix the standard of weights and measures:

To provide for the punishment of counterfeiting the securities and current coin of the United States:

To establish post-offices and post-roads:

To promote the progress of science and useful arts, by securing, for limited times, to authors and inventors, the exclusive right to their respective writings and discoveries:

To constitute tribunals inferior to the Supreme Court:

To define and punish piracies and felonies committed on the high seas, and offences

against the law of nations:

To declare war, grant letters of marque and reprisal, and make rules concerning captures on land and water:

To raise and support armies: but no appropriation of money to that use shall be for a longer term than two years:

To provide and maintain a navy:

To make rules for the government and regulation of the land and naval forces:

To provide for calling forth the militia to execute the laws of the Union, suppress insurrections and repel invasions:

To provide for organizing, arming, and disciplining the militia, and for governing such part of them as may be employed in the service of the United States, reserving to the States respectively, the appointment of the officers, and the authority of training the militia according to the discipline prescribed by Congress:

To exercise exclusive legislation, in all cases whatsoever, over such district (not exceeding ten miles square) as may, by cession of particular States, and the acceptance of Congress, become the seat of the government of the United States, and to exercise like authority over all places purchased by the consent of the legislature of the State in which the same shall be, for the erection of forts, magazines, arsenals, dock-yards, and other needful buildings. And,

To make all laws which shall be necessary and proper for carrying into execution the foregoing powers, and all other powers vested by this Constitution in the government of the United States, or in any department or officer thereof.

Section 9. The migration or importation of such persons as any of the States now existing shall think proper to admit, shall not be prohibited by the Congress prior to the year one thousand eight hundred and eight; but a tax or duty may be imposed on such importation, not exceeding ten dollars for each person.

The privilege of the writ of *habeas corpus* shall not be suspended, unless when in cases of rebellion or invasion the public safety may require it.

No bill of attainder or *ex post facto* law shall be passed.

No capitation, or other direct tax, shall be laid, unless in proportion to the *census* or enumeration herein before directed to be taken.

No tax or duty shall be laid on articles exported from any State.

No preference shall be given by any regulation of commerce or revenue to the ports of one State over those of another; nor shall vessels bound to, or from, one State be obliged to enter, clear, or pay duties in another.

No money shall be drawn from the treasury, but in consequence of appropriations made by law; and a regular statement and account of the receipts and expenditures of all public money shall be published from time to time.

No title of nobility shall be granted by the United States; and no person holding any office of profit or trust under them, shall, without the consent of the Congress, accept of any present, emolument, office, or title of any kind whatever, from any king, prince, or foreign state.

Section 10. No State shall enter into any treaty, alliance, or confederation; grant letters of marque and reprisal; coin money; emit bills of credit; make any thing but gold and silver coin a tender in payment of debts; pass any bill of attainder, *ex post facto* law, or law impairing the obligation of contracts, or grant any title of nobility.

No State shall, without the consent of the Congress, lay any imposts or duties on imports or exports, except what may be absolutely necessary for executing its inspection laws; and the net produce of all duties and imposts, laid by any State on imports or exports, shall be for the use of the treasury of the United States: and all such laws shall be subject to the revision and control of the Congress. No State shall, without the consent of Congress, lay any duty of tonnage, keep troops, or ships of war, in time of peace, enter into any agreement or compact with another State, or with a foreign power, or engage in war, unless actually invaded, or in such imminent danger as will not admit of delay.

Article II.

Section 1. The executive power shall be vested in a President of the United States of America. He shall hold his office during the term of four years, and together with the Vice-President, chosen for the same term, be elected as follows:

Each State shall appoint, in such manner as the legislature thereof may direct, a number of electors equal to the whole number of Senators and Representatives to which the State may be entitled in the Congress; but no Senator or Representative, or person holding an office of trust or profit under the United States, shall be appointed an elector.

The electors shall meet in their respective States, and vote by ballot for two persons, of whom one at least shall not be an inhabitant of the same State with themselves. And they shall make a list of all the persons voted for, and of the number of votes for each; which list they shall sign and certify, and transmit sealed to the seat of the government of the United States, directed to the President of the Senate. The President of the Senate shall, in the presence of the Senate and House of Representatives, open all the certificates, and the votes shall then be counted. The person having the greatest number of votes shall be the President, if such number be a majority of the whole number of electors appointed; and if there be more than one who have such majority, and have an equal number of votes, then the House of Representatives shall immediately choose by ballot one of them for President; and if no person have a majority, then from the five highest on the list the said House shall in like manner choose the President. But in choosing the President, the votes shall be taken by States, the representation from each State having one vote; a quorum for this purpose shall consist of a member or members from two thirds of the States, and a majority of all the States shall be necessary to a choice. In every case, after the choice of the President, the person having the greatest number of votes of the electors shall be the Vice-President. But if there should remain two or more who have equal votes, the Senate shall choose from them by ballot the Vice-President.

The Congress may determine the time of choosing the electors, and the day on which they shall give their votes; which day shall be the same throughout the United States.

No person except a natural born citizen, or a citizen of the United States, at the time of the adoption of this Constitution, shall be eligible to the office of President; neither shall any person be eligible to that office who shall not have attained the age of thirty-five years, and been fourteen years a resident within the United States.

In case of the removal of the President from office, or of his death, resignation, or inability to discharge the powers and duties of the said office, the same shall devolve on the Vice-President, and the Congress may by law provide for the case of removal, death, resignation, or inability, both of the President and

Vice-President, declaring what officer shall then act as President, and such officer shall act accordingly until the disability be removed, or a President shall be elected.

The President shall at stated times, receive for his services, a compensation, which shall neither be increased nor diminished during the period for which he shall have been elected, and he shall not receive within that period any other emolument from the United States or any of them.

Before he enter on the execution of his office, he shall take the following oath or affirmation:

"I do solemnly swear (or affirm) that I will faithfully execute the office of President of the United States, and will, to the best of my ability, preserve, protect, and defend the Constitution of the United States."

Section 2. The President shall be Commander-in-Chief of the Army and Navy of the United States, and of the militia of the several States, when called into the actual service of the United States; he may require the opinion, in writing, of the principal officer in each of the executive departments, upon any subject relating to the duties of their respective offices, and he shall have power to grant reprieves and pardons for offences against the United States, except in cases of impeachment.

He shall have power, by and with the advice and consent of the Senate, to make treaties, provided two thirds of the Senators present concur; and he shall nominate, and by and with the advice and consent of the Senate, shall appoint ambassadors, other public ministers and consuls, judges of the Supreme Court, and all other officers of the United States, whose appointments are not herein otherwise provided for, and which shall be established by law. But the Congress may by law vest the appointment of such inferior officers, as they think proper, in the President alone, in the courts of law, or in the heads of departments.

The President shall have power to fill up all vacancies that may happen during the recess of the Senate, by granting commissions which shall expire at the end of their session.

Section 3. He shall, from time to time, give to the Congress information of the state of the Union, and recommend to their consideration such measures as he shall judge necessary and expedient. He may on extraordinary occasions, convene both Houses, or either of them; and in case of disagreement between them, with respect to the time of adjournment,

he may adjourn them to such time as he shall think proper. He shall receive ambassadors and other public ministers. He shall take care that the laws be faithfully executed; and shall commission all the officers of the United States.

Section 4. The President, Vice-President, and all civil officers of the United States, shall be removed from office on impeachment for, and conviction of, treason, bribery, or other high crimes and misdemeanors.

Article III.

Section 1. The judicial power of the United States shall be vested in one Supreme Court, and in such inferior courts as the Congress may, from time to time, ordain and establish. The judges, both of the Supreme and inferior courts, shall hold their offices during good behaviour; and shall, at stated times, receive for their services, a compensation, which shall not be diminished during their continuance in office.

Section 2. The judicial power shall extend to all cases, in law and equity, arising under this Constitution, the laws of the United States, and treaties made, or which shall be made, under their authority; to all cases affecting ambassadors, other public ministers, and consuls; to all cases of admiralty and maritime jurisdiction; to controversies to which the United States shall be a party; to controversies between two or more States, between a State and citizens of another State, between citizens of different States, between citizens of the same State claiming lands under grants of different States, and between a State, or the citizens thereof, and foreign states, citizens or subjects.

In all cases affecting ambassadors, other public ministers and consuls, and those in which a State shall be party, the Supreme Court shall have original jurisdiction. In all the other cases before mentioned, the Supreme Court shall have appellate jurisdiction, both as to law and fact, with such exceptions, and under such regulations, as the Congress shall make.

The trial of all crimes, except in cases of impeachment, shall be by jury; and such trial shall be held in the State where the said crimes shall have been committed; but when not committed within any State, the trial shall be at such place or places as the Congress may by law have directed.

Section 3. Treason against the United States, shall consist only in levying war against them, or in adhering to their enemies, giving them aid and comfort. No person shall be convicted of treason unless on the testimony of two witnesses to the same overt act, or on confession in open court.

The Congress shall have power to declare the punishment of treason, but no attainder of treason shall work corruption of blood, or forfeiture, except during the life of the person attained.

Article IV.

Section 1. Full faith and credit shall be given in each State to the public acts, records, and judicial proceedings of every other State. And the Congress may by general laws prescribe the manner in which such acts, records, and proceedings shall be proved, and the effect thereof.

Section 2. The citizens of each State shall be entitled to all privileges and immunities of citizens in the several States.

A person charged in any State with treason, felony, or other crime, who shall flee from justice, and be found in another State, shall, on demand of the executive authority of the State from which he fled, be delivered up to be removed to the State having jurisdiction of the crime.

No person held to service or labour in one State, under the laws thereof, escaping into another, shall, in consequence of any laws or regulation therein, be discharged from such service or labour, but shall be delivered up on claim of the party to whom such service or labour may be due.

Section 3. New States may be admitted by the Congress into this Union; but no new State shall be formed or erected within the jurisdiction of any other State; nor any State be formed by the junction of two or more States, or parts of States, without the consent of the legislatures of the States concerned, as well as of the Congress.

The Congress shall have power to dispose of and make all needful rules and regulations respecting the territory or other property belonging to the United States; and nothing in this Constitution shall be so construed as to prejudice any claims of the United States, or of any particular State.

Section 4. The United States shall guarantee to every State in this Union a republican form of government, and shall protect each of them against invasion; and on application of the legislature, or of the executive (when the legislature cannot be convened), against domestic violence.

Article V. The Congress, whenever two thirds of both Houses shall deem it necessary, shall propose amendments to this Constitution, or, on the application of the legislatures of two thirds of the several States, shall call a convention for proposing amendments, which, in either case, shall be valid to all intents and purposes, as part of this Constitution, when ratified by the legislatures of three fourths of the several States, or by conventions in three fourths thereof, as the one or the other mode of ratification may be proposed by the Congress; provided that no amendment, which may be made prior to the year one thousand eight hundred and eight, shall in any manner affect the first and fourth clauses in the ninth section of the first article; and that no State, without its consent, shall be deprived of its equal suffrage in the Senate.

Article VI. All debts contracted, and engagements entered into, before the adoption of this Constitution, shall be as valid against the United States, under this Constitution, as under the confederation.

This Constitution and the laws of the United States which shall be made in pursuance thereof, and all treaties made, or which shall be made, under the authority of the United States, shall be the supreme law of the land: and the judges, in every State, shall be bound thereby, any thing in the constitution or laws of any State to the contrary notwithstanding.

The Senators and Representatives before mentioned, and the members of the several State legislatures, and all executive and judicial officers, both of the United States and of the several States, shall be bound, by oath or affirmation, to support this Constitution; but no religious test shall ever be required as a qualification to any office or public trust under the United States.

Article VII. The ratification of the conventions of nine States, shall be sufficient for the establishment of this Constitution between the States so ratifying the same.

TEN ORIGINAL AMENDMENTS: THE BILL OF RIGHTS

(These first 10 amendments were adopted in 1791.)

Article I. Congress shall make no law respecting an establishment of religion, or prohibiting the free exercise thereof; or abridging the freedom of speech, or of the press; or the right of the people peaceably to assemble, and to petition the government for a redress of grievances.

Article II. A well regulated militia being necessary to the security of a free State, the right of the people to keep and bear arms shall not be infringed.

Article III. No soldier shall, in time of peace, be quartered in any house without the consent of the owner; nor in time of war, but in a manner to be prescribed by law.

Article IV. The right of the people to be secure in their persons, houses, papers, and effects, against unreasonable searches and seizures, shall not be violated; and no warrants shall issue, but upon probable cause, supported by oath or affirmation, and particularly describing the place to be searched, and the persons or things to be seized.

Article V. No person shall be held to answer for a capital or otherwise infamous crime, unless on a presentment or indictment of a grand jury, except in cases arising in the land or naval forces, or in the militia, when in actual service, in time of war or public danger; nor shall any person be subject for the same offence to be twice put in jeopardy of life or limb; nor shall be compelled, in any criminal case, to be witness against himself; nor be deprived of life, liberty, or property, without due process of law; nor shall private property be taken for public use without just compensation.

Article VI. In all criminal prosecutions the accused shall enjoy the right to a speedy and public trial, by an impartial jury of the State and district wherein the crime shall have been committed, which district shall have been previously ascertained by law, and to be informed of the nature and cause of the accusation; to be confronted with the witnesses against him; to have compulsory process for obtaining witnesses in his favour; and to have the assistance of counsel for his defence.

Article VII. In suits at common law, where the value of controversy shall exceed twenty dollars, the right of trial by jury shall be preserved; and no fact tried by a jury shall be otherwise re-examined in any court of the United States than according to the rules of the common law.

Article VIII. Excessive bail shall not be required, nor excessive fines imposed, nor cruel and unusual punishments inflicted.

Article IX. The enumeration in the Constitution of certain rights, shall not be construed to deny or disparage others retained by the people.

Article X. The powers not delegated to the United States by the Constitution, nor prohibited by it to the States, are reserved to the States respectively or to the people.

AMENDMENTS SINCE THE BILL OF RIGHTS

Article XI (1795). The Judicial power of the United States shall not be construed to extend to any suit in law or equity, commenced or prosecuted against one of the United States by citizens or subjects of any Foreign State.

Article XII (1804). The electors shall meet in their respective States, and vote by ballot for President and Vice-President, one of whom, at least shall not be an inhabitant of the same State with themselves; they shall name in their ballots the person voted for as President, and in distinct ballots the person voted for as Vice-President; and they shall make distinct lists of all persons voted for as President, and of all persons voted for as Vice-President, and of the number of votes for each, which list they shall sign and certify, and transmit sealed to the seat of the government of the United States, directed to the President of the Senate; the President of the Senate shall, in the presence of the Senate and House of Representatives, open all the certificates, and the votes shall then be counted: the person having the greatest number of votes for President shall be the President, if such number be a majority of the whole number of electors appointed; and if no person have such majority, then from the persons having the highest numbers, not exceeding three, on the list of those voted for as President, the House of Representatives shall choose immediately, by ballot, the President. But in choosing the President, the vote shall be taken by States, the representation from each State having one vote; a quorum for this purpose shall consist of a member or members from two thirds of the States, and a majority of all the States shall be necessary to a choice. And if the House of Representatives shall not choose a President whenever the right of choice shall devolve upon them, before the fourth day of March next following, then the Vice-President shall act as President, as in the case of the death or other constitutional disability of the President.

The person having the greatest number of votes as Vice-President shall be the Vice-President, if such number be a majority of the whole number of electors appointed; and if no person have a majority, then from the two highest numbers on the list the Senate shall choose the Vice-President: a quorum for that purpose shall consist of two thirds of the whole number of Senators, and a majority of the whole number shall be necessary to a choice.

But no person constitutionally ineligible to the office of President shall be eligible to that of Vice-President of the United States.

Article XIII (1865).

Section 1. Neither slavery nor involuntary servitude except as a punishment for crime whereof the party shall have been duly convicted, shall exist within the United States, or any place subject to their jurisdiction.

Section 2. Congress shall have power to enforce this article by appropriate legislation.

Article XIV (1868).

Section 1. All persons born or naturalized in the United States, and subject to the jurisdiction thereof, are citizens of the United States and of the State wherein they reside. No State shall make or enforce any law which shall abridge the privileges or immunities of citizens of the United States; nor shall any State deprive any person of life, liberty, or property, without due process of law, nor deny to any person within its jurisdiction the equal protection of the laws.

Section 2. Representatives shall be apportioned among the several States according to their respective numbers, counting the whole number of persons in each State, excluding Indians not taxed. But when the right to vote at any election for the choice of electors for President and Vice-President of the United States, representatives in Congress, the executive and judicial officers of a State, or the members of the legislature thereof, is denied to any of the male inhabitants of such State, being twenty-one years of age, and citizens of the United States, or in any way abridged, except for participation in rebellion or other crime, the basis of representation therein shall be reduced in the proportion which the number of such male citizens shall bear to the whole number of male citizens twenty-one years of age in such State.

Section 3. No person shall be a Senator or Representative in Congress, or elector of President and Vice-President, or hold any office, civil or military, under the United States, or under any State, who having previously taken an oath, as a member of Congress, or as an officer of the United States, or as a member of any State legislature, or as an executive or judicial officer of any State, to support the Constitution of the United States, shall have engaged in insurrection or rebellion against the same, or given aid or comfort to the enemies thereof. But Congress may by a vote of two thirds of each house remove such disability.

Section 4. The validity of the public debt of the United States, authorized by law, including debts incurred for payment of pensions and bounties for services in suppressing insurrection or rebellion, shall not be questioned. But neither the United States nor any State shall assume or pay any debt or obligation incurred in aid of insurrection or rebellion against the United States, or any claim for the loss or emancipation of any slave; but all such debts, obligations, and claims shall be held illegal and void.

Section 5. The Congress shall have power to enforce, by appropriate legislation, the provisions of this article.

Article XV (1870).

Section 1. The right of citizens of the United States to vote shall not be denied or abridged by the United States or by any State on account of race, color, or previous condition of servitude.

Section 2. The Congress shall have power to enforce this article by appropriate legislation.

Article XVI (1913). The Congress shall have power to lay and collect taxes on incomes, from whatever source derived, without apportionment among the several States, and without regard to any census or enumeration.

Article XVII (1913). The Senate of the United States shall be composed of two Senators from each State, elected by the people thereof, for six years; and each Senator shall have one vote. The electors in each State shall have the qualifications requisite for electors of the most numerous branch of the State legislatures.

When vacancies happen in the representation of any State in the Senate, the executive authority of such State shall issue writs of election to fill such vacancies: *Provided,* That the legislature of any State may empower the executive thereof to make temporary appointments until the people fill the vacancies by election as the legislature may direct.

~~This amendment shall not be so construed as to affect the election or term of any Senator chosen before it becomes valid as part of the Constitution.~~

Article XVIII (1919).

~~Section 1. After one year from the ratification of this article the manufacture, sale, or transportation of intoxicating liquors within, the importation thereof into, or the exportation thereof from the United States and all territory subject to the jurisdiction thereof for beverage purposes is hereby prohibited.~~

~~Section 2. The Congress and the several States shall have concurrent power to enforce this article by appropriate legislation.~~

~~Section 3. This article shall be inoperative unless it shall have been ratified as an amendment to the Constitution by the legislatures of the several States, as provided in the Constitution, within seven years from the date of the submission hereof to the States by the Congress.~~

Article XIX (1920).
The right of citizens of the United States to vote shall not be denied or abridged by the United States or by any State on account of sex.

Congress shall have power to enforce this article by appropriate legislation.

Article XX (1933).
Section 1. The terms of the President and Vice-President shall end at noon on the 20th day of January, and the terms of Senators and Representatives at noon on the 3rd day of January, of the years in which such terms would have ended if this article had not been ratified; and the terms of their successors shall then begin.

Section 2. The Congress shall assemble at least once in every year, and such meeting shall begin at noon on the 3rd day of January, unless they shall by law appoint a different day.

Section 3. If, at the time fixed for the beginning of the term of the President, the President elect shall have died, the Vice-President elect shall become President. If a President shall not have been chosen before the time fixed for the beginning of his term, or if the President elect shall have failed to qualify, then the Vice-President elect shall act as President until a President shall have qualified; and the Congress may by law provide for the case wherein neither a President elect nor a Vice-President elect shall have qualified, declaring who shall then act as President, or the manner in which one who is to act shall be selected, and such person shall act accordingly until a President or Vice-President shall have qualified.

Section 4. The Congress may by law provide for the case of the death of any of the persons from whom the House of Representatives may choose a President whenever the right choice shall have devolved upon them, and for the case of the death of any of the persons from whom the Senate may choose a Vice-President whenever the right of choice shall have devolved upon them.

Section 5. ~~Sections 1 and 2 shall take effect on the 15th day of October following the ratification of this article.~~

Section 6. ~~This article shall be inoperative unless it shall have been ratified as an amendment to the Constitution by the legislatures of three fourths of the several States within seven years from the date of its submission.~~

Article XXI (1933).
Section 1. The eighteenth article of amendment to the Constitution of the United States is hereby repealed.

Section 2. The transportation or importation into any State, Territory, or possession of the United States for delivery or use therein of intoxicating liquors, in violation of the laws thereof, is hereby prohibited.

Section 3. ~~This article shall be inoperative unless it shall have been ratified as an amendment to the Constitution by conventions in the several States, as provided in the Constitution, within seven years from the date of the submission hereof to the States by the Congress.~~

Article XXII (1951).
Section 1. No person shall be elected to the office of the President more than twice, and no person who has held the office of President, or acted as President, for more than two years of a term to which some other person

was elected President shall be elected to the office of the President more than once. ~~But this Article shall not apply to any person holding the office of President when this Article was proposed by the Congress, and shall not prevent any person who may be holding the office of President, or acting as President, during the term within which this Article becomes operative from holding the office of President or acting as President during the remainder of such term~~.

Article XXIII (1961).

Section 1. The District constituting the seat of Government of the United States shall appoint in such manner as the Congress may direct: A number of electors of President and Vice-President equal to the whole number of Senators and Representatives in Congress to which the District would be entitled if it were a State, but in no event more than the least populous State; they shall be in addition to those appointed by the States, but they shall be considered, for the purposes of the election of President and Vice-President, to be electors appointed by a State; and they shall meet in the District and perform such duties as provided by the twelfth article of amendment.

Section 2. The Congress shall have the power to enforce this article by appropriate legislation.

Article XXIV (1964).

Section 1. The right of citizens of the United States to vote in any primary or other election for President or Vice-President, for electors for President or Vice-President, or for Senator or Representatives in Congress, shall not be denied or abridged by the United States or any State by reason of failure to pay any poll tax or other tax.

Section 2. The Congress shall have the power to enforce this article by appropriate legislation.

Article XXV (1967).

Section 1. In case of the removal of the President from office or his death or resignation, the Vice-President shall become President.

Section 2. Whenever there is a vacancy in the office of the Vice-President, the President shall nominate a Vice-President who shall take office upon confirmation by a majority vote of both houses of Congress.

Section 3. Whenever the President trans-

mits to the President *Pro Tempore* of the Senate and the Speaker of the House of Representatives his written declaration that he is unable to discharge the powers and duties of his office, and until he transmits to them a written declaration to the contrary, such powers and duties shall be discharged by the Vice-President as Acting President.

Section 4. Whenever the Vice-President and a majority of either the principal officers of the executive departments or of such other body as Congress may by law provide, transmit to the President *Pro Tempore* of the Senate and the Speaker of the House of Representatives their written declaration that the President is unable to discharge the powers and duties of his office the Vice-President shall immediately assume the powers and duties of the office as Acting President.

Thereafter, when the President transmits to the President *Pro Tempore* of the Senate and the Speaker of the House of Representatives his written declaration that no inability exists, he shall resume the powers and duties of his office unless the Vice-President and a majority of either the principal officers of the executive departments or of such other body as Congress may by law provide, transmit within four days to the President *Pro Tempore* of the Senate and the Speaker of the House of Representatives their written declaration that the President is unable to discharge the powers and duties of his office. Thereupon Congress shall decide the issue, assembling within 48 hours for that purpose if not in session. If the Congress, within 21 days after receipt of the latter written declaration, or, if Congress is not in session, within 21 days after Congress is required to assemble, determines by two-thirds vote of both houses that the President is unable to discharge the powers and duties of his office, the Vice-President shall continue to discharge the same as Acting President; otherwise, the President shall resume the powers and duties of his office.

Article XXVI (1971).

Section 1. The right of citizens of the United States, who are eighteen years of age or older, to vote shall not be denied or abridged by the United States or any state on account of age.

Section 2. The Congress shall have the power to enforce this article by appropriate legislation.

GLOSSARY
OF KEY WORDS AND TERMS

act of Congress. What a bill is called after it has been approved by both houses of Congress. (p. 121)

adjourn. To suspend a meeting or a session. (p. 122)

administrator. Public official who carries out the terms of a law. He/she usually directs the work of many other people. (p. 51)

agency. One of the smaller working units of a department of the Executive Branch. (p. 49)

ambassador. A government official who represents his/her country in the capital of a foreign country. (p. 28)

amendment. A change in a bill, an act of Congress, or the Constitution. (p. 13)

appeal. To ask a higher (more powerful) court to hear arguments for overruling the decision of a lower court. (p. 190)

apportion. To assign the seats in the House of Representatives to different states, according to the size of each state's population. (p. 108)

appropriations. Tax money set aside by law for specific purposes. (p. 108)

benefits. Money or services given to individuals by an insurance or welfare plan. (p. 50)

biased. Prejudiced or slanted. (p. 96)

bill. A written statement presenting an idea for a new law. (p. 25)

bipartisan. Of both political parties. A bill that the Republicans and the Democrats support is bipartisan. (p. 165)

bonds. Certificates which state and local governments or businesses sell to raise money. The government or business promises to pay back the buyer, with interest, over a given time. (p. 57)

branch. One of the three major parts of the U.S. government (the executive, legislative and judicial branches). (p. 10)

bureaucracy. A way of organizing a large number of government offices. (Small offices may be grouped together into bureaus. Bureaus may be grouped together into divisions.) (p. 51)

Cabinet. A group of officials chosen by the President to help run the Executive Branch. Most of the members of the President's Cabinet head a different department of government. (p. 16)

census. An official report, made every 10 years, about the population of the U.S. (p. 113)

chairperson. Person in charge of a committee or a subcommittee of Congress. (p. 146)

checks and balances. How the U.S. system of government limits the power of the three branches. Each branch of government is able to check the actions of the other two branches. (p. 67)

Circuit Court. A court that has the power to overrule the decisions of judges in the U.S. District Courts. Same as U.S. Court of Appeals. (p. 190)

cloture. A vote in the Senate to end debate on a bill. (p. 161)

committee. A small group of Senators or Representatives who meet regularly to discuss certain types of bills. (p. 25)

compromise. A way in which two or more people or groups reach an agreement by each giving up a part of their desires. (p. 106)

confirm. To approve. A President's choice of judge, ambassador, or other appointed official needs to be confirmed by the Senate. (p. 108)

Congress. The legislative branch of the U.S. government. It is made up of two houses—the Senate and the House of Representatives. (p. 10)

constituents. The people who are represented and served by an elected official. (p. 106)

constitutional. Allowed by the Constitution. (p. 134)

debate. A controlled form of public argument and speech. In Congress, people with different opinions on a bill present arguments for and against it. (p. 116)

defendant. The person who is accused or held accountable in a civil or criminal trial. (p. 191)

delegation. A group of representatives from a particular place or organization. (Example: the New Jersey delgation to the national convention of bricklayers.) (p. 152)

desegregation. Segregation is the separation of people of different races. Desegregation is getting rid of segregation, allowing people of different races to mix. (p. 217)

democracy. Form of government in which those who govern are elected to office by the free choice of all citizens. (p. 19)

deport. To send someone out of a country. A person may be deported if he/she is not a citizen of the country and is not legally allowed to be there. (p. 187)

diplomat. A government official trained in communicating with foreign governments. (p. 28)

dissenting opinion. The written statement of a Supreme Court or an appeals judge who disagrees with his/her court's decision in a case. (p. 216)

district. An area served by a single government agency or official. People living within a Congressional district are served by the same Representative. (p. 105)

district attorney. The lawyer employed by the government to present the government's case in a trial. (p. 110)

duty. A tax on imported goods. (p. 57)

economy. Production, distribution, and use of all goods and services in a country. (p. 26)

elastic clause. Section of the Constitution that allows Congress to do all things "necessary and proper" to carry out its other powers. (p. 135)

equal protection of the laws. A guarantee in the Constitution that all citizens shall receive equal treatment from government officials and laws. (p. 218)

excise. A tax on the sale, manufacture, or use of goods. For example, Congress has placed an excise tax on tobacco. (p. 134)

Executive Branch. The branch of the federal government headed by the President, who is responsible for enforcing the laws of the land. (p. 10)

federal system. The system that gives some powers to the national government in Washington, DC and other powers to the 50 state governments. (p. 214)

filibuster. A method of defeating a bill in the Senate by dragging out the debate over it. (p. 115)

floor. The place where Senators and Congresspersons gather to debate and vote on bills. (The floor of the House is separate from the floor of the Senate.) (p. 115)

foreign aid. Money, services, and goods given or loaned by the U.S. government to foreign governments. (p. 26)

foreign policy. The idea or plan behind our government's dealings with other nations. (p. 28)

grand jury. A group of citizens who decide whether there is enough evidence to hold a suspected lawbreaker for trial. (p. 189)

grant. A sum of money given by the U.S. government to a person or organization for a specific purpose. (p. 59)

House of Representatives. The lower house of Congress whose members are elected for two-year terms. Each state is represented in the House according to its population. (p. 82)

immigrant. A citizen of a foreign country who comes to live permanently in another country. (p. 134)

impeachment. Charges against a public official of failing to perform his/her duty. A vote to impeach always occurs before there can be another vote to remove the official from office. (p. 82)

import. To bring into a state or nation (especially goods made in another state or nation). (p. 57)

inaugurate. To install into office with a special ceremony. (p. 80)

independent agency. An agency that does not belong to any of the 13 departments of the Executive Branch. The President appoints members of the agency but does not control their decisions. (p. 54)

indict. To formally accuse. A statement of the accusation or charges (indictment) is made by a grand jury in a U.S. court. (p. 189)

injunction. A court order not to do something. (p. 228)

judicial review. The power of the Supreme Court to decide whether acts of Congress and the President are allowed by the Constitution. (p. 215)

judicial restraint. The tendency of the courts to rule in favor of upholding legislation rather than overruling it. When practicing judicial restraint, judges are restraining, or holding back, from using their power. (p. 202)

judiciary. The branch of government that interprets the laws. It is made up of a system of courts, the highest one being the U.S. Supreme Court. (p. 187)

larceny. Stealing. (p. 189)

legislature. A group of elected officials who debate bills and enact laws. (p. 13)

lobby. An organized attempt to persuade lawmakers to vote a certain way on a bill. (p. 137)

lobbyist. Someone whose job is to try to influence lawmakers to vote a certain way on a bill. (p. 172)

logrolling. The practice of trading favors in Congress. (I'll support your bill if you support mine.) (p. 146)

militia. Citizens trained and equipped by state governments for local defense. (Another name for the state militia is the National Guard.) (p. 176)

nominate. To formally recommend a person for public office. (p. 214)

offense. The breaking of a law. (p. 189)

omnibus bill. A bill with many amendments which may cover many different issues. (p. 160)

parole. The freeing of a prisoner upon the promise of good behavior. (p. 190)

patent. A government document giving an inventor exclusive rights to his/her invention for a specified number of years. (p. 134)

patronage. The power to make appointments to government jobs. (p. 202)

petition. A formal written request. (p. 229)

plaintiff. Someone who starts a lawsuit against another person. (p. 191)

pocket veto. The President may exercise a pocket veto if Congress ends its session less than 10 days after passing a bill. In that case, the President may simply leave the bill unsigned, and it will not become law. (p. 126)

point of order. A term often used in committee meetings and floor debates. It is a request to know what the rules of debate allow. (p. 115)

political action committee (PAC). An organization that funnels money from the supporters of a particular cause or interest to the campaigns of candidates that support that cause. (p. 174)

political activist. One who takes direct action in support of his or her side of an issue. A political activist might protest, petition, or strike. (p. 59)

political party. A large group of citizens and politicians who try to elect their candidates to office. (p. 29)

precedent. Something similar that happened before (especially a previous court case). (p. 228)

President pro tempore. A majority-party Senator who is elected to lead the Senate when the Vice President is absent. (p. 85)

presiding officer. Someone who runs the formal debates of a committee meeting or a session of Congress. (p. 107)

pressure group. An organization that tries to persuade government officials to support their ideas and needs. (p. 172)

probation. Supervision of a convicted offender outside of prison. A person found guilty of a crime may be placed on probation instead of being sent to prison. Or a person may be released from prison on probation (also called parole) before he or she has served a full sentence. (p. 196)

public hearing. An open meeting of a committee of public officials to hear evidence for or against a bill or plan of action from interested citizens or organization representatives. (p. 138)

public opinion. What different groups of citizens think about public problems. (p. 91)

reasonable doubt. The phrase used to describe the degree to which someone must be proven guilty before the court can consider them to be guilty. If there is a reasonable doubt about whether someone has committed a crime, he/she should not be considered guilty. (p. 190)

regulate. To set rules. For example, the U.S. government requires private organizations, such as businesses and labor unions, to follow certain rules. (p. 134)

regulatory agencies. Independent agencies of the Executive Branch that have the power to make rules about certain matters of public concern. For instance, the Federal Communications Commission makes rules about radio and television, and the Food and Drug Administration regulates the contents of food, medicine and other products. (p. 54)

roll (roll call). Asking the members of a house of Congress to vote on a bill as their names are called. (p. 115)

Senate. The upper house of Congress whose members are elected for six-year terms. Each state is represented by two Senators. (p. 13)

seniority. The traditional method of choosing committee chairpersons in Congress. The member who has served on a committee for the longest period of time takes the chair. (p. 146)

session. The period of time that Congress meets each year. (p. 115)

social security. A government insurance program that provides money for people when they retire or are disabled. Benefits are also paid to the survivors (widows and children) of workers covered by the program. Funds for the program come from contributions that employers and employees are required to make. (p. 49)

Speaker of the House. The presiding officer in the House of Representatives. (p. 85)

staff. The group of people who work directly for the President, Senator, or other official. (p. 54)

State Department. The part of the Executive Branch of the U.S. government that has the main responsibility, along with the President, of carrying out foreign policy. (p. 26)

statistics. Numbers which give information, such as how many people live in an area, how much rain fell last year, and what kinds of crime occur most often in cities. (p. 55)

subsidy. A sum of government money given to private persons or organizations to help maintain an activity considered beneficial to the public. (p. 55)

treaty. A formal agreement between two or more countries. (p. 10)

U.S. Code. A complete collection of the laws of the United States. (p. 188)

urban renewal. The attempt to improve old and rundown sections of a city. (p. 56)

vest. To give authority. When someone has a particular authority, or power, it is said to be vested in them. For example, the power to control the armed forces is vested in the President. (p. 10)

veto. Refusal to approve. The President's veto is the refusal to sign an act of Congress. (p. 29)

INDEX

Abraham, Henry J., 209, 225
Abzug, Bella, 152-153, 155
Adams, John, 40
Adams, John Quincy, 40
Advise and Consent, 183
Agencies, independent, 54
Agencies, regulatory, 54
Agnew, Spiro, 84
Agriculture, Department of, 55
Air Force, U.S., 29
Air Line Pilots Association, 138-141
Ambassadors, 28
American Bar Association (ABA), 202, 205
American Heritage, 99
America in Search of Itself: The Making of the President 1956-1980, 101
Amtrak, 139
Anderson, Glenn, 128-129
Anderson, Robert, 16
Appeals, Courts of (Circuit Courts), 190, 192, 194, 202, 228, 235,
Armstrong, Scott, 221, 236
Army of the Potomac, 19
Army, U.S., 29, 50
Arthur, Chester A., 41
Attorney General, 26, 54, 207

Bailey, F. Lee, 237
Bass, Jack, 237
Bentley, Judith, 237
Benton, Hart, 183
Bill of Impeachment, 82, 84
Bishop, Jim, 24
Black, Hugo, 209, 212-213, 221, 223
Blair, Montgomery, 16
Blessing, Tim H., 96
Block, Herbert, 101
Blood River, 121-122
Boller, Paul F., 100, 101
Bork, Robert, 203, 209
Brademas, John, 122, 124-126
Brandeis, Louis, 209
Breaux, John, 139-141
Brennan, William J. Jr., 207, 232-234
Brethren, The, 221, 236
Brezina, Dennis, 122
Brown, Henry, 219
Brown v. Board of Education, 207, 218, 221, 237
Buchanan, James, 40

Bureaucracy, federal, 51-57
Burger, Warren, 221-223, 237
Burns, James MacGregor, 72

Cabinet, 16, 25-26, 52-53, 85
Came the Revolution: Argument in the Reagan Era, 183
Capital punishment, 213-214
Cardozo, Benjamin, 203
Carey, Hugh, 152
Carp, Robert A., 230, 231
Carswell, G. Harrold, 209
Carter, Jimmy, 21, 41, 63, 75, 100-101, 204-205
Cartoons, political, 157-163, 166
Censorship, 228-229, 232-233
Central Intelligence Agency (CIA), 28
Certiorari, 229
Chief Justice, 78-80, 211, 215-217, 229
China, 83
Choosing the President 1984, 101
Christopher, Maura, 164
Circuit Courts, *see* Appeals, Courts of
Civil Service Commission, 52
Civil War, 14-19
Clark, Tom, 207
Cleveland, Grover, 41
Cloture, 161
Collins, Cardiss, 105-106, 109, 118, 119
Colombia, Panama Canal and, 70-71
Commerce, Department of, 55
Congress, 10, 18, 54, 105-118, 121-129, 183, 188; campaign expenses for, 162, 171, 174; chart, 108; commerce power, 134; committees, 109; Congressional district size, 107, 109; Congressional bills and, 25; criticism of, 157-163; democracy of, 160-161; enacting law, 122-127; honesty of, 162; influence on, 169-176; makeup of, 106; military power, 134; party politics in, 159; power in, 145-150; President and, 29; Presidential power and, 65-69; rules governing, 159-162; salaries of, 162; seniority system, 146-148; slowness of, 158-160; staff size, 159; taxing power, 134-135, 137; terms of members, 167; war power, 134 *see also* House of Representatives, Legislative Branch, Lobbying, lobbyists; Senate
Congress in Action: The Environmental Education Act, 122

Congressional bills, 121-129, 130-131; chart, 123; judging of, 133-137
Congressional Directory The, 119, 155
Congressional Quarterly, 182, 183, 209, 225
Congressional Record, 128, 131
Constitution, U.S., 12, 13, 29, 96, 140, 207, 213, 215, 225; amendments to—1st: 134, 216; 2nd: 176; 8th: 213; 14th: 218, 219, 220; 22nd, 82; Article I, 106, 134; Article II, 66, 74, 106; Article III, 106, 187-188; balance of power, 107; Congress, 106-109; Congressional bills and, 122, 134-137; Louisiana Territory, 11-13; Presidential duties and powers described in, 9-10, 65-69; Presidential replacement, 77; Supreme Court and, 231;
Constitution: That Delicate Balance, The, 237
Contras, 165
Controversial Court: Supreme Court Influences on American Life, The, 237
Coolidge, Calvin, 41, 66
Courts, U.S., 10, 187-237; chart, 193; Constitution and, 187-188; sentencing and, 196-197; tracking a case through, 227-231; *see also* Appeals, Courts of; District Court; Supreme Court
Coy, Harold, 183

Day in the Life of President Johnson, A, 24-27
Defense, Department of, 25, 49-50, 55, 152
Defense Never Rests, The, 237
Defense, Secretary of, 50
Democracy, 19
Democratic party 26, 83, 105, 124, 147-148
Depression, Great, 44, 96
Desegregation, 207, 217, 221-224
Diplomats, 28
Dissenting opinion, 216, 232
District attorney, 110, 189-190
District court, 192, 196, 202-204, 222, 227-228
Docket, 229
Dole, Robert, 164-165
Dorsey, John, 33
Douglas, William O., 216
Drug testing, 138-141
Drury, Allen, 183

Economy, 29
Education, Department of, 55
Ehrenhalt, Alan, 183
Eisenhower, Dwight D., 41, 66, 78, 80-81, 82, 87, 96, 207
Eisenhower, Mamie, 78, 80-81
Elastic clause, 135
Elliot, Martha J. H., 237
Energy, Department of, 56

Environmental Education Act, 122-126
Equal protection of the laws, 220, 224
Executive Branch, 10, 13, 26, 27, 28, 49-63, 96, 106, 184

Facts on File, 225
Federal Aviation Administration (FAA), 141
Federal Bureau of Investigation (FBI), 28, 54, 83, 189
Federal case, 227
Federal Communications Commission (FCC), 54
Federal Courts, The, 230
Federal deficit, 165
Federal Reserve System, 54
Feinberg, Barbara, 101
Filibuster, 115, 160, 164, 166-167
Fillmore, Millard, 40
Food and Drug Administration (FDA), 54
Ford, Gerald R., 41, 84, 205
Foreign policy, 28, 165
Fort Donelson, 18
Fort Henry, 18
Fort Sumter, 15-16, 17
France, 11-13
Francis, Willie, 213-214
Frankel, Marvin, 196
Frankfurter, Felix, 211-213
Franking privileges, 162
Franklin Roosevelt, Gallant President, 101
Freedom: of religion 134; of speech and the press, 134, 215, 216, 225, 228-229
Free Speech, Free Press, and the Law, 236
Friendly, Fred W., 237
Furgurson, Ernest B., 182

Garfield, James, 40, 89
Ginsburg, Donald, 209
Goldman, Sheldon, 205
Goldwater, Barry, 75
Goode, Stephen, 183, 237
Goss v. Lopez, 235
Government, U.S., services guide, 58-59; *see also* specific listings for branches and agencies
Grant, Ulysses S., 18-19, 40
Gray, Kenneth, 128-129
Great Britain, 61
Green, Garry, 139, 141
Greenberg, Jack, 221-223
Gun control, 175

Hall, James, 121-122, 126
Hard Right: The Rise of Jesse Helms, 182
Harding, Warren, 41, 66
Harlan, John Marshall, 222-223

Harrison, Benjamin, 41
Harrison, William Henry, 40
Harry S Truman, 35, 101
Hatch, Orrin, 105-106, 109, 118
Hazelwood case, 227-229, 232-235
Hayes, Rutherford, B., 40
Health and Human Services, Department of, 56
Hebert, Edward, 152
Helms, Jesse, 182
Herblock Through the Looking Glass: The Reagan Years in Words and Pictures, 101
Hitler, Adolf, 45
Hollings, Ernest, 138-140
Holmes, Oliver Wendell, 207, 209
Hoover, Herbert, 41, 66, 203
House of Commons, British, 157
House of Representatives, 118, 128-129, 157; Appropriations Committee, 146; Armed Services Committee, 152-53; Banking and Currency Committee, 153; Committee on Committees, 152; Government Operations Committee, 153; House Rules Committee, 125, 149-150; impeachment, 82, 84; Judiciary Committee, 84; Labor and Education Committee, 124-125; makeup of, 106; Senate comparison, 107-109; Speaker, 85, 107, 149-150, 182; *see also* Congress
Housing and Urban Development, Department of, 56
Howard, James, 128-129
How Congress Works, 182
Hughes, Charles Evans, 207, 211, 217
Humphrey, Hubert H., 26

Impeachment, U.S. judges, 202; U.S. President 82-83; *see also* Bill of Impeachment
Inauguration 82, 88, 89; Eisenhower: 80-81; Kennedy: 86-87; Truman, 78-81
Ingram v. Wright, 235
Injunction, 228
Interior, Department of, 56
Iran-Contra scandal, 165
In re Gault, 235
Internal Revenue Service (IRS), 57

Jackson, Andrew, 40
Jackson, Robert, 216
Japan, 44
Jefferson, Thomas, 11-13, 14, 20, 40, 96
Johnson, Andrew, 40, 82
Johnson, Lady Bird, 26-27, 35
Johnson, Lyndon B., 24-27, 35, 41, 77, 182, 205
Journal of American History, 96
Judges, U.S. 201-204; chart, 205; Constitution and, 202; criteria for selection, 201-203;

impeachment of, 202; President and, 202-205
Judicature, 205
Judicial Branch, 106, 187, 189, 211
Judicial restraint, 202, 208, 230
Judicial review, 215
Jury, 187, 190; grand, 189
Justice Sandra Day O'Connor, 237
Justice, system of, 188-193
Justice, Department of, 26, 54, 56, 75, 221-222
Justices and Presidents: A Political History of Appointments to the Supreme Court, 209, 225

Keeping the Faith: Memoirs of a President, 100
Kennedy, Edward, 208
Kennedy, John F., 41, 77, 86-87, 89, 149-150, 183
Kennedy, Robert F., 21
Kuhlmeier, Cathy, 227, 234

Labor, Department of, 57
LaFollette, Fola and Belle, 116
LaFollette, Robert, Jr., 116-117
LaFollette, Robert, Sr., 109-111, 114, 116-117, 166
Landry, James, 138-140
Law of Delay, The, 60-61
Leahy, Patrick, 165
League of Women Voters, 101
Legislative Branch, 106
Legislatures, state, 13
Leonard, Jerris, 221-223
Lieberman, Jethro K., 236
Lincoln, Abraham, 9, 14-16, 18-19, 20, 39, 40, 73, 79, 96, 100, 203
Lincoln, 100
lobbying, lobbyists, 137, 172-173
logrolling, 146
Louisiana Territory, 11-13

Madison, James, 40
Maps and charts: America in 1803, 11; Fort Sumter and Southern Forts, 17; Guide to Government Services, 55-57; Panama in 1903, 70; Two Houses of Congress, 108; U.S. Court System, 193; Who Are the Presidents?, 40-41
Majority opinion, 216, 224, 232
Management and Budget, Office of, 54
Man of the House — The Life and Political Memoirs of Speaker Tip O'Neill, 182
Marbury v. Madison, 215, 225
Marcos, Ferdinand, 27
Marines, U.S., 29
Marshall, John, 209, 215, 217, 225, 231

Marshall, Thurgood, 203, 221, 223
McClure, Alexander, 18-19
McKim, Eddie, 33
McKinley, William, 41, 89
Medicare, 165
Merrimack River, 121
Monroe, James, 40
Moynihan, Daniel Patrick, 183
Murray, Robert K., 96

Nangle, John, 228
National Association for the Advancement of
    Colored People (NAACP), 221
National Safety Council, 129
National Transportation Safety Board, 140
Navy, U.S., 29, 44, 51
Nelson, Gaylord, 122, 124-125
New Congress, The, 183
New Jersey v. T.L.O., 230-231
New York Times, The, 30
Nicaragua, 165
Nixon, Richard M., 21, 41, 83-84, 124, 126, 205
Non-Proliferation Treaty, 29
Novak, William, 182
Nuclear disarmament, 24

Oberdorfer, Louis, 221-223
O'Connor, Sandra Day, 201-203, 237
Omnibus bills, 159
O'Neill, Tip, 182
Oval Office, 25, 26
Overmeyer, Allen, 122

Pack, Robert, 101
Panama Canal, 70-71, 75
Parkinson, C. Northcote, 60
Patronage, 203
Pearl Harbor, 44, 45
Pentagon, 50
Peters, Mike, 157
Petitions, 229
Pierce, Franklin, 40
*Plain Speaking: An Oral History of Harry S
    Truman,* 207
Plessy v. Ferguson, 218-220, 222
Political action committees (PAC's), 174
Political parties, 29, 147-150; role in selecting
    judges, 203; *see also* Democratic party;
    Republican party
*Politics in America: Members of Congress in
    Washington and at Home,* 183
Polk, James, 40
Postal Service, U.S., 189
Precedent, legal, 228, 232
President, U.S., 6-47, 49, 165; background of
    (chart), 40-41; Constitution lists powers

and duties of, 9-10, 65-69; impeachment
    of, 82-85; judging, 91-97; power of, 65-75;
    qualifications of, 37-39, 46-47; replacing,
    77-87; roles of, 23-27, (chart) 28-29, 30,
    34-35; Senate and, 13; Supreme Court
    and, 206-207; veto power 126, 131; *see
    also* names of individual Presidents
President pro tempore of the Senate, 85
Presidential Campaigns, 100
Presidential Government, 73
Presidential Wives, 101
Pressure groups, *see* lobbying, lobbyists
Profiles in Courage, 183
Public hearing, 138
Public opinion, 91

Rayburn, Sam, 150-151
Reagan, Nancy, 101
Reagan, Ronald, 21, 24, 30-31, 32, 41, 44-45,
    51, 96, 101, 202, 204-206
Rehnquist, William, 202
Republican party, 105, 124, 147-148; *see also*
    Political parties
Reynolds, Robert, 227, 228
Richardson, Bill, 128-129
Roe, Gilbert, 117
Rooney, John, 152
Roosevelt, Eleanor, 79
Roosevelt, Franklin D., 41, 79, 82, 86, 96, 101,
    212, 213
Roosevelt, Theodore, 41, 72-73, 207
Rossiter, Clinton, 51

Scott, Winfield, 15-16
Search and seizure, 230
Secret Service, 33
Segregation, racial, 218-223
Senate, 118, 138-141; Commerce Committee,
    142; debate in, 116-117; Judiciary Com-
    mittee, 203, 208, 209; House of Represen-
    tatives comparison, 107-109; impeach-
    ment, 82, 84; Labor and Public Welfare
    Committee, 125; makeup of, 106; Presi-
    dent and, 13; Supreme Court and, 203;
    Vice-President and, 108; *see also* Con-
    gress
Separate but equal, 219-220, 224
Sherwood, Robert, 44
Shiloh, Battle of, 18-19
Slavery, 14
Smart, Leslie, 227
Smith, Howard, 149-150
Social Security, 165
Social Security Administration, 50
Speaker of the House, 85, 107, 149-150, 182
Speakes, Larry, 101

Speaking Out: The Reagan Presidency from Inside the White House, 101
Special interest groups, 158
Split decision, 235
State, Department of, 26, 51, 56
Stidham, Ronald, 230, 231
Stone, Richard, 138-140
Supreme Court, New Jersey, 230
Supreme Court, The, 237
Supreme Court, U.S., 84, 187, 192, 201-203, 208-209, 211-228, 230-235; Bork nomination, 203; cases, screening of, 229; Chief Justice of, 217; Constitution and, 231; Justices of, 206-207; nomination to, 214; "packing" of, 206-207; power of, 192; President and, 206-207; role of, 214; Senate and, 206; Watergate and, 84
Switzer, Carroll, 201, 203

Taft, William Howard, 41
Taylor, Zachary, 40
Terminiello v. Chicago, 216
Thirteen Days, 21
Time Magazine, 86
Tinker v. Des Moines Independent Community School District, 228, 232-233, 235
Tippet-West, Lee Ann, 227
Transportation, Department of, 57
Treasury, Department of the, 51, 57
Treaties, 10, 13
Trial by jury, 187, 190
Truman, Bess, 32, 78-80
Truman, Harry S., 20, 21, 32-33, 41, 78-80, 82, 88, 101, 201, 207
Truman, Margaret, 32-33, 35, 78, 101
Tyler, John, 40

Union of Soviet Socialist Republics (U.S.S.R.), 24, 83
Unlikely Heroes, 237
Update Magazine, 164
U.S. Code (USC), 188
U.S. Courts, *see* Courts, U.S.; Supreme Court

Van Buren, Martin, 40
Veto, 29, 131; pocket, 126
Vice-President, U.S., 26, 77, 82, 85, 88, 99, 107
Vidal, Gore, 100

Warren, Charles, 206
Warren, Earl, 207, 217, 220, 237
Washington, George, 39, 40, 66, 73, 74, 96,
Washington Lobby, The, 183
Watergate scandal, 83-84
White, Byron, 232-233
White, Theodore H., 101

White House Diary, A, 35
White House Office, 54
Wilson, Woodrow, 41, 114-115
World Almanac, The, 89, 119, 194
World War I, 114
World War II, 96
Woodward, Bob, 221, 236
Wright, Jim, 178

You and Your Congressman, 178